MW01487208

BETH CHATTO'S
GREEN TAPESTRY
revisited

BETH CHATTO'S GREEN TAPESTRY
revisited

A guide to a sustainably planted garden

Photography by Steven Wooster

BERRY&**CO**

Beth Chatto's Green Tapestry Revisited

First published as *The Green Tapestry*, 1989

This revised and updated edition published in 2021 by
Berry & Co (Publishing) Ltd
47 Crewys Road
London NW2 2AU
UK
www.berrypublishing.co.uk

© Berry & Co (Publishing) Ltd 2021
Text © Beth Chatto/Beth Chatto Education Trust 1989, 2021
Photography © Steven Wooster 2021 except pp 9, 26, 43, 136, 145, 171, 199 br, 201 tr, 202 tr, 203 tr, 208 tr & br, 209 tr, 220, 221 tr & bl, 234 tr & cr: © Beth Chatto Education Trust

All rights reserved. No part of this publication may be reproduced, stored in a retrieval system or transmitted, in any form or by any means, electronic, mechanical, photocopying, recording or otherwise, without the prior permission in writing from the publisher.

Additional text **David Ward** and **Åsa Gregers-Warg** (Beth Chatto's Plants and Gardens)

Designer **Steven Wooster**
Planting plans **Jacob Pettersson**
Editor **Susan Berry**
Plant checking & index **Tony Lord**

A catalogue record for this book is available from the British Library

ISBN 978-1-9999631-6-3

Reproduction by Pixywalls Ltd, UK
Printed and bound in China

CONTENTS

Foreword **6**

INTRODUCTION **8**

PRINCIPLES OF PLANTING **18**

THE GRAVEL GARDEN **34**

THE WATER GARDEN **62**

THE OPEN WALKS **90**

THE SHADE GARDENS **108**

THE RESERVOIR GARDEN **134**

THE WOODLAND GARDEN **152**

THE SCREE GARDEN **172**

OTHER AREAS OF INTEREST **186**

Plant directory **196**

Index **250**

Acknowledgments **7, 256**

Garden Plan **256**

PAGE 1 Lush, contrasting, early summer foliage in the damp soils around the ponds.

PAGES 2-3 Looking up through the original Mediterranean Garden, the planting framed by *Verbena bonariensis* and punctuated with vertical sages and white mulleins.

LEFT Ground-hugging stonecrops, thyme and fleshy houseleeks form a year-round tapestry of interconnecting foliage in the raised beds of the Scree Garden.

Foreword

AS BETH CHATTO'S granddaughter and as a director of her business, Beth Chatto's Plants and Gardens, I am delighted to introduce this revised reprint of her original book, *The Green Tapestry*, in which she guided visitors around her gardens, explaining her philosophy of planting in the very different conditions in each area of it.

Beth's approach to her planting, namely of choosing the right plant for the right place, was unusual and ground-breaking at the time but it has become infinitely more relevant with climate change and the pressing need to plant sustainably. Her desire to spread the word saw a decade of consecutive Gold Medal winning displays at the Chelsea Flower Show in the 1970s and '80s, along with many books (almost all still in print) and international lectures.

My grandparents, Beth and Andrew, spent their lifetimes studying and learning about plants and this consuming interest, combined with enthusiasm and original thinking, resulted in their 7.5-acre informal garden – a unique and beautiful example of sustainable, naturalistic planting. The significance of Beth's work was recognized in 2020 when the gardens were awarded a Grade II listing by Historic England.

So, some 30 years after the *The Green Tapestry* was published, the time is right for a fully revised and updated edition. It has given the opportunity not only to bring Beth's original discussion of her gardens to a new audience, but to include descriptions, in photographs and words, of how the garden has developed since, both under her careful eye in her lifetime and following her principles since then. As Beth would say, 'a garden is not a picture' – it is ever changing, requiring editing and refreshing at times. We have been careful to include in this revised edition the ways in which it has and will continue to develop. The section on the Scree Garden is rather short, owing to the ongoing replanting of a major bed in that area.

Thankfully, Beth's achievement in turning the nursery and gardens into a successful business has ensured that her dedicated team can continue to nurture her beloved garden, making it available to visitors as a source of inspiration and education, and to propagate and make available thousands of varieties of plants for today's gardeners.

Beth Chatto, at the age of 91, decided she wanted to share the results of hers and Andrew's life work by founding the Beth Chatto Education Trust. Its aim is to provide horticultural education to all, from toddlers to the elderly, from beginners to advanced gardeners, and for private and public area planting that is beautiful, ecological and sustainable. Royalties from her books go to this Trust, which funds visits from schools and organizations that would not normally have the necessary resources.

We have got a lot to live up to!

Julia Boulton, March 2021

Low shafts of sunlight on a summer evening highlight the vertical elements in the mixed planting in the Gravel Garden.

Acknowledgments to special contributors
Revising and updating this book would not have been possible without the following people:

Beth's right-hand man, Garden and Nursery Director, **David Ward**, who has painstakingly gone through the original text and added hugely to the content. It now includes both the Woodland Garden and Beth's iconic Gravel Garden, which he worked alongside her to create.

Åsa Gregers-Warg, Head Gardener, in particular for her contribution on the Reservoir Garden – which she designed and planted, and which Beth officially opened.

Steven Wooster, a key photographer of the gardens during Beth's lifetime. It has been wonderful to have him here taking new pictures – his photographs have illustrated many of Beth's books.

Introduction

This is Beth's original introduction to The Green Tapestry.
*It is illustrated principally with images from the gardens
as they are today.*

I HAVE LIVED all my life in Essex – I was born in Good
Easter near Chelmsford and brought up near Saffron
Walden. Gardening, I suppose, is in my blood. My father
was a good gardener, and my mother too, and even as quite
a small child I had a garden of my own. I bought packets
of seed and grew annuals. My parents had an interesting
garden and grew a number of species plants among the
typical collection of cottage garden plants, which in those
days was unusual.

After teacher training college during the war, I married
Andrew Chatto, a fruit grower. As a child he had lived
for several years on the West Coast of America and it
was during that time, when he saw California poppies
(*Eschscholzia*) and *Ceanothus* and lupins growing wild, that
his interest in plant ecology started. He had previously seen
these plants in England and when he saw them in America,
his first thought was, 'How did all the plants get here?'
Much later, when Andrew took me to Switzerland, it was
my turn to have my breath taken away by sheets of flowers
growing wild that I had previously only seen cultivated in

Beth and Andrew at Col de Sevi, Corsica, in 1951 on one of their early holidays to explore the wild flowers of the mountain regions of Europe. The breathtaking sight of sheets of alpine flowers that she had previously only seen cultivated in gardens inspired Beth to share Andrew's passion for plants.

gardens. The Swiss Alps looked like a huge rock garden, grazed short by the cattle and conditioned by the climate. Long rank grass does not grow in the chilled air in thin, shallow soils but the latter are the ideal growing conditions for plants with small brilliantly coloured flowers. To see the turf studded with gentians and the rocks covered with cobwebbed houseleeks (*Sempervivum*), and the dry slopes bright with *Dianthus* and many other familiar plants, was a revelation.

I think for us both the significance of seeing plants growing together in association and in different situations

A harmonious group of plants in partial shade alongside the ponds in late spring. This area offers both sun on the open side of its borders and shade under the trees. Bowles's golden sedge, *Carex elata* 'Aurea', on the right and *Euphorbia palustris*, in flower on the left, both thrive in these conditions. The naked flower stems of *Darmera peltata* precede their soon-to-emerge large, parasol-like leaves.

was what really fired our idea of making a garden based on ecological ideas. But when it comes to putting it into practice, you cannot be a complete purist. Gardening is the art of combining plants from many different areas of the temperate world to provide pleasure and interest for a much longer season than that of the flowering meadows of the Swiss Alps. Furthermore, there are many plants, such as stinging nettles or running twitch grass, that may be part of a natural association but are not desirable in the garden. However, if I ignore too many of the principles I have learnt from Andrew's teaching and my own observation, I find that either the plants do not perform well or the planting lacks harmony.

We are often surprised by the way the plants themselves do not always grow as we would expect. Something that astounded my husband is the way I can grow *Helleborus × hybridus*. Andrew had read that these hellebores grow wild in the Caucasus among bushes and trees around the foothills in mountainous country, so when I first put them in an open site in well-prepared but light, well-drained soil, he was sure they would suffer from the full exposure. To his surprise and my relief, they flourished. We are, in some cases, able to grow plants in the open in our temperate climate that in nature would normally be found in the shade. In their native home, the summer sun would be considerably hotter than it is here, so some shade is essential. Today, these plants have retreated into scrubby places where they are safe from grazing animals and from man's scavenging of the land in order to grow crops. In most cases these are the only places where they have survived extinction.

As a beginner, of course, I did not realize that plants have their preferences and are adapted to special conditions. Let us take, for example, cultivated garden plants, such as pyrethrums or double zinnias. These plants need what is generally termed 'good garden soil' and open sunny conditions, as they have been developed and evolved from plants that originally liked and grew in open sunny places, so they cannot be expected to perform well in dim, shady backyards where they would become pale and leggy, reaching for the light.

The majority of cultivars grown for their flowers could be planted in straight rows in the vegetable garden, where they would have full sunlight and air all around them, and where they would provide good-quality flowers for picking. But there is an increasing interest among gardeners to use more plants as they are found growing in the wild, so you really do have to find out what the 'wild' is like. It is not enough to know that the plant came from China or Japan or America. Was it from the north, east, south or west? Was it from a hot, dry, gravelly slope or was it found in a boggy place? Many well-known herbaceous plants like rudbeckias, Michaelmas daisies and goldenrod are mainly found in the damp meadowlands of North America, while asphodels and many euphorbias are found in stony soil in countries around the Mediterranean, which habitually have hot, dry summers.

As far as plants grown mainly for their foliage are concerned, at the beginning of the 20th century William Robinson was using many of them. They were grown in the gardens of the wealthy and the discerning, and slowly they spread into other gardens but, on the whole, it was just a small circle of people who travelled and mixed socially who knew of them. There were still many typical Victorian gardens full of salvias and other plants from the greenhouse put out in rows like guardsmen, but William Robinson and Gertrude Jekyll began the movement towards a more natural style of planting. The writings of Vita Sackville-West carried that further, but the problem for many of their followers was where to find such plants.

Achilleas are native to central and south-western Asia but *Achillea filipendulina* has become naturalized in Europe and North America. This cultivar, *A. f.* 'Gold Plate', an easy and adaptable plant, makes an eye-catching feature for full sun and also an ideal dried flower when picked.

At that time, many wealthy people did not involve themselves in their gardens; they relied on their gardeners to do it all for them, but Miss Ellen Willmott was an exception. A wealthy woman and a great gardener, she collected species plants and made a garden at Warley Place, near Brentwood in Essex, where she employed over 150 gardeners whom she trained herself with discipline and zeal. She brought from Switzerland 'a man of the mountains' to create and tend her alpine garden, but I suspect few of her treasures percolated into the cottage gardens around.

After the Second World War, the situation changed. Many more people were seeking new interests after years of austerity. During the war we read and were enthralled by the inspired writing of both Vita Sackville-West and Margery Fish. In the mid-1950s, I made the acquaintance of the late Sir Cedric Morris and his wonderful garden on

Many of Beth's plants came to her from her friend, Sir Cedric Morris. Irises and poppies were two particular favourites of his, immortalized in his paintings. *Papaver* (Oriental Group) 'Cedric Morris' takes centre stage in a typical grouping in the Gravel Garden, the blue-mauves of catmints in the forefront and *Iris pallida* subsp. *pallida* beyond, contrasting with the lime-greens of euphorbias.

the outskirts of Hadleigh in Suffolk. It was full of irises, poppies, tall verbascums and alliums, along with many other plants that we grow in our gardens today but which were rarely seen then. I think that for those of us who could visit his garden he became for us what Vita had been to the readers of her articles in the *Observer*. No doubt up and down the country there were people like them who were influencing a small circle of gardeners around them, which gradually grew and spread through all sections of society.

The idea of making a nursery of unusual plants came to me through my association with the Flower Club movement when it first began, not long after the Second World War. Women were depressed after years of making do and needed something to relieve the austerity of rationing, still in use five or six years after the end of the war, and felt frustrated by shortages of materials. Flower arranging suddenly arrived as a pastime, largely initiated by Constance Spry with her fresh and individual style. She, too, had the advantage of knowing Cedric Morris and would stay with him occasionally in Suffolk, returning to London with her car full of flowers, seed-heads and wonderful leaves not seen in London flower shops before.

When I was about thirty years old, with two young children, Mrs Pamela Underwood, the founder of the Colchester Flower Club, came into my life. She was our neighbour at our first married home at Braiswick, Colchester, where we gardened alongside the ancient Roman ramparts on the outskirts of the town. Through the flower club, my eyes were opened to things I had never properly seen before, even though I thought I was an observant gardener. I became aware of plants in a new way, not only in the garden but on wasteland and on the salt marshes, and of their foliage as well as their flowers.

I discovered that it was possible to create an attractive design with many unexpected things. This was meat and

Seed-heads like those of *Aster amellus* 'King George' play a key role in the garden in autumn. Beth often preferred to leave them to stand through the winter rather than rushing to tidy up and cut back.

drink to many women who had no gardens at all and who were being taught how to put together two or three leaves, a bud and a flower to make something attractive for their homes when previously if they did not have a bunch of roses or gladioli, they felt they had nothing to arrange.

At that time I was very fortunate because I was able to enjoy nearly twenty years of creative activities around the home, which not only enriched my life at the time but also proved to be helpful later on. I was much involved with the flower garden but also ran the kitchen garden, and grew unusual vegetables, encouraged by my old friend Sir Cedric. From him I obtained seeds of vegetables like blue-podded beans (instead of the common scarlet runner beans), 'Avocadella' marrows, chicory, several kinds of radish like 'China Rose' and 'Black Spanish Long', and asparagus peas – none of which were then in seedsmen's catalogues.

At the same time, I brought home from Sir Cedric's garden all kinds of seeds and cuttings, and tiny scraps of this and that, and set about teaching myself how to propagate unusual plants. This discipline was good preparation for becoming a nurserywoman.

THE NURSERY

I started the nursery with just one girl who had been working for my husband on the farm. By this time, we had lived for about seven years in the new farmhouse we had built on the edge of wasteland between our neighbour's farm and ours, and the garden (the subject of the main chapters of this book) was taking shape. After a couple of years other women came along to help. Then, when the farm was sold, Harry, the youngest man on the farm, came and joined me, and remained with us ever since.

The flower arranging movement was transforming the nursery business in this country at that time, as people like myself and Mary Pope, who started the first Flower Club

An unusual range of gourds and squashes are grown on our large compost heap in the summer. It has become a tradition of the gardens to create a display of their wonderfully varied forms and colours in autumn.

in Dorchester, began to use more species plants. When I first started my own nursery, I would give demonstrations at flower clubs using only garden plants, which became my best publicity.

Mrs Pamela Underwood rang me one day and said, 'I want you to open a new flower club at Framlingham', in Suffolk. I could not drive a car, but I quickly learned, and just as quickly had to teach myself to do flower demonstrations. Before long I was doing them up and down the country, always taking flowers and foliage from the garden. The garden gave me confidence, although I knew the majority of demonstrators used florists' material. The response was astonishing. I, who had been growing these plants for fifteen years, had forgotten how unlikely it was that other people would know and grow euphorbias, hellebores and other green flowers with unusual foliage and textures. So, the seed was sown in my mind that if ever I had the chance, I would have a business one day selling them, and would call it 'Unusual Plants'.

Today the nursery (now called 'Beth Chatto's Plants and Gardens') relies very much on the garden and the garden on the nursery. I could never have made the enterprise so large or so full of interesting plants without the money

ABOVE Beth was among the first to promote green-flowered plants like euphorbias for flower arrangements.

LEFT The nursery stock beds are an important source of propagating material for the nursery. Most of these grasses are divided in the spring, with the added benefit of providing plumes for autumn flower arrangements.

OPPOSITE In the nursery, plants for sale, like these agapanthus, are propagated in the ever-expanding polytunnels needed to cater for a business that has grown to offer one of the widest ranges of perennials, grasses and ferns in the country, purchased both on site and online.

that comes from the nursery or the help of my dedicated staff. We need each other, and the visitors, too, make another contribution because they inspire me to make new plantings or redesign areas past their best. Gardens become elderly, just as we do, if we carry on doing the same things and fail to see them afresh. Although it is not my main intention to make a garden for the public, since I feel the appropriateness of the planting must come first, I am both inspired and sometimes chastened by comments I hear around me.

I look for sources of interesting plants all the time. Some people will occasionally say that we have so many plants here there cannot be any more we could want. Sometimes I feel there is not enough space for more, but then I realize that all I have to do is renovate an area of the garden to create the room.

Principles of Planting

MANY GARDENERS are full of enthusiasm, but at the same time are often very conscious that they are not getting their planting right, and that they need some guidelines. Perhaps they are dissatisfied with the effect they create – for some reason, the plants do not look well together. Often they have very little idea of plant grouping and dot plants around the garden like pins in a pincushion; where there is a space, they put in the latest acquisition without even stopping to think whether it is the sunny or the shady side of the garden and whether this matters or not.

I was recently asked to write an article on planting for problem situations by a journalist who felt other readers might value advice on where and how to plant. She herself was having trouble with the planting in the sunny part of her garden. Curiously enough, she was doing quite well with the shady, cool side, which she had realized could look very attractive, but on the hot, dry side the plants were dying. She was probably planting things like hostas, primulas or gentians: plants not adapted to such conditions. In most gardens, the design effect depends on flowers rather than foliage. Once flowering is over, the plants either stand there looking bedraggled because the conditions are too dry or they are cut down, leaving a gap in the planting. In either case, the garden may end up looking characterless and

This rich mixture of form and texture demonstrates Beth's hallmark planting style. The eye is drawn from the smaller plants at the front to the taller shrubs behind, with contrasts of foliage from soft, rounded silvery-grey leaves to narrow, strap-shaped green ones, with verticals and seed-heads creating a more naturalistic effect.

ragged. The disastrous results make you think you have a 'problem' situation when all you have is a site that different species of plants would enjoy.

Perhaps another reason why people sometimes make mistakes is that they fail to work from the right end of the equation. Instead of accepting that what they have is a sunny site, working out what will grow on it and making the most of that, they collect ideas about plants from books. Inspired by beautiful pictures of blue this and yellow that, they then go to the garden centre and buy plants they cannot resist, thinking that all the plants require is to be put into the earth. It does not occur to them that the plant may not like the situation. Even when they are not seduced by flower colour but commendably look for good foliage form, they may be no more successful. If you have a hot, sunny garden and plant ferns or hostas, or other plants with delicate foliage that scorches in the sun, the effect will be depressing because the leaves will be damaged. There are plenty of colourful annuals like French marigolds and larkspur that will grow in that hot, dry soil, provided you water them in and go on watering them, but there is then no background to the planting. All you have is hot, garish colours and the garden lacks what I call the 'furniture' – the permanent planting. I feel that the garden should be attractive as far as possible all year round. It is easiest to do this in a hot, dry garden if you plant many of the grey-leaved plants and those with tough leathery leaves that will last through the winter. Although in this part of the world it can be very cold indeed in winter, many Mediterranean-type plants will usually survive in well-drained gravel.

ATTITUDES TO PLANTING

The art of gardening has changed considerably over the centuries. In the 17th century, garden designers like André Le Nôtre (who created the great garden at Versailles for

A self-seeded *Verbascum bombyciferum* with its large silver-felted leaves and the fleshy-leaved spurge, *Euphorbia characias* subsp. *wulfenii*, are ideally adapted to life in dry, sunny, well-drained soil and are often seen in combination in very much those same conditions in the Gravel Garden.

'Nowadays many people travel and have the opportunity to see plants growing in their natural habitat. Some may feel the urge to try to cultivate these same plants to bring something of the peace and tranquillity of nature into their gardens.'

Louis XIV) were pushing nature back, sweeping the forest away from the great, stately chateaux. In those days, this had a practical reason: the forest was still full of wolves and bears, and so there had to be a barrier of walls and hedges around the garden. Everything else in the garden was formal too – long stretches of water echoed the straight lines of the boundary fences and the architecture. There were none of the wild grasses and foliage plants that we enjoy using today. On the contrary, almost everything was clipped and manicured into formal shapes and designs. It was an age when gentlemen paraded up and down between geometrically designed parterres. They needed to feel safe and civilized; nature was not something to be enjoyed but something to be tamed or kept at bay. Nowadays we are trying hard to return to nature, perhaps because we are overcivilized. Also, many people travel and have the opportunity to see plants growing in their natural habitat. Some may feel the urge to try to cultivate these same plants to bring something of the peace and tranquillity of nature into their gardens.

Many gardeners are not aware that the most well-known garden plants have been developed by hybridization and

A native of the Himalayas, Wallich's wood fern, *Dryopteris wallichiana*, can also be found in parts of Central America. This stately fern remains evergreen here along the Shady Walk that runs along boundary of the Water Garden. Its finely divided foliage adds to the contrast in form and texture in this largely evergreen planting.

selection from plants found growing in the wild. They tend to think of them as products of the horticulturists. We do not, after all, go out and pick carrots from the hedge; we have tamed vegetables and made them palatable for human use. Equally, man has made ornamental plants for the garden appropriate for his use and ideas of what 'appropriate' is have changed from generation to generation. The mop-headed chrysanthemums, huge dahlias and statuesque gladioli so popular with generations of plant breeders are, after all, only cultivated and 'improved' forms of plants that all originated in the wild in a much simpler form.

When they begin gardening, many people, particularly city dwellers, are often almost totally ignorant of nature. They think of wildflowers as weeds like dandelions and bindweed. If you have not learned much botany at school, the plants that grow wild and those that grow in garden centres seem poles apart.

THE INFLUENCE OF CLIMATE

It would be wrong to frighten people off by suggesting there is a mystique about planting – that you must put plants in exactly the right situation. Many of them will tolerate quite a wide range of conditions, but certainly when you come to using species plants you cannot go too far beyond their natural range. Take, for example, rhododendrons that come from mountainous areas throughout Asia and northern America. They receive ample rainfall and although they are growing at high altitudes where the power of the sun will be great, the constant accumulation of clouds will also keep their foliage moist. If you try to grow rhododendrons in the drier parts of the British Isles, the leaves will scorch and wither. The same is true of azaleas. These are under-storey plants – that is, they are found growing in the shade of woodland trees. Many of them are from Japan, and again the Japanese islands are affected by moisture-laden air.

The European *Rhododendron ponticum*, which needs acid soil and ample rainfall, has adapted only too well in parts of the British Isles, where it has become a serious problem, suckering and seeding on acidic soils, and effectively crowding out the native flora. Fortunately, the gardeners here keep it in check, digging out any layered branches and errant seedlings.

They have a climate more like the south-west peninsula of Devon and Cornwall. (Incidentally both azaleas and rhododendrons are adapted to acid, peaty conditions and will not tolerate chalky soil.)

The hardiness of plants is conditioned by the type of soil you have because this exaggerates or counteracts the climatic conditions. Poor sandy or gravelly soil is warmer in winter because it is not full of icy water. In summer, the plants grow tough and wiry in such soils. If they were in better soil, they would grow soft and sappy and would then collapse in the first frost. When I first came here, I planted cistuses in some of my more retentive soil. They grew wonderfully well, but I lost them in a hard winter. Heathers, on the other hand, do not like the driest of conditions. They grow on moors – a very different habitat from East Anglian gravel. Heathers from Dartmoor or Scotland will not do well on a soil with very low rainfall. But on certain East Anglian sandy soils, ling and bell heather form a peat layer and thus do survive and create heathland.

I am writing and gardening to help people grow plants in the climate and conditions that exist for them. To pour water on the garden in times of drought is now almost impossible: as soon as there is a drought, watering in gardens is usually banned to keep the reserves of water for the population and the food crops. Provided you choose your plants carefully, you do not need to go in for regular watering. I certainly do not subscribe to it.

If you do as much as you can to improve the soil texture before planting and protect it with mulches like chipped bark (or even less attractive but equally useful ones like straw, paper and black polythene) until the plants can become established, you will help the garden to mature more quickly. At the end of the first season the plants themselves will already cover much of the ground. If you lift a plant even in dry weather, there will always be some

One of the best drought-resistant grasses, the golden oat grass, *Stipa gigantea*, contrasts well with equally drought-resistant silver-leaved plants such as *Lychnis coronaria* and *Verbascum bombyciferum*.

moisture under it. But even mulching will not get you very far if you do not use plants that are adapted to drought.

If you have energy, time and enthusiasm you can always improve the conditions in the garden to enable you to grow a wider range of plants. Most of us, however, have to live, more or less, with what we have. In my first married home, on the outskirts of Colchester, I had a garden on chalky boulder clay which, when it dried out, set hard. There was no way I could grow bog-loving plants yet, when offered wonderful plants like *Astilbe* and *Lysichiton,* I thought in my youth and ignorance that I could grow them. I tried and I lost them. No matter how much compost I put into the soil, those plants could not survive such low rainfall, their distress aggravated by drying winds.

SOIL

Many gardening books discuss endlessly the acidity and alkalinity of the soil but fail to talk about its texture. For some plants, like the azaleas and rhododendrons I mentioned, the acidity or alkalinity of the soil is important – but there are only a few of them. People who live on chalky soil and want to grow acid-loving plants have to add certain chemicals to the soil to neutralize it, but this has to be a continuing process, since rain will wash the chemicals out, and more dissolved chalk will upset the balance. I prefer not to go down that route and instead choose plants that suit the conditions. You can grow a far wider range of plants if you do something about the texture of the soil – and you can forget about whether it is acid or chalk. You just need to find out which plants are lime-haters and avoid them if you have calcareous soil or, if you have very acid, peaty soil, add chalk.

It is the texture of the soil – the blend of air, drainage and nutrients – that really matters. You have three basic soil types – sand and gravel, silt, and clay. If you hold the

The soil in Beth's gardens varies in different areas, from a very dry, almost sandy soil (above) which, as Beth would say, 'runs through your fingers like sand in an egg-timer' in the Scree and Gravel Gardens to much more moisture-retentive organic soil around the spring-fed pools in the Water Garden and near the ditch in the Woodland Garden (opposite).

soil in your hand, a light gravel or sandy soil will probably fall apart, even when wet, and, when dry, it runs through your fingers like sand in an egg-timer. In long periods of drought these types of soil are disastrous for many plants as they simply dry out. Obviously, they drain only too well, and what you need is some kind of moisture-retaining material like humus, which also adds nutrients to the soil. Mulching the surface after planting also helps to prevent excess moisture evaporation.

Once you have improved a light soil so it will hold together, you can grow a wider range of plants. Many of my woodland plants – hostas, pulmonarias and cranesbills – are growing in the same kind of soil as my drought-loving plants just a few yards away, but the shade from a huge oak and holly protects the woodland plants for much of the day when the little Mediterranean Garden lies in full sun.

On the lower side of the oak-holly bed we have a different soil – poor and fine-textured – which is a dense silt. To this you need to add a lot of grit, for although it has good water-

Both dense and dappled shade, provide shelter for the many foliage plants that thrive in this damp corner of the Woodland Garden, making it the perfect home for plants such as hostas, *Lysichiton* and moisture-loving ferns.

holding properties, plants with fine roots cannot push their way through it when it becomes compacted. What it needs is a generous application of grit to the top spit, otherwise it cannot breathe. I also use bonfire waste, which is gritty, to open up the texture.

In areas of heavy clay – the most difficult soil to improve – you have to wait until the soil is in a manageable state. If it has dried as hard as concrete or has become as soft as butter, you cannot handle it. Ideally you need to dig it in the autumn to allow the frost to break it up, and then dig in plenty of grit and humus in the spring. If you live in an area that has solid clay from one end of the county to the other, and cannot lay your hands on gravelly soil to mix with it, you will have to come to terms with it and concentrate on those plants with penetrating roots. Gardeners on very light soils will be envious of clay's water-retention and feel equally frustrated.

People sometimes ask me how often they should try to tackle the job of improving their soil. Obviously, you are not going to do this every year to an established bed, but every six or seven years I remove plants from part of a border, divide the ones that have become overgrown and rejuvenate the entire bed – both the soil and the planting.

The asymmetrical triangle between earth, man and sky, regarded as the golden principle of design by the Japanese, was a key principle of Beth's in her planting schemes in the island beds. The diagram (below left) shows the design in elevation, with smaller plants at the base, medium ones in the centre leading to the tallest, set slightly off-centre to create the asymmetry. It is demonstrated in a photograph (below) of an actual planting group with a triangle imposed upon it.

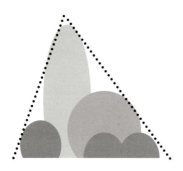

I take the herbaceous plants out and leave in the ones that hate being moved (those with very deep roots which, in any case, can cope with the soil). I dig the soil to at least a spit's depth and put in whatever it happens to need – grit, compost or well-rotted farm manure. Minor renovation of a small planting area can pay too – you do not have to dig up a whole border.

DESIGNING

Two influences have helped me in design. First has been my husband, with his studies of plant ecology which demonstrate that plants prefer to be in an environment similar to the one they have in the wild, so you do not simply jumble plants up according to whim. Secondly, when I was involved in the flower-arranging movement (which I talk about in the Introduction on page 15), I made friends with an old lady whose husband had connections with Japan. She had a great many books on flower arranging in Japan, and I studied them with great interest. You cannot translate the arrangements directly into western-style houses, as they would not suit our style and taste in furniture, but looking at them I began to appreciate the golden principle of design – the asymmetrical triangle between earth, man and heaven – which is so beautiful and gives such a wonderful feeling of balance. The art is in making everything flow together in harmony. Although my garden is in no way Japanese, because I could not make one in this landscape even if I wanted to, I have assimilated some of their principles and ideas. I hope overall there is a balance and a harmony of shape, form, outline and texture.

I never realized at the time that these principles would have such a profound and long-lasting influence, but they underpin all my ideas about planting. Take my Mediterranean Garden, which is full of many different types of plant, but which I hope no-one would find garish or

'The way you group plants together is the whole essence of gardening. There are many ways of doing this, which is just as it should be – it would be very dull if everybody put their plants together in the same way.'

bitty. Why not? Because the plants are all adapted to much the same conditions. They blend well together while any monotony arising from having so many small-leaved plants together is broken by the use of handsome architectural ones, like cardoons and tall imposing fountains of grasses like *Stipa gigantea*.

'Harmonious' is a word I would like to apply to the garden, meaning that overall there is a feeling of simplicity and continuity, with wide grass curves and gentle walkways. I hope there is nothing abrupt or startling. I always prefer to plant in groups and to leave spaces in between the groups so that the design has greater depth, providing glimpses of different areas of the garden beyond. Big full-stop plants punctuate the design and add contrast, but never in a way that shocks or startles. Surprise elements are necessary; shock tactics are not.

The see-through tall plumes of *Stipa gigantea* make a great counterpoint to the lower-level, dense planting surrounding it.

PLANNING FOR COLOUR

Although I have views on which colours go well together in the garden (as discussed on pages 30-31), I would never deliberately plan a white garden, for instance. If you do, the danger is that you are going to take white plants requiring very different conditions and try to grow them all in one area. That goes against my theories of gardening. A white *Persicaria* needing moisture and heavy clay is not going to perform well if it is planted in the dry soil that suits *Oenothera lindheimeri* and white-flowered *Dianthus*. In my opinion, they just do not go together and I would be surprised if they all survived the same conditions.

I am not drawn to a garden planned in this way, as I find it artificial. It is heresy to say so, but the White Garden at Sissinghurst is not something I can totally admire. I first saw it many years ago and although my impression of it then was that it was very romantic, seeing it again recently I was not sure that I liked it, and I certainly did not feel

'What I enjoy most in my garden is the contrast of leaf and form, and, of course, the promise always of the flowers to come. If you go along a border and see everything flowering at the same time, you get that sickening feeling about what is going to be here in three weeks' time.'

The garden borders have no straight edges, but gentle curves invite the visitor to explore with expectation, whilst still offering a vista beyond. In this border, the big clump of tall Joe Pye weed, *Eupatorium maculatum* Purpurea Group, creates the 'full stop' punctuation point that Beth recommends for border planting.

at home in it even though I was very interested in the individual plants and excited by the great variety of white-flowering ones.

Equally, although I know that they are an integral part of classically styled gardens, I am not keen on clipped box hedges forming a barrier between me and the plants they enclose. I prefer plants to merge and flow together to soften the edges of the paths. When I say I do not like box hedges, it does not mean that I cannot accept them somewhere else, in the same way that one can enjoy many different styles of painting. Take a garden like Hidcote. Although I admire the combination of colours, the planting and design, with the compartments of the garden spread like rooms with Persian carpets of plants, I would never choose to make a garden like that.

Here I am never concerned if the colour has gone out of a border. I would not rush in to remedy the lack with begonias and dahlias. My style of gardening does not depend too much on colour and, where it does, it is in a more subtle way. Throughout spring and summer waves of soft colour ebb and flow through the basic patterns of foliage plants, which all produce flowers in their turn. Then, as the season wanes, little jewel-like autumn flowers

This delightful combination of foliage plants, where blue *Hosta* (Tardiana Group) 'Halcyon' contrasts with the yellow and green leaves of *Hakonechloa macra* 'Aureola', and softens the edge of a border below the clay bank in the Shady Walk.

add sparkle. A feeling for shape is just as important as a sense of colour. Often people who use colour very well fail to pay sufficient attention to form and outline.

When thinking of colour schemes for planting, you must again consider the situation. Where you have overcast skies, soft light most of the time and green that almost hurts because it is so bright, then the really savage reds, purples and blues of certain cultivars simply do not look right. Set against stonework, they look fine but in most temperate gardens the softer colours and smaller flowers of the species plants blend more sympathetically with the green environment.

The flowers of shade-loving plants are less brightly coloured on the whole than those of sun-loving ones. You are not going to get brilliant scarlet flowers on shade-loving plants – they tend to be more pastel-coloured on the whole. Many of the really brightly coloured flowers come from the desert areas of the world, where you have a deep-blue sky and a coppery sun bearing down. If you used pale colours in such a situation, they would look washed out but the contrast of brown or red soil with the scarlets, yellows and bright purples of big, brash flowers can be dramatic.

I find it difficult to use some strong flower colours. However, if I use them in small groups and if the flowers themselves are not huge, they can be successful. Take *Crocosmia* 'Lucifer', for instance, which I am just finding out how to place. I cannot mix it with my grey planting, which tends to have a lot of mauves and pinks and pale colours. But elsewhere I have found a way of combining it with acid yellows of euphorbias and with the dark blues of salvias, which balance its intensity. So, you can use intense colours, but preferably in small amounts. Too large a group of strongly coloured plants can be off-putting. They are best used as an accent, preferably with paler shades of the same colour grouped around them. You need to avoid a series

TOP Cool colours, like the pale lilac of the delicate flowers of *Anemonella thalictroides*, are typical of woodland plants that prefer a shady situation.

ABOVE The hotter colours, like the strong reds and oranges of *Crocosmia* cultivars, are more commonly found in those plants that prefer full sun.

of plants fighting each other in blocks of primary colours. Two strong shades together virtually cancel each other out, as your eye does not know where to turn. Each flower colour should enhance those nearby, either by blending in tone or by providing subtle contrast. If you use colour in this way, it enables you to see the other colours better. If they are all there in the same degree, the impact is so much less. Although it pays to lead in gradually to stronger colours, there are exceptions to the rule. I think the big blocks of guardsman-like rows of vividly coloured tulips in our public parks look wonderful, but you do need to be careful when using colour to observe its level of intensity, as it can be overpowering in a small garden.

'I always prefer to plant in groups and to leave spaces in between the groups so that the design has greater depth, providing glimpses of different areas of the garden beyond. Big, full-stop plants punctuate the design and add contrast, but never in a way that shocks or startles. Surprise elements are necessary; shock tactics are not.'

PLANNING FOR SMALL GARDENS

If my garden were smaller, I would have to think differently about the planting. In small gardens it is particularly important that you choose plants that offer more than just attractive flowers. At the risk of becoming a bore on the subject (it is a topic I keep returning to, both in this book and in others), I think all the plants in the garden, and even more so in a small garden, must have interesting or valuable leaf texture, colour or form. I think the same principles of planting for foliage first apply there too. You can have colour – but not sheets of colour – in small gardens. You have to give up the idea of great drifts of primulas, you may not even have roses (apart from one or two climbing or specimen roses), and you certainly will not be planting in clumps of fives or tens. If, on the other hand, the garden is completely overshadowed by tall buildings or trees, you can grow only the shade-loving plants, which gives your planting natural harmony.

In a very small garden, your aim has to be to cover every available surface with leaves that harmonize with one another. On the sunny side you will have the drought-

Evergreens can look heavy and dull, but when grouped using contrasts of leaf form, texture and colour, as with these two evergreen shrubs, *Fatsia japonica* and *Skimmia japonica* 'Rubella', the result is much more lively.

loving varieties with grey, succulent or leathery leaves, and on the shady side you will have ferns, hostas, dicentras – the more delicate-foliaged plants.

There is hardly a garden that does not have two different climates, created by the shade of house walls. When a garden is in full sun most of the day, you can add shade by planting suitable trees and shrubs. (You can also create new environments for smaller plants by making raised beds.) However, if you have a new house on a housing estate, you probably will not have any shade except under the walls – perhaps a boundary wall, or the north- or east-facing walls of the house. If the road runs east to west, which side of the street you live on is important: gardens on one side will all be south-facing and those on the other side of the street will all be north-facing. The gardens on the sunny side of the street (which get the hot afternoon sun) will be able to grow very different plants from those on the north, cool side of the street. The north-facing back gardens will provide ideal homes for hostas and hydrangeas, while the houses on the other side of the street will be able to grow these in their front gardens, and vice versa.

A good solution for a town garden is to use water to create a very different atmosphere. Even a small pool can bring an extra dimension to the garden. Being able to touch water, watch reflections or sit in the shade of arching bamboos (provided their roots are restricted) blots out the buildings beyond by concentrating the mind on a tiny oasis of green.

THINKING AHEAD

Gardeners rarely become bored, but even the most enthusiastic of us become exhausted from time to time, not just physically but emotionally and mentally as well. We get frustrated, as does everyone else, by the weather, or pests, or whatever problem may be paramount. No-one can live on a topnote all the time. If I am downcast

about something or other, a walk round the garden almost any day of the year will usually restore me, though I must confess that after the freak hurricane in October 1987 there were times on gloomy November mornings when I did not want to go into the garden at all. But once I started thinking about how I would actually tackle the damage from both the storms and the unusually wet summer, the enthusiasm came back. I believe it is working in and re-making the garden that gives the most enjoyment, far more than simply admiring the results. It can well be the digging and delving on a miserable winter's day that starts to lift the spirits, as you suddenly see a way to make something fresh, to bring new vitality into the garden.

The small paved garden near Beth's house. Her design for this small area would translate well into a town garden. Following the suggestions she makes in this chapter, the area with the feature vase could easily be turned into a small formal pool to bring an extra dimension to the garden.

The Gravel Garden
formerly the Entrance Garden

Beth's description (from pages 36-44) is of the Entrance Garden, the precursor to her Gravel Garden (created over 1991 and 1992 after The Green Tapestry *was published). David Ward introduces the reasons for the change and, at the end of Beth's discussion about the original Entrance Garden, summarizes how the Gravel Garden subsequently developed from it.*

IT WAS IN 1990 that Beth was given the opportunity to purchase three acres of the neighbouring farmland. The Entrance Garden, and the west-facing border Beth described in her original text, ran along the length of the old, grassed car park. With increasing numbers of visitors, the additional area would allow Beth to find a home for her ever-growing selection of sun-loving, drought-resistant plants. A famously dry area of the garden, the redesign and replanting gave her the scope to expand on the lessons she had learned on combining drought-resistant plants that would flourish in these conditions,

Not only is this area of the garden dry, but so is the region, with an average annual rainfall barely over 20in/51cm. So Beth decided that, apart from initial watering when planting, this part of the garden would never be artificially watered. Therefore, plant choice was critical.

Early summer sees the Gravel Garden at its most colourful. Here
Iris 'Jane Phillips' is underplanted with a delightful self-seeding
hardy annual, *Omphalodes linifolia*. The soft yellow of *Erysimum
pulchellum* sets off the irises and the purple flowers of a shrubby
sage, *Salvia lavandulifolia*.

THE ENTRANCE GARDEN

When you come in through the main gate, the first impression is of the great sweep of the west-facing border on your left-hand side. Originally, I had intended to put in only shrubs here, and began by planting deciduous trees at the back of the border as a windbreak, with laurels, hollies and cotoneasters to form groups of drought-resisting evergreens. A few years after that I planted the long hedge of × *Cuprocyparis leylandii* behind as extra protection. At the time of writing (Note: in 1989), the border is very mixed, with trees, shrubs, perennials and bulbs as the wider the contrast of shapes and forms, the better it looks.

I consider the planting of this very large border to be 'coarse' planting as opposed to the type of planting in my little Mediterranean Garden behind the house (see page 184) where the groups are smaller in scale and the plants themselves are smaller. This is a big entrance garden, deliberately planned to be a low-maintenance one, because

The Leyland cypress hedge that formed the east boundary to the Entrance Garden still remains, now sheltering the Gravel Garden from the cold winds. The border is now much deeper than when it was fronted by the grassed car park. A self-seeded mullein, *Verbascum bombyciferum*, adds height where the lower level planting merges with the gravelled path.

Unlike the achilleas that were formerly used in this area but did not fare well under the no-watering regime of the new Gravel Garden, bergenias thrive in the dry soil and open position, flowering abundantly in spring and colouring as well as ever in winter.

we do not have the time to spend on a border far away from the rest of the garden. Rather than fussy planting with hundreds of varieties, I initially put in large groups of a few varieties of bold and easy plants, like bergenias and achilleas. Although I have concentrated on creating contrast in leaf form, the planting is not without colour. On a sunny day in winter, the big glistening bergenia leaves, showing many tones of red, make exciting contrast with other evergreens.

Bergenias need the right setting. I use them as major 'full-stop' plants among small-leaved foliage plants. Their big round leathery leaves catching the light in the sun make a marvellous foil to the crinkly, fussy leaves of *Cistus*, *Santolina* and Spanish gorse, *Genista hispanica*. They look good, too, against the verticals of *Iris foetidissima* with its strap-shaped leaves, and they all provide different tones and colours – especially in winter, when many leaves are reddened by cold. The hebe nearby makes a lovely contrast of scale and texture. (Note: As the new Gravel Garden took shape, several plants from the original long border in the Entrance Garden were saved to be replanted in the Gravel Garden. The bergenias proved invaluable in forming large groups throughout the newly planted beds.)

' Throughout spring and summer waves of soft colour ebb and flow through the basic patterns of foliage plants, which all produce flowers in their turn.'

Quite often people fail to be bold enough in their plant groupings and then do not get the full effect. Of course, if you have a very small garden and you love collecting plants, it is tempting to try and put as many in as you can, but one plant alone rarely looks good. One clump of *Iris foetidissima* can be very effective, but you need at least three plants of *Bergenia* to form a bold clump. Again, if bergenias are left year after year they become leggy, with long woody stems. It is better to dig them up and divide and replant them every few years.

The way you group plants together is the whole essence of gardening. There are many ways of doing this, which is just as it should be – it would be very dull if everybody put their plants together in the same way. Designing a garden is rather like painting. Two painters will take the same pigments but will produce an entirely different picture, just as we do with our plants. But there are some rules. The soil here is very poor – the same dry gravel that I have in the Mediterranean Garden. Over the years I added humus and a mulch of straw at the back of the borders, which helps to feed the soil and improve the texture. But it is a free-draining gravel and, if we have a drought in summer, these plants may have no measurable water from June till September. They have all been chosen because they can withstand these conditions – with leathery leaves (like bergenias), or finely cut leaves (like santolinas), or 'fat' leaves (like sedums – now *Hylotelephium*) to help them retain moisture. Although they may suffer in times of prolonged drought, they will not die and this is the main consideration behind my choice of plants – here you will see no asters, goldenrods, hostas or delphiniums, all of which need retentive soil and adequate rainfall to thrive.

The border is backed, as I said, by a × *Cuprocyparis leylandii* hedge. I always swore I would not have any more hedges to cut, but we had to have a boundary between us

The crown imperial fritillary, *Fritillaria imperialis*, comes in shades of yellow, red or fiery orange. It rapidly shoots up and by April is a magnificent sight in full flower, before the top growth starts to yellow and die back in mid-summer.

and our neighbour's fruit farm. (Note: this is now the car park.) We also needed shelter from the north-east winds sweeping across the North Sea from the Russian Steppes. Even when young, at 3m/10ft high and around 45cm/18in wide, it makes a good, protective background.

(Note: This hedge still remains a vital backdrop to the Gravel Garden and although its height has been kept in check, its width has increased enormously. In 2020, two massive free-standing leylandii at the top of the Gravel Garden had to be removed, something we had been putting off for years. The space and light created 'gives us the opportunity to replant some old favourites as well some new introductions. For small gardens, there are slow-growing hedging plants on a more compact scale that would be preferable.)

Tall stands of crown imperial fritillary, *Fritillaria imperialis*, shoot up rapidly in April, while the taller alliums, such as *Allium hollandicum*, make interesting verticals in May and June. Large bulky masses of *Euphorbia characias* subsp. *wulfenii* and the lower-growing *E. epithymoides* (syn. *E. polychroma*) illuminate the border from March until June with vivid lime-green heads. Woven through many green-leaved plants, including Oriental poppies,

An ever-narrower gap in the leylandii hedge serves as the entrance from the car park beyond but this area is now full of form and texture all year round (seen here in autum), with its rivers of gravel interspersed with island beds of planting.

OVERLEAF High summer in the Gravel Garden sees it at its most spectacular. A stately *Yucca gloriosa* in full bloom dominates the scene. The silvery Miss Willmott's ghost, *Eryngium giganteum*, a long-term resident of the old Entrance Garden, is allowed to seed among stands of the Mexican feather grass, *Stipa tenuissima*, and clumps of yet-to-flower agapanthus.

spurges and bergenias, are grey and silver mounds of *Ballota, Santolina* and *Artemisia*. I scattered seed of the Peruvian lily, *Alstroemeria ligtu* hybrids, which flourish in the warm, free-draining soil and seed themselves into their neighbours. Other interesting verticals are formed with *Asphodelus albus* followed by the yellow asphodelines. The foxtail lily, *Eremurus robustus*, stands out well against the clipped leylandii hedge, and so, too, do great cloudy masses of honey-scented *Crambe cordifolia*.

Additional background trees and shrubs have been chosen to provide good form and contrast of foliage. They include a Chinese wild apple, *Malus hupehensis*, *Rosa glauca, Genista aetnensis* and *Crataegus persimilis* 'Prunifolia', whose polished leaves turn the most vivid red in autumn. (Note: As this long border became integrated into the new Gravel Garden, many of these trees and shrubs were removed and replaced with plants more suited to the

Looking down the long hedge-side border serves as reminder of just how many of the same type of plants from the original planting found their way into the Gravel Garden. Most, such as catmints, euphorbias and lamb's ears, go from strength to strength but a few, such as this lovely pink *Papaver* (Oriental Group) 'Cedric Morris', have unfortunately died out, falling victim to a destructive form of mildew disease.

changing conditions and look. For example the *Malus* and *Crataegus* were removed, whereas the *Rosa glauca* and *Genista* were incorporated into the design.)

Most of the autumn tidying-up is for aesthetic reasons, but in some cases it is better to leave the tops of the plants for protection in winter. It can be quite difficult to decide what should be left so that the garden retains some interest. But if you have planted the garden with forethought, it should still look good even when most of the summer performers have died down or been removed. When I walk round the water gardens in winter, I have to rely entirely on my memory of what was there, but almost all the bones of the planting of the entrance border remain and the only things to have disappeared will be the collapsing stems of the summer-flowering plants.

One of the summer-long features in this border is the artichoke-like plant, the cardoon, *Cynara cardunculus*, with graceful arching sprays of silver-grey foliage. When these become battered and damaged, they have to be removed, as do the fern heads before they have seeded. *Hylotephium* 'Herbstfreude' still has good form and deep colour even in January, and sometimes I leave it standing all winter. Bergenia leaves also look attractive all winter, with luck. Some of them turn red and yellow in late autumn before they die, but others remain throughout the winter, turning rich shades of cherry-red and plum at the first winter chill.

When I first made this bed, I did not necessarily use the usual wide backbone structure of trees and shrubs because at the time I could not afford to buy a great quantity. I tended, as I have done so often, to grow what I could from seeds or from cuttings. But over the years the plants have grown, and changes have been made. Some were too close together, while others were damaged by storms and had to be removed.

The large stonecrop, *Hylotelephium* 'Herbstfreude' has the bonus of good structural seed-heads in autumn and winter as the striking brick-red flowers gradually lose their colour.

'If you have planted the garden with forethought, it should still look good even when most of the summer performers have died down or been removed.'

Once you have finished mourning the loss of favourite plants, it can be exciting to realize that you now have the space for something new. At the end of the border nearer the house is an enormous pollarded oak. It is a magnificent tree with several secondary trunks springing from its pollarded main trunk. Underneath its canopy, I planted a number of good, tough ground-cover plants. In summer, the oak leaves make a complete umbrella so the soil can become very dry. For years I struggled to establish plants in it. Eventually I planted the golden, variegated-leaved holly, *Ilex × altaclerensis* 'Golden King' which made a handsome bush. In spring, the floor is carpeted with aconites and snowdrops – *Galanthus elwesii* is such a good, bold snowdrop – with colchicums to follow them in autumn.

Very good with the snowdrops are arums, *Arum italicum* subsp. *italicum* 'Marmoratum' (syn. *A. i.* subsp. *i.* 'Pictum'). In one place in the gardens it seems to have crossed with our native *Arum maculatum*, giving a new plant with much larger leaves but with the beautiful veining of the former. These leaves, at least 30cm/1ft long and almost as much across, start coming up in the autumn and are at their best in spring, when the green spathes of the flowers appear, and then there is nothing until the red berries in autumn.

(Note: These now get removed as, 30 years on, Beth's favourite arums have become the bane of the garden, having spread everywhere. While they still provide valuable winter interest, they smother smaller plants and the bulbs and bulbils produced are impossible to eradicate. Removing the berries before they ripen has become an annual chore to prevent birds from eating them and dropping the seeds.)

THE GRAVEL GARDEN

At this point, Dave Ward picks up the story:
Beth had been growing drought-resistant plants for around 40 years but in 1991 she was faced with a new challenge.

The backlit flowers of *Stipa gigantea* are the focal point in this early-morning view towards the house, taken in late November. On the right is the enormous pollarded English oak, *Quercus robur*, possibly 400 years old, balanced on the left by one of the remaining eucalyptus.

The decision to move the visitors' car park, on the west side of the leylandii hedge, to ground beyond it added around three-quarters of an acre to the gardens. In addition to the poor, compacted soil, the gardens experienced low rainfall and drying winds. Beth then decided that this new part of the garden would never be artificially watered, emphasizing the need to choose only plants that were naturally adapted to these conditions and so the concept of a gravel garden was born. Beth's design inspiration was that of a dried-up-river bed: a flowing sequence of island beds in sinuous curves around gravel paths. She executed it by means of her time-honoured technique of using hosepipes to lay out her plans on the ground, rather than planning it in advance on paper. This enabled her to consider the relationship of one bed to another, while looking ahead to the next

Everywhere in the gardens you can find Beth's much-loved, but now contentious *Arum italicum* subsp. *italicum* 'Marmoratum'. Its wavy-edged, attractively marbled leaves still provide good ground cover but preventing it from spreading too vigorously has become a major task.

section to make sure the major and minor pathways flowed unobtrusively. It was important, she realized, to consider the whole picture and the detail simultaneously, to get the balance right.

Because the ground was so heavily compacted, Beth abandoned her usual process of hand-digging for the new beds. A subsoiler was hired to break up the compacted soil and the area was then ploughed, turning in the dug-up grass. After that, the ploughed furrows were rolled. Because the soil was so poor, it was essential to conserve any moisture, and to this end Beth decided to cover the the beds with homemade and mushroom compost, as well as bonfire waste, all of which was incorporated to a depth of two spits. While this might be thought excessive for drought-tolerant plants on more standard soil, Beth felt the aim should never be to expect plants to put up with the worst you can offer, but to give them the best possible start so that they build up a good root structure and thus tolerate greater extremes of drought and cold.

KEY

1 *Agapanthus* (×1)
2 *Allium × hollandicum* 'Purple Sensation' (drift)
3 *Allium sphaerocephalon* (drift)
4 *Ballota pseudodictamnus* (×1)
5 *Bergenia* (×14)
6 *Cistus × argenteus* 'Peggy Sammons' (×1)
7 *Euphorbia characias* subsp. *wulfenii* (×3)
8 *Oenothera lindheimeri* (×1)
9 *Hylotelephium* 'Herbstfreude' (×1)
10 *Juniperus scopulorum* 'Blue Arrow' (×1)
11 *Nepeta* (×3)
12 *Origanum vulgare* 'Thumble's Variety' (×5)
13 *Scilla* (drift)
14 *Stachys byzantina* (×7)
15 *Stipa gigantea* (×1)
16 *Stipa tenuissima* (×6)
17 *Teucrium × lucidrys* (×7)
18 *Thymus* (×8)

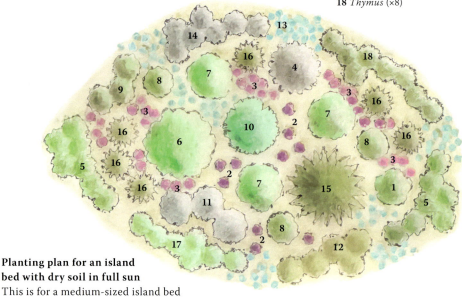

Planting plan for an island bed with dry soil in full sun
This is for a medium-sized island bed approx. 8m/26ft wide by 5m/16ft deep.

Planting the Gravel Garden

Beth's preference in her planting for creating a rich tapestry-like effect that varied over the seasons was achieved by planting vertically as well as horizontally, so that as one group of plants died back, the first leaves of a new group were pushing through. An important element of this is to encourage a fluid intermingling of plants and allowing plants to self-seed, where they can find their own space. Many visitors ask if a membrane is used to help control weeds. As well as being highly impractical on such a scale, the plan was for the plants themselves to smother the weeds, so we needed the plants to self-seed. Obviously, this was managed originally by the skilled and experienced eye of Beth and her gardeners, and is still carried on by the latter today.

The dominant plants

Each of the beds was organized using Beth's key principle of beginning with the dominant plants, around which a chorus of smaller plants could be added. She also chose to position a few well-placed light trees to provide a sense of scale to the area, while not creating too much shade. To break up the density of the background border of the leylandii hedge and being keen, as always, to paint the sky as well as the ground, Beth planted several eucalyptus trees, three of which now dominate the skyline in this part of the gardens. One of these mountain gums, *Eucalyptus dalrympleana*, which she originally kept cut back to form a handsome background shrub, now forms a striking feature, towering over the Gravel Garden (although the mountain gum should never be planted anywhere near buildings, due to its questing roots). Smaller trees were chosen to create punctuation points, without casting too much shade. Several specimens of *Genista aetnensis*, the Mount Etna broom, with its graceful form and showers of scented yellow

A pair of stately verbascums frame the view of the planting beyond. Both a vertical and a dominant plant, the indispensable *Verbascum bombyciferum* often self-seeds. As it is easy to remove the seedlings, gardeners choose to leave only the best-placed ones in the permanent planting.

flowers in summer, were planted to provide structure to the Gravel Garden beds. But it is important not to plant too many shade-casting trees or shrubs, as drought-resistant plants are invariably sun lovers. Verticals, in the form of conifers, are also a good choice along with the blue junipers, such as *Juniperus scopulorum* 'Blue Arrow'.

The under-storey

Planting the island beds called for lower-growing plants that would survive in free-draining soils with little in the way of summer rainfall. These can be predominantly found on the borders of the Mediterranean. They include many of the silvery-leaved plants, like various forms of lavender, white-felted *Ballota pseduodictamnus* and the woolly leaves of *Santolina chamaecyparissus*, as well as artemisias in many different shapes and sizes, ranging from large feathery shrubs to silky mat-formers spreading over the gravel. As too many rounded bun-like shapes look monotonous, Beth added dramatic vertical perennials, like *Verbascum bombyciferum*, with its rosette of felted silvery leaves at the base crowned with spires of small yellow flowers in summer. The spires of *Salvia* 'Blue Spire' add a soft haze of colour in the summer, as do the mauve flower-heads of *Verbena bonariensis,* from summer into autumn.

Bulbs also perform a similar function. Beth liked to place the cricket-ball sized heads of various alliums at the back of the borders where their rosy mauve flowers were set off by the dark contrast of the hedge. Other good bulbs for vertical interest in early summer are *Nectaroscordum siculum* subsp. *bulgaricum* (syn. *Allium siculum* subsp. *dioscoridis*), *Gladiolus communis* subsp. *byzantinus* and *Fritillaria persica.*

The Gravel Garden includes many drought-resistant plants whose leaves have adapted in one way or another to conserve moisture and resist scorching. Some plants

'My approach to the Gravel Garden was to achieve the layers of interest over time, allowing the seasonal effect to build up as my experiment progressed.'

Two dominant trees of the Gravel Garden. In July, the yellow pea-like flowers of the Mount Etna broom, *Genista aetnensis,* spread their delicious scent. Behind it, the quick-growing mountain gum, *Eucalyptus dalrympleana,* is not a tree for smaller spaces, as it has now reached around 20m/65ft in 30 years.

adapt to dry conditions by having finely cut leaves. Big soft leaves, like those of hostas or the delicate trails of *Tiarella* all scorch easily and must be grown in shade. There are very few plants in this part of the garden which have large plain leaves, apart from yuccas, with stiff, sword-shaped leaves, and bergenias, with tough, leathery leaves. A final adaptation with many bulbs and a few plants is to appear early in the year but then lose their leaves and return to a dormant state before the onset of drought.

While most people accept that they will put their small plants at the front of a bed and their large plants at the back, this principle is boring if adhered to too rigidly. To have the occasional plant which breaks that habit and comes forward as a mound or even a small vertical on the front edge of the bed creates an element of surprise, rather than the inevitable flat mat. To depart from these basic principles will help to create a much more lively, three-dimensional element.

The other principle Beth used in planting is based on the asymmetric triangle (see page 26). As she said, 'This is difficult to explain but easy to understand when you see it.' Looked at it in profile, it passes through tiny-leaved, sweetly

OPPOSITE *Verbascum bombyciferum* is ideally adapted to survive these dry conditions, its felted silver-white leaves both reflecting light and trapping moisture in the hairy coating. With all these plants originating from drier regions around the world, and requiring similar conditions, they naturally associate well together.

Bulbs are ideally suited to being grown in dry conditions as they are often dormant by mid-summer. The unusual *Nectaroscordum siculum* subsp. *bulgaricum* (syn. *Allium siculum* subsp. *dioscoridis*), with its attractively drooping heads of two-tone flowers, is later than most to do so in June, by which time its foliage will have died back.

scented thymes, and groups of low-growing euphorbias, through larger mounds of silvery-grey lavender and ballota, to *Euphorbia characias* subsp. *wulfenii*, say, which is taller still, until we meet a taller shrub, perhaps an amelanchier. But the eye has been lifted, and the line leads up to the sky, perhaps to a *Cupressus arizonica* beyond – a useful drought-loving coniferous tree. The skyline should not look as though the plants had been pushed in like walking-sticks in a hallstand; they should carry a profile. This may not happen everywhere, but where it does, it makes an effective frame for the view beyond.

A loose, informal tapestry of foliage and flower, as well as verticals and levels. The round purple heads and stiff stems of *Allium sphaerocephalon* contrast well with the feathery grass, *Stipa tenuissima*, while the rigid spikes of *Verbascum chaixii* are setting seed above a lone opportunistic seedling of the silvery Miss Willmott's ghost, *Eryngium giganteum*.

It was of equal importance, according to Beth, to consider the contribution that foliage shape, texture and colour add to the mix, 'It is a never-ending pleasure making patterns with leaves, regardless of the flowers. In the drier parts of the garden, even in November, when there is not a flower in sight, there is still plenty of colour with silver and grey, grey-blue and glaucous green. Bronze tangles of shrubby potentillas add warmth. There is still a lot of colour without flowers. Just as interesting are the many forms and textures, with very feathery leaves and larger simpler leaves which you must have for contrast. If the overall design is fussy, made with only tiny leaves like those of thyme and lavender, there is no impact. To create impact, look for striking leaf forms like *Euphorbia characias* subsp. *wulfenii*, and, in the background, the fine bright sword-shaped leaves of *Iris foetidissima. Ballota* is another good contrast plant, with its mounds of velvety, almost suede-like white leaves. If we have a really severe winter, we may lose most of the top growth, but it always comes back again from the base.'

Billowing lime-green heads of *Euphorbia characias* subsp. *wulfenii* complete the line of the border, running down from the taller conifer beyond, creating a perfect contrasting frame for the blues and purples of the irises and alliums.

As part of the plan for creating contrast in the planting, Beth often chose to add accents of very bright colour among the softer palette, for which she found kniphofias to be very effective. She had selected good forms from seedlings over many years, so she had a wide range of sizes and colours to choose from, from deep reds and bright oranges to softer apricot, lemon or even green tones. Contrasting red with an acid yellow green was another favourite. In spring, that could be created with the bright red flowers of *Anemone × fulgens* and the yellow-greens of euphorbias or, in the summer, from the scarlet flowers of crocosmias growing amongst the seeding stands of *Bupleurum falcatum*.

Beth persisted with bedding out certain half-hardy plants, not only nicotiana, but plants such as cosmos, particularly the white *Cosmos bipinnatus* 'Purity' and the trailing *Bidens ferulifolia*, which she loved to see trailing

In general, a bright but soft palette of colours works best for the style and feel of the Gravel Garden. In fact, few drought-resistant plants are not in pastel shades. Here an unknown cultivar of *Alstroemeria* creates a pool of softly contrasting colour among the greys and greens of *Ballota*, euphorbias and bergenias, with the tall, arching plumes of the long flowering grass, *Ampelodesmos mauritanicus*, bringing the eye up to the shrubs and trees behind.

over the green summer foliage of the bergenias, but, as gaps were filled with more permanent planting, she stopped.

We continue with the practice of planting out large, specimen *Agave americana*. These are particularly useful for adding a more structural focus point to some areas of the Gravel Garden, as well as giving it a more 'arid' feel.

THE SEASONAL CHANGES

Walking through the Gravel Garden as I do on an almost daily basis, it will often strikes me how interesting it still looks throughout the winter months. Even with fresh growth emerging as the year progresses, Beth's commitment to the key principles of structure, form, and texture are never more apparent than in this part of the garden, no matter what the season.

Spring

The intrinsic qualities of winter notwithstanding, the arrival of spring sunshine and warmth are always welcome. Carpets of established spring bulbs in this part of the garden start to flower with scillas, puschkinias and ipheions in shades of blue, whilst self-seeding groups of *Anemone pavonina* in pink, red, white, and even salmon, pop up where the fancy takes them. The emerging foliage of later-flowering bulbs – alliums and species tulips in particular – can be seen among the small bushes and ground cover with the promise of more soon to follow.

Unless March remains cold, as it often can in the east of England, the Gravel Garden is tidied up, grasses cut down and spent seed heads removed. As the daylight increases, those bergenias that have lit up the winter garden with their burnished-plum foliage now revert to green as their April blossoms come and go, often in harmony with the light apple-green heads of *Helleborus argutifolius*. The slowly developing buds of *Euphorbia characias* subsp.

'I was surprised and delighted how well everything has grown. The hot dry spell in May and June 1996 was a testing time, but welcome rain came in time while it was still warm for everything to put on new growth, so that already this new garden has an established look. During the summer I used several half-hardy plants like the green-flowered tobacco, Nicotiana 'Lime Green' *to fill in gaps... there will be much to learn from this experiment.'*

wulfenii finally unfurl to provide bright splashes of yellowy-green, often accompanied in April by the scarlet flowers of *Fritillaria imperialis*, a survivor of the original Entrance Garden border. On a smaller scale, this eye-catching colour combination can be repeated with *Euphorbia epithymoides* 'Major' contrasting with the brilliant scarlet flowers of *Anemone × fulgens*.

Summer

As spring merges into early summer, the alliums have come and gone but we leave their seed-heads for as long as we dare (they are prolific seeders in this dry, warm soil). The gravel mulch, so apparent in the spring, disappears, having been covered by the lush growth of plants racing to flower before it gets too hot and dry. Beth's bun-shaped plants, ballota, santolinas, lavender, rock and sun roses for example, are now fully furnished and create domes through which vertical spikes of plants arise, such as *Asphodelus albus*, *Verbascum bombyciferum*, or the giant Greek fennel, *Ferula communis*.

Over the years, self-seeding hardy annuals have established themselves, although heavily edited and controlled lest they become too out-of-hand. An unusual silver-veined thistle, *Galactites tomentosa*, in its white form always draws comment from visitors, as does our insistence in allowing only the creamy-yellow form of the typically orange poppy, *Eschscholzia californica*.

Annual poppies suit the dry east Anglian climate, with Cedric Morris's much treasured pastel selection of our native field poppy, *Papaver rhoeas* 'Mother of Pearl', encouraged to form colonies, although any wild red forms are diligently removed, as they would soon dominate if allowed to seed. Recent times have given us *Papaver dubium* subsp. *lecoqii* 'Albiflorum', now known as Beth's poppy, although its origins are unclear.

This shorter form of giant fennel, *Ferula tingitana* 'Cedric Morris', has much shinier foliage and provides a useful, medium-sized vertical with branching heads of small yellow flowers on slender stems.

While some of Beth's original choices have not survived the harsh, dry conditions, others have thrived. This is true even within a genus, such as *Anthemis*, where those with grey foliage have become stalwarts, while those with green foliage, such as *Anthemis tinctoria* 'E. C. Buxton', struggle. Other mainstays of the Gravel Garden throughout the summer include *Oenothera* (formerly *Gaura*) *lindheimeri* and *Verbena bonariensis*, which achieves only half its normal height. Agapanthus thrive too, flowering well in the warm soil. Grasses create an important long-lasting feature here and we simply could not do without *Stipa tenuissima* or the tall golden oat grass, *S. gigantea*, both lasting well into the winter.

This wider view of the scene shown in detail on pages 34-35 demonstrates just how well that group blends with its surrounding planting. The delight of this part of the garden lies in its interest at several different levels: from the sprawling plants at the forefront through to taller plants behind and the shrubs and trees above.

Autumn

In the autumn months the Gravel Garden sees a gradual return to the dominance of structure while flowers still come and go. Autumn bulbs, after a summer of dormancy – the ideal way to survive summer drought – pop up unexpectedly, creating a mini-spring-like effect before the onset of winter. Crocus-like colchicums flower along the shadier side of the Gravel Garden during September and October, while the true autumn crocus is represented by *Crocus speciosus* 'Albus' with its sharply pointed petals just waiting for a mild day to display their full glory. Sedums (now renamed *Hylotelephium*) and grasses must be mentioned as key players at this time of year, as the scene once again is of fresh seed-heads intermingled with splashes of autumn foliage colour

For many years, a stag's horn sumac, *Rhus typhina*, provided a blaze of shrubby autumn colour adjacent to our tearoom, but eventually it became less and less healthy and had to be removed. Close by, growing beneath the ever-encroaching canopy of the ancient pollarded oak, is *Amelanchier lamarckii*, turning spectacular shades of orange-red. This was a favourite shrub of Beth's, adaptable and widely used throughout the garden. At the foot of a shrubby *Euphorbia characias* subsp. *wulfenii*, its buds tightly furled at the tip of each stem, can be found *Bergenia* 'Mrs Crawford' as the first bergenia leaves beginning to change colour when, once again, the days shorten and the temperature drops.

THE GRAVEL GARDEN TODAY

Beth often referred to the Gravel Garden as 'starting out like a baby, needing constant care and attention, then becoming an unruly teenager, which needed to be kept in check, before maturing into an adult, and settling down'. Now, I guess, the adult has become middle aged

Once the planting is reduced to its bare bones in winter, its intentionally river-like flow becomes much more apparent; the foreground bed was planted in 2019 when the two original beds were joined together.

In late summer the garden wears a different coat. The palette moves to soft golds and browns, when the Mexican feather grasses, *Stipa tenuissima*, are at their best on a sunny day, the light catching their feathery plumes and glinting on the bright yellow flowers of the Mount Etna broom, *Genista aetnensis*, in the background.

and constant repair and replanting have become more of a theme of recent years as we try to manage this and all the other areas of the garden. Two recent dry summers (in 2018 and 2020) have made us aware we need to plant more sustainably and to look closely at the range of plants we now consider to be drought-resistant.

We are always looking to introduce new plants and extend the palette of those we use. On reviewing the plant lists contained in *The Gravel Garden*, published in 2000, it was interesting to note that Beth did not mention two plants that are now a major summer feature of the Gravel Garden: a grass, *Stipa barbata*, and the Californian tree poppy, *Romneya coulteri*, while many plants from the original planting have not proved sufficiently drought-resistant over the years, including anthemis, achilleas or Beth's lovely, self-selected seedling, *Kniphofia* 'Little Maid'. We are always slightly wary of introducing any new plants that might cause problems further down the line (being keen to avoid another *Arum* situation) so we will not be replanting *Euphorbia cyparissias* 'Fen's Ruby' here again, as it has proved to spread way too enthusiastically.

The recent removal of the two large leylandiis has exposed, as we knew it would, an unsightly telegraph pole with its associated cables. The reason Beth planted the conifers there was to hide this eyesore. (As she later admitted, she probably chose the wrong plant, as leylandiis cannot be cut back into old wood because they will not grow back.) In their place, to do the same job, but positioned well away from the pole and its attendant cables, we have planted a fast-growing, narrow-leaved black peppermint, *Eucalyptus nicholii*.

But, as Beth herself would say, 'Not all plants will be successful. Some may die, others may prove unsuitable... making the garden is like working on a canvas, painting in highlights and shadows – never can one say, it is finished!'

The Water Garden

The Water Garden remains largely unchanged from its original concept. Apart from the cycle of renewal of herbaceous planting every few years and the loss of the occasional tree or shrub, the main structure has continued to mature. Unsurprisingly, many of the issues Beth writes about here still cause concern, including the build-up of silt in the ponds, the battle against blanket weed, the pond edges collapsing and the overly vigorous natives (celandines), to mention a few. One constant has been the peace and tranquillity that perhaps only a water garden can achieve.

I DOUBT whether I would have made a water garden if I had not had a naturally wet site, and I have no experience of making such a garden in any other way – for example, by using pond liners and so on. Plants suitable for water gardens range from those adapted to growing in the water itself, such as waterlilies and certain irises, through those found around the water's edge – marginal plants, like bog primulas – and finally to large perennials like astilbes, ligularias and persicarias, which need soil that is not waterlogged but remains damp throughout the summer. For a water garden to look natural, this transition of soil conditions must already exist or be provided.

The naturally wet conditions around the water's edge come alive in late spring. Below ground for most of the winter, the emerging plants race ahead as the season progresses. Foliage dominates here, with large-leaved ligularias and gunneras contrasting well with the grassy clumps of *Miscanthus*. Yellow globes of *Trollius × cultorum* 'Helios' pick up the lime-green of the mounds of *Euphorbia palustris*, as the grassed walkway leads across the ponds.

In the shallow depression between the south-west boundary and the house, we had a spring-fed ditch which formed the basis of the water garden we eventually made here. We started by widening part of the ditch into a single pond and initially we thought, 'Wonderful, now we can have sheets of primulas and sheaves of water iris'. But since we had not done nearly enough to improve the heavy clay soil, the sheets of primulas never materialized. Only a few big and hefty plants survived the original planting and it was several years before I realized I would have to start all over again.

One cold February morning, the drag line (a machine with a great bucket on the end of a chain) arrived on its caterpillar tracks to make a new pond. Suddenly, I had to be crystal clear in my mind about what I wanted to have done, since these large machines can excavate so quickly that the geography of the garden can be transformed in

Mixed colonies of orange and apricot Candelabra primulas, mainly *Primula bulleyana*, colonize the damp soil around clumps of shallow-rooted astilbes, for which summer moisture is a must. Here, a careful eye is kept on the large parasol-shaped leaves of *Darmera peltata*, its thick, green rhizomes slowly but surely creeping over the muddy soil.

a very short space of time. It is not possible to be totally exact about creating ponds. I knew what I wanted, but as the scene changes so quickly and everywhere is reduced to oozing mud, it has to be done with hope and faith in both yourself and the operator. By making several ponds on gently dropping levels, I planned to drown a lot of my problems where the land was very waterlogged and full of all kinds of scrubby bushes and weeds, including willows, marsh thistles and rushes. We excavated fairly shallow pools because the deeper you excavate, the greater the piles of clay you have to remove. Some of the soil was used to make dams, thus forming four large pools. Because the clay was so dense down in the hollow there was no need to line the ponds or even to puddle the sides to make them watertight. We removed some clay from the top spit of land around them and added lighter soil from elsewhere plus copious dressings of any organic matter we could find to create planting areas around the water's margins. We have such a diversity of soils here that we can often utilize one type to improve another. The clay that came out of the bottom of the ponds was carted away to make the west boundary, where newly established trees and shrubs now grow very well.

You can make a boggy area in gravel or other non-retentive soil by sinking plastic sheeting some way down beneath the soil surface, just as your pond itself will also need to be lined with plastic sheeting, but you would have to put the polythene at least 60cm/2ft under the surface of the soil. A gunnera, for example, would not be supported in only that depth of soil. It would need a deep, damp, rich soil although its roots do not necessarily need to be in water. It can be grown on the edge of a lawn as a specimen, or in a damp hollow, but it must not dry out. You need an annual rainfall of about 75-100cm/30-40in; otherwise you will have to water it. And never try to grow it in dry, light soil.

Connecting the ponds, as the levels drop through the Water Garden, this ditch slowly meanders its way around the rising bole of a swamp cypress, *Taxodium distichum*. Above the gulley, an ageing white cherry, *Prunus* 'Tai-haku', sheds is autumn leaves.

OVERLEAF Grasses reflect well in the open water of the pump pond. On this bankside, dark flowered *Miscanthus sinensis* 'Poseidon' dominates while the unusual New Zealand toetoe grass, *Cortaderia richardii*, becomes established.

Many gardeners feel the urge to make a small artificial pool with a few suitable plants around it. You can make very pretty water gardens using just half a wine cask let into the ground (allowing it to leak a little to moisten the soil around the outside). Use plants that look appropriate to water such as rush- or iris-like plants, or those with big, round leaves. Make one or two good contrasts of shape but leave it at that and avoid fussy planting. For goodness sake, do not put in petunias! Garish colour is completely unsuitable. I saw an example of it the other day in a garden that I originally designed and planted. Unfortunately, without a firm hand to hold them back, the owners had slid back into their passion for strong colour. Where I had created a mixed planting of predominantly foliage plants (which was too subdued for their taste) they ripped these out and filled the area with pink, red and orange bedding plants. It looked just like chicken pox against the green grass and flowing river beyond.

PLANTING THE WATER GARDEN

It is interesting to notice how many of the waterside plants have large handsome leaves. This does not mean that they necessarily always need a bog. It is sometimes enough to plant them in a sheltered area, such as a protected hollow or in a dell in a woodland. These make ideal places for some of the large-leaved hostas, as do the north- or east-facing sides of the garden. In hot, dry exposed conditions these soft, large leaves will suffer, just as someone with a delicate skin will burn if they are exposed to too much sun. You can see a similar kind of distress in the garden. A period of ample rainfall will sometimes be followed by hot sunshine, when large leaves will wilt, even though they have all the moisture they need at their feet. Their stomata, or pores, are wide open because they have been accustomed to gentle, soft moist days, so they have no protection against

Planting plan for moisture-retentive soil in full sun
This is for an area approx. 7.5m/25ft wide by 5m/16ft deep. Here, it borders a medium-sized pool.

KEY

1 *Astilbe* (×5)
2 *Carex elata* 'Aurea' (×1)
3 *Cornus alba* Baton Rouge = 'Minibat' (×1)
4 *Darmera peltata* (×3)
5 *Eupatorium maculatum* Atropureum Group (×1)
6 *Euphorbia palustris* (×3)
7 *Fritillaria meleagris* (×14)
8 *Iris pseudacorus* (×3)
9 *Leucojum aestivum* 'Gravetye Giant' (×2)
10 *Ligularia* (×3)
11 *Lysimachia nummularia* 'Aurea' (×10)
12 *Lythrum* (×3)
13 *Miscanthus sinensis* (×1)
14 *Myosotis* (×9)
15 *Onoclea sensibilis* (×5)
16 *Osmunda regalis* (×1)
17 *Primula* (×5)
18 *Trollius* (×3)

OPPOSITE Groups of coloured dogwoods (*Cornus alba*) will enhance dormant winter planting in moist conditions. There are many useful varieties, such as *C. a.* Baton Rouge = 'Minibat'.

LEFT *Primula bulleyana* makes a colourful choice for the water's edge and will form drifts in the right conditions.

the sudden heat. That does not mean that they will die. Wilting is their way of protecting themselves. After the cool of evening they will stand erect again. *Persicaria bistorta* 'Superba', with large dock-like leaves, behaves like this, and some of the ligularias will suddenly wilt in hot sunshine even though they may have their feet in water or in very damp soil. You may think how awful the garden must look because of all these big wilting leaves. But if they have been conditioned over the season to gradually drying conditions, and do not have regular rainfall, they will send

ABOVE Gunneras needs winter protection in a cooler climate. Here, their upturned leaves provide useful insulation for the soft crowns.

RIGHT The Chilean gunnera, *Gunnera tinctoria*, emerging from around the base of the dawn redwood, *Metasequoia glyptostroboides*. Now this gunnera is considered an invasive alien species, we have to remove its seeds to prevent it from spreading.

their roots deeper, close up their stomata and adapt to the conditions as they arise over the season.

To sit on one of the grass-covered dams, surrounded by almost tropical-looking plants, watching little schools of fish sunning themselves among the water-weeds, and listening to the splash of water as it falls from one level to another is an unexpected luxury in the heart of dry Essex farmland. Lush though the water-garden planting is in summer, during the winter almost none of it is visible. It is not easy to find plants that remain evergreen by the

'It is interesting to notice how many of the waterside plants have large handsome leaves. This does not mean that they necessarily always need a bog. It is sometimes enough to plant them in a sheltered area, such as a protected hollow.'

waterside. Most disappear completely and there is a great contrast between the wonderful rich green of the summer planting and the bareness of the water garden in winter. In a typically English spring, gunnera is one of the first plants to struggle to emerge from the winter gloom. The plants are covered during the winter months to protect them from the severe frosts but in April the shoots of the young leaves start to push through the blanket of old leaves mounded over them. Although they may be burnt a little by spring frosts, they usually start to recover by May and produce fresh green leaves from inside their great crowns.

The foliage of gunnera and lysichiton forms some of the grandest architectural features of the water garden. *Lysichiton americanus* is also one of the first flowers to appear in spring. Its foot-high spathes of bright butter-yellow emerge through the bare mud at the water's edge, where they are reflected in the dark water. (Note: Both *Lysichiton americanus* and *Gunnera tinctoria* have since been added to an ever-growing list of potentially invasive species that, given ideal conditions, could spread into the wild and compete with our native flora; they are now banned for sale in the United Kingdom. Fortunately, we are not obliged to remove existing plants but we do have to remove the seed-heads before they mature and make sure plants are stable and cannot drift downstream – in fact, this is highly unlikely to occur as both plants have extremely deep root systems.)

They are joined soon after by the flower-packed posies of marsh marigolds (*Caltha*), both single and double forms, followed by the Candelabra primulas, their colours veiled among marsh ferns and little patches of silky, white-haired cotton grass. Crimson tapers of knotweed and feathery spires of astilbe are the next to flower, while the rush-like daylilies (*Hemerocallis*) have not only attractive young leaves in spring but rich-toned flowers in late summer.

Visitors are often surprised to see the florist's arum lily, *Zantedeschia aethiopica* 'Crowborough', growing quite happily in the water. This hardier cultivar is ideal in colder climates and the shallow water helps protect the crown from frosts.

OPPOSITE This particular combination of foliage, form and texture illustrates Beth's preferred planting choices. Dominant horse chestnut-like leaves of *Rodgersia* 'Herkules' are underplanted with the filigree-like fern, *Onoclea sensibilis*, and backed by the fine-leaved *Miscanthus sinensis* 'Morning Light'. The pink flowers of the rodgersia provide height until the miscanthus rises up to claim the apical point in Beth's triangular planting shape (see page 26).

The damp garden is spangled with wild celandines in early spring. I try to control them where planted among small plants, but here in their native habitat by the waterside they do little harm and the sheets of shining yellow flowers are a delight early in the year while we wait for the main waterside plants to appear. Huge plants like rodgersias, hostas, globe-flowers (*Trollius*) and knotweeds will later push their way through from a lower depth. Celandines are as pretty as aconites, but aconites themselves (if they will grow well for you, and they do not for everyone) can be invasive, so they, too, can sometimes be in the wrong place. All gardeners have to make up their own minds about what they consider to be a weed in their garden and whether they can tolerate it. What decides the issue is whether the plant in question harms the rest of the planting. A weed is simply a plant in the wrong place.

Around the edges of my pools I have extended some of the beds to provide places for moisture-loving plants. At the pond edge, the 'marginal' plants may actually have their feet in water, those like *Caltha*, the marsh marigold, among them. *Caltha palustris* var. *radicans* is a later-flowering form, with smaller flowers. The double form of the common marsh marigold, *C. palustris* 'Flore Pleno', makes a good show, but I find the flowers of the single form more attractive. *Caltha palustris* var. *palustris* has much bigger flowers but you do need a larger pond to grow it successfully. It does not have as many flowers as *C. palustris*, which is more commonly grown, but it blooms over a longer period – there is hardly a month of the year when it does not have a flower. The leaves are larger, too, making handsome green mounds or rafts, eventually flopping into the water from the bank edges and continuing to root and shoot in shallow water. *Calla palustris* is another marginal, a little white arum-like plant that floats in the water. There are several kinds of iris, including the beautiful *Iris pseudacorus* 'Variegata' with its

emerging yellow leaves which by summer will have turned green, that will grow in shallow water.

At the edge of the pond are fine colonies of pickerel weed, *Pontederia cordata*, which slowly spreads into deeper water, forming crowded stems of spear-shaped leaves and spikes of small blue flowers in late summer. At the very edge in the squelchy sodden mud are the two magnificent bog arums, *Lysichiton americanus* (already mentioned) and

Young fronds of *Matteuccia struthiopteris* emerge in late spring before *Darmera peltata* spreads its large, scallop-edged foliage. To the right is the handsome royal fern, *Osmunda regalis*, with its head-high fronds just emerging, seen here with the flag iris, *Iris pseudacorus*.

the white-flowered species that comes from Siberia and Japan, *L. camtschatcensis*. (Note: Over the years, these two species have hybridized, resulting in the truly magnificent *Lysichiton × hortensis* with large creamy-yellow spathes in spring and huge leaves in summer. It does not seed itself so will not cause a problem as its yellow parent has done.)

Plants needing the most moisture must be planted either in the shallow water or within a short distance of

An autumn scene just below the house, overlooking the second of the two house ponds. The golden larch, *Pseudolarix amabilis*, lights up in a golden blaze, the needle-like leaves retaining their colour as they fall and carpet the ground beneath.

the water's edge. Water does not travel very far sideways in the soil. The water forget-me-not (*Myosotis scorpioides*) makes a good edging plant against the water, its bright blue flowers blooming for weeks on end in summer. In places I have widened the border so that I can grow more damp-loving plants but, as you move farther away still from the water's edge, the conditions are more like the borders in the Open Walks (which I talk about on page 90) – they are retentive of moisture, but not waterlogged.

Near the edges of the pools there are plants that must have constant moisture, like the big ligularias, whose large, round leaves may be green or purple; several different kinds of knotweed, and many forms of water iris, as well as *Zantedeschia aethiopica*, the handsome white arum lily that you often see in church flower arrangements at Easter. This plant does well in 30-60cm/l-2ft of water where deep mud protects the roots from winter cold. Rodgersias enjoy the wet soil in open conditions but will also grow well in part-shade in damp situations. They are among the most handsome of foliage plants. *Rodgersia aesculifolia* has broad bronze-tinted leaves rather like a horse chestnut's, followed in midsummer by pyramidal spires of soft cream or pink flowers. Other species have variously cut leaves, some more finely divided than others, but one former rodgersia, now *Astilboides tabularis*, has circular leaves the size and shape of a dinner plate (or even a tea-tray when grown in rich moist soil), with heavy drooping clusters of star-shaped creamy flowers held high on 1.2m/4ft stems as an additional bonus.

Under a willow, beside one of the pools, I have created an irregularly shaped bed that slopes several feet up from the water's edge to the mown grass walk on the opposite side. There, different degrees of shade and proximity to the water create very different planting conditions. In wet shade beneath the weeping willow close to the water's edge I have planted *Onoclea sensibilis*, a marsh-loving fern, and spring-flowering primulas, hostas and the yellow creeping Jenny (*Lysimachia nummularia* 'Aurea'). Higher up, perhaps 60cm/2ft above the water level, over the roots of the willow, I grow *Tiarella cordifolia*, snowdrops, other hostas and plants that do not need a lot of sun to produce flowers. Farther away from the tree, though not where the soil is waterlogged, there are astilbes, persicarias, *Euphorbia palustris*, ligularias, *Angelica archangelica* and *Scrophularia aquatica* 'Variegata' – the big water figwort whose leaves, vividly variegated in cream and green, are among the first to appear in spring. This plant illuminates the border throughout summer as its rigid branching stems continue to produce leaves of smaller size, but almost totally cream. On the upper side of the border by the mown grass edge, low clumps of a pretty variegated grass, *Molinia caerulea* subsp. *caerulea* 'Variegata', repeat this light colouring and remain a feature until the autumn when their knitting-needle-like flower stems and soft, arching leaves will have bleached almost to ivory. When the flower colour has gone from this border, a good display of interesting foliage still remains.

Reviewing the situation

It is important to assess the planting situation carefully. You cannot simply say this is the waterside so any damp-loving plant will grow here. Even in this relatively small bed, approximately 9 × 4.5m/30 × 15ft, there are different conditions – in sun or in shade, boggy, or comparatively dry at the top of the slope. As far as the ponds themselves are concerned, I would like to plant more waterlilies, but the biggest single problem with my water is the amount of blanket weed that covers the surface as the weather becomes warmer. The conditions are aggravated by too much nitrogen, and I cannot get the ecological balance of

Keeping the flow running between the garden ponds is an almost daily task, especially once the autumn leaves start to fall.

OPPOSITE A never-ending battle is fought against blanket weed, seen here 'bubbling' to the surface. Whilst we have tried every means available to control the problem, none is a long-term solution and we invariably resort to manual removal. Owing to silt build up, the water is now shallow and consequently warms up quickly, further encouraging the blanket weed seen here on the surface..

the pond right. Unfortunately, the nitrogen comes from the farmland around. Algicides would control it, but then I fear I would lose some of my oxygenating plants as well. (Note: A fine dusty chalk has proved effective when applied on a still, calm day. A highly porous form of calcium carbonate, it is completely harmless to plants and wildlife, and reduces the organic silt build up, as well as lowering the acidity of the water.) We have experimented with two people dragging a rope across the surface of the ponds. This removes much of the weed, greatly improving the appearance, but needs to be done frequently in the summer. The gardeners often don their waders to do a more thorough job and those confident enough to use a boat will do so.

Along some edges of the pond I now grow the bog-loving primulas that first fired my imagination when I started the water garden. Among them are *Primula bulleyana*, with its whorls of rich orange flowers, and *P. japonica*, the first Candelabra primula to flower, with heads of pink, magenta or white flowers with golden eyes standing above the huge rosettes of lettuce-like leaves. There are others, but the last to flower in late summer is the lovely giant Himalayan cowslip (*P. florindae)*, whose buds and stems are powdered with palest green dust. Drooping heads of creamy-yellow bell-shaped flowers eventually make elegant seed-heads.

THE CANAL BED

The Canal Bed is a large oval area of heavy wet land lying at the bottom end of the original boggy meadow, with the remains of the ditch (widened now – hence its name) running through the centre. The whole area is about 28m/90ft long by 14m/45ft wide. It is partially shaded by two oaks, the native oak, *Quercus robur*, that was here when we arrived and a pin oak, *Q. palustris*, which we planted. Some years the pin oak turns red in autumn, especially its growing shoots, and it is doing better than the native

In the Canal Bed, foliage can often be the only feature. Self-seeded *Lythrum salicaria* provide a hint of vertical colour, plus seed-heads later on.

OPPOSITE Looking from the bridge back up the Water Garden, the canal is lined with various moisture-loving perennials including this beautiful sedge, *Carex elata* 'Aurea', known as Bowles's golden sedge, seen here in early May.

oak. Beneath these are mixed shrubs to give bulk to the planting, including *Acer palmatum* and the beautiful lace-cap viburnum, *Viburnum plicatum* 'Mariesii'.

Initially I made narrow borders along the banks on either side of the ditch, but immediately I ran into two problems. The first was the quality of the soil, which was harsh and sticky and very unkind to the plants. I did my best by putting compost into the holes where I was putting water irises, primulas, marsh marigolds and so on. I also planted *Rheum palmatum* because I had read that ornamental rhubarbs like to be on the edge of the water, but their starchy crowns rotted away, as it was too wet for them. If you want to have rheums near water, where their large leaves look so effective, put them some distance from the water itself so that they are not going to be flooded in winter or overly wet at any time, and provide them with good, rich, vegetable-type garden soil. *Gunnera*, on the other hand, comes to no harm from the wet conditions.

The second problem I found was that the soil on the sloping banks slid into the water. Native weeds, like rushes, certain forms of grass and the form of willowherb called codlins and cream, *Epilobium hirsutum,* quickly carpeted the soil, and I spent my time pulling out great barrow-loads to rescue the plants I hoped to establish. By doing so, I pulled off what little topsoil there was, and the sloping sides of the banks crumbled and fell into the water. We overcame this by supporting the pond edges with hollow concrete blocks, standing two or three on top of each other to form a wall against the bank, and then driving angle-irons through them into the firm soil below the wet mud. The angle-irons were rescued from the farm and we bought hollow concrete blocks from a builders' supplier. If they are available and not prohibitively expensive, wooden stakes driven to within a few inches of the surface of the water do the job just as effectively and look most attractive. We have

Early morning sun on a winter's day backlights the swamp cypress, *Taxodium distichum*. This photogenic old wooden boat finally had to be retired but it will need replacing. In the interim, the gardeners can be seen regularly wading in the water, but never alone.

Pink pokers of *Persicaria bistorta* 'Superba' with the yellow globeflower, *Trollius europaeus*, in the Canal Bed, flanked by Candelabra primulas (a mixture of *Primula japonica* and *P. pulverulenta*). The distant grassy path leads up to the Reservoir Garden, past a fine *Rhododendron* 'Sappho'.

now managed to prevent the topsoil sliding down into the water and the concrete edging, just above the water, has eventually weathered to an unobtrusive mossy green.

We can now stand on the firm block edging to weed, plant or dig without the soil tumbling into the water. Ideally the blocks or wooden piles should be hardly visible above the water level but, if not, use bold plants that will disguise the hard edge when it shows too conspicuously.

We now have *Salix repens* var. *argentea* forming a feature beside the grassed dam that was made to form the pool above the canal – this shrub looks charming all summer with long sprays of tiny grey leaves. In spring, the bare branches are covered with little cotton-wool buds that burst into fluffy yellow catkins. Contrast is provided by large clumps of iris and tall Japanese grasses – various forms of *Miscanthus*. Even in early autumn, after a wet summer, there is still colour in the foliage and interesting texture. There are two moisture-loving ferns, the ostrich plume fern (*Matteuccia struthiopteris*) and the sensitive fern (*Onoclea sensibilis*), that do well here because they enjoy the shade from the oaks.

There is also a form of the native iris, *Iris pseudacorus* 'Bastardii', which has pale creamy-yellow flowers. It has grown rather too big for its position, so a certain amount of renovating is going to be needed here, but without removing everything. There will be certain features that I would not be able to move even if I wanted to, for example the *Lysichiton americanus*. If I stood against a clump of foliage in midsummer you would see that the leaves are as tall as I am – enormous, beautiful, spinach-shaped leaves, held in a great rosette. These plants could only be removed by killing them with weedkiller, which would be a sin. Probably some of the other plants will stay. The big beds of *Rodgersia* are fine, but in the foreground is a bed of *Vinca minor* 'Bowles's Blue' which was put here for two reasons: firstly, I needed

ground cover and, secondly, I did not have help to cope with a more intricate planting scheme. Now I can remove it and improve the soil, giving some space to furnish with new plants that have come in. The maintenance of this area will be kept down largely with pulverized bark as a mulch.

I will certainly use more primulas, because originally primulas were planted next to the water's edge and have been driven out by more rampant plants. In a way planting is like creating a painting. I will scrub out a piece here, saying perhaps that I could improve this by putting in a focal point here, or calm that by using something simpler. I am also acquiring new plants that need homes, but I find you cannot just take two or three plants and put them in among established ones. It is almost as if the old club will not accept new members. I think from time to time you need to renew your enthusiasm for a garden by making changes here and there sufficiently so that you can make a really good job of digging. If you have thick solid clay, you must do what you can to improve it – there is no easy way out. To improve the texture is every bit as important as feeding the soil, if not more so.

OPPOSITE This bed under the pin oak, *Quercus palustris*, proved too dry during the summer so the rampant wood spurge, *Euphorbia amygdaloides* var. *robbiae*, took advantage to colonize this area to great effect. A variegated cultivar of *Phormium tenax* creates a focal point of contrasting form. The stripes in the lawn never met with Beth's approval but she did concede that any lawn needed to be well maintained.

BELOW The Willow Room overlooks the Pump Pond (in the area formerly part of the nursery stock beds). In late spring, it is surrounded by some harmonious planting, including seeding aquilegias and yellow *Smyrnium perfoliatum*.

LEFT The water from the Canal Bed drops down into the neighbouring farm reservoir, where the curious zigzag canes of *Phyllostachys aureosulcata* f. *aureocaulis*, the golden crookstem bamboo, stand guard. The reservoir was created to irrigate the apple orchards that once surrounded the gardens.

OPPOSITE The reservoir viewed from the bottom of the Woodland Garden. (The green duckweed on its surface is a recent phenomenon, turning the pond into a green lawn-like expanse during summer). This larger area of water gave Beth the opportunity, in her own words, 'to paint the sky' and to plant trees that would create the perfect backdrop to the gardens. The fine swamp cypress, *Taxodium distichum*, colours well in early November while the relatively well-behaved bamboo, *Phyllostachys bambusoides*, is allowed to grow unchecked at the water's edge.

THE RESERVOIR BEYOND

The ditch running through the Canal Bed finally tumbles into a large farm reservoir. Although it has its attractions (a sheet of water holding about 2 million gallons), it is part of a commercial enterprise and used to irrigate crops. During long weeks of summer drought, pumping will reduce the level considerably, so any planting around it must be predominantly of trees and shrubs. I was glad to be allowed to plant them around the expanse of water to create a pleasant view from the garden, and they also help to create shelter from wind.

There are oaks, hollies, field maples and willows – mostly British native trees. They must be given a good start; it is useless to plant them straight into soil with the consistency of plasticine. Holes need to be dug with drainage sloping outwards so they do not fill with water, which rots the roots. I gradually add a new soil layer on top, using grit, bonfire waste, compost and spent soil from nursery pots for the mixture.

I did most of the planting in the mid-'70s. But the hard work was well worthwhile. It is a lovely sight now, with a slight mist over the water, reflecting the fringe of trees and shrubs. It is not exactly Sheffield Park, but at least it is improving gradually every year.

'You cannot just take two or three plants and put them in among established ones. It is almost as if the old club will not accept new members.'

The Open Walks

ON THE gentle slope between the south-west boundary and the Water Garden the soil does not dry out, helped partly by the fact that it is very close-textured silt over clay and partly by its being fed by moisture that comes from springs deep down underneath.

This area, which I call the Open Walks, has three large beds, each with a wide sunny border facing the Water Garden and backed by trees and shrubs, leaving a narrow shady side facing the farm boundary. I divided the planting area into three sections because I thought it would have been boring to have had one very long border, and also you would not have been able to walk round each section and enjoy it in the same way.

SOIL IMPROVEMENTS

When I first began to garden here, I thought this area had good growing soil – it remained damp far longer than the lighter soil and felt wonderful in my hands. It turned out to be far from ideal, however. It is what is often called a 'structureless' soil because it is very close-textured, has very few stones, and the drainage and the amount of air passing through is inadequate for many plants. The cure is to trench the beds – to dig them a couple of spits deep, spread gravel across the face of the trench, then cover it

The three island beds, each with a more open sunnier side, as well as a shady side. As surrounding trees grow, ever more shade is cast. In the furthest island bed, *Euphorbia griffithii* 'Fireglow' sits comfortably at one corner, while, in the Canal Bed opposite, its cousin, the lime-green *Euphorbia amygdaloides* var. *robbiae*, lives up to its reputation as a rapid colonizer.

with soil from the next trench. As a result the soil will be better aerated and able to absorb rainwater down new channels created by the stones.

I first discovered that this type of soil would need improvement when ground-cover plants like *Tiarella* and *Tellima*, which normally like a leafmould soil, failed to thrive. I thought they would do wonderfully well on this soil, but they did not. Nor did any plants with fine hairy roots. In times of drought, they were unable to penetrate the packed soil and simply sat on top of it like a cushion, their roots shrivelled in the top layer – you could lift them off like a piece of ragged carpet. At first I did not realize that silt is so very different from leaf-mould, but obviously it is. I've seen *Tiarella* growing wild in the woodlands in America, but two factors are different there. One is that since the leaf-mould is not so dense as silt, delicate little roots can penetrate it, and the second is that it rains there more frequently than it does here, and that make a great difference to what grows well. Here in East Anglia three months can pass by in summer with scarcely a drop of rain.

The brilliant deep red plumes of false goatsbeard, *Astilbe × arendsii* 'Fanal'. It needs a moisture-retentive, humus-rich soil.

CLIMATE CONSIDERATIONS

No matter where you live, you are going to be faced with some soil and rainfall problems, although not necessarily the same as mine. I saw a programme on television once about a garden in the west of Scotland where it so obviously hardly ever stopped raining that I felt almost sodden watching it. Some of the plants were similar to the ones I grow here around the pool margins – there were sheets of bog primulas that had seeded in the paths, with blue Himalayan poppy, *Meconopsis*, and spires of white *Actaea*. A whole host of attractive plants grew there just like weeds because they were ideally suited to those conditions, but the poor owner did not stand a chance of growing the grey-leaved plants that do so well in a dry garden. We gardeners

opposite This shows the curving design of this part of the garden, the borders separated by grassed pathways, with more open areas that set off the borders perfectly. Beautiful though they are, these grassed areas are subject to constant wear and require regular maintenance.

are all perverse: we want to try to grow what we cannot. Much of my life in East Anglia I have wanted to grow moisture-loving plants like astilbes, but in my previous garden I had difficulty even with delphiniums, which will fade and fail without adequate moisture. All the time you wish you could grow the plants you see doing well in other people's gardens. When you first start gardening, this is often exactly what you try to do, without stopping to think about the conditions in your own garden. Perhaps you see something like lady's locket (*Lamprocapnos spectabilis*) looking marvellous outside a cottage door in the West Country, and rush home to plant one in your dry, sunny gravel. Naturally enough, it fails to perform. What you have not asked yourself is: are the conditions the same? We have 50cm/20in average rainfall in East Anglia as opposed to 150cm/60in in the West Country, and this makes the world of difference. Even a small amount of extra rainfall a year – at the right time – can affect which plants you can grow well and which you cannot.

'All the time you wish you could grow the plants you see doing well in other people's gardens. When you first start gardening, this is often exactly what you try to do, without stopping to think about the conditions in your own garden.'

THE SUNNY BORDERS

The east-facing front of all three beds contain plants that enjoy retentive soil and an open sunny site. In spring, there are bulbs, including our own native fritillary, *Fritillaria meleagris*, which is a damp-meadow plant. Before we started a garden here, that is exactly what this area was – a damp meadow – so they could have been growing wild here, although, in fact, there were none. But there were colonies of spotted orchid (*Dactylorrhiza fuchsii*) which we have since struggled to preserve. There are also several species of narcissus and snowdrops (*Galanthus*) as well as erythroniums, like *Erythronium dens-canis*, *E. californicum* 'White Beauty' and *E.* 'Pagoda' All these plants like deep rich soil that does not dry out, although they would not

KEY

1 *Acer negundo* 'Flamingo' (×1)
2 *Ajuga reptans* (×6)
3 *Aster × frikartii* 'Mönch' (×3)
4 *Astrantia* (×5)
5 *Camassia leichtlinii* (drift)
6 *Euphorbia griffithii* 'Fireglow' (×3)
7 *Geranium* Rozanne = 'Gerwat'(×3)
8 *Hemerocallis* (×3)
9 *Lilium martagon* (×3)
10 *Lysimachia ciliata* 'Firecracker' (×3)
11 *Molinia* (×1)
12 *Narcissus* 'Rijnveld's Early Sensation' (drifts)
13 *Pennisetum alopecuroides* 'Hameln' (×2)
14 *Persicaria affinis* (×6)
15 *Persicaria amplexicaulis* (×3)
16 *Phormium tenax* (×1)
17 *Rudbeckia fulgida* (×3)
18 *Symphyotrichum novi-belgii* 'Heinz Richard' (×5)

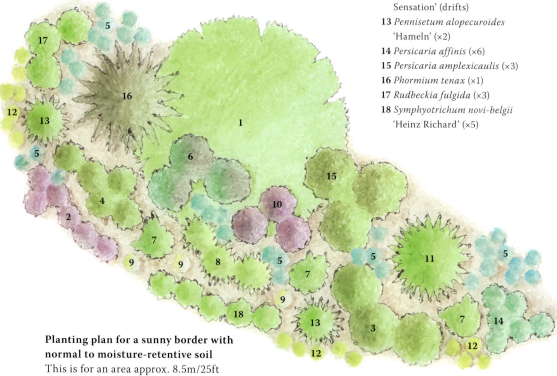

Planting plan for a sunny border with normal to moisture-retentive soil
This is for an area approx. 8.5m/25ft long by 3m/10ft deep.

tolerate the boggy conditions lower down the slope nearer the water's edge. The bulb season is extended into June and July in these borders with camassias, from North America, either cream- or blue-flowered, which rise up elegantly alongside the soft tomato-red flower-bracts of *Euphorbia griffithii* 'Fireglow'.

But the principal planting here is made up of herbaceous perennials and, of course, there are many plants to choose from that like these conditions. If you live in a part of the country with a good average rainfall, then even in a poorer, less retentive soil than this you could grow the campanulas, astrantias and epimediums that flourish here, but as we have such a low rainfall in East Anglia then the heavier, retentive soil is imperative.

For ground cover in these borders I like to use *Tiarella cordifolia,* which grows well both here in the shade, as well as the various cranesbills. Most are quite tolerant of a wide range of soils, but there are a few, such as *Geranium psilostemon* – a great big flamboyant plant with crimson flowers – that I would not put in the damp or shady parts of the garden. It goes far better with old-fashioned roses, or grey-leaved plants in the drier areas, and the reliable *Geranium macrorrhizum* would be a much better choice.

ACHIEVING HEIGHT IN PERENNIAL BORDERS

In spring, flowering bulbs and emerging plants create a low pattern of colour and cover, but by midsummer it is virtually a jungle as, apart from the edges, most of the planting in the bed will be from waist to head high.

Along with some other handsome architectural plants, I use the big yellow gentian from central Europe, *Gentiana lutea.* Its young foliage looks a little like *Veratrum viride,* which, in turn, is often mistaken for a hosta when its basal clusters of leaves first emerge in the spring. Veratrums make narrow columnar plants set with stiffly pleated leaves

The imposing pyramidal flower-heads of *Veratrum album.* The late summer-flowering false helleborine appreciates the deep, retentive soil found in the beds around the Open Walks area.

and topped with branching spires of green, plum-coloured or white flowers in late summer. Fortunately, green flowers are more appreciated now than they were when Reginald Farrer wrote such seductive descriptions of alpines in *The English Rock Garden*. He gave a mouth-watering description of the leaves of *Veratrum*, which built you up to anticipate a marvellous plant, and then dismissed the flowers as being of 'unmitigated dinginess', because he, of course, was looking for the bright colours so typical of alpines.

Nowadays, though, we appreciate bold forms for the contrast they create with smaller plants. Those that make this kind of impact include Solomon's seal, *Polygonatum*, and the giant ornamental rhubarb, *Rheum palmatum*, which makes such a splendid full-stop plant in this border. Rheums are sometimes described as being ideally positioned by the waterside, but, as I explained before, they have to be planted on a free-draining slope. *Rheum palmatum* needs rich, deep soil – what I call good vegetable-garden soil – to grow well. All these plants must be able to get through the droughts we have in high summer, when they would die if they did not have a good retentive soil.

Jacob's ladder, *Polemonium caeruleum*, a very pretty plant with sheaves of small saucer-shaped blue flowers and arching mid-green feathery foliage, looks well towards the front of the border. There are several species of *Polemonium*, providing flowers over a long season. *Polemonium carneum* tends to flop about a bit, but although that might put some people off, I think that plants which droop gracefully, without doing harm to their neighbours, add such a pretty, natural look to the border. *Polemonium carneum* is exquisite and flowers throughout June with silky textured, saucer-shaped flowers, the buds opening creamy-white, then changing to pink before finally fading to lavender.

I do not like to see all the plants standing stiffly to attention, like soldiers on parade. I particularly dislike

OPPOSITE Between the house and the garden ponds, this fine Chinese golden larch, *Pseudolarix amabilis*, takes centre stage in late autumn. Underneath, an established group of spangle grass, *Chasmanthium latifolium*, with its flattened oat-like seed-head, will last throughout the winter.

BELOW The same scene beneath the Chinese golden larch earlier in the summer, with the arching plumes of the New Zealand tussock grass, *Chionochloa flavicans*.

seeing them tied up to canes and prefer not to stake my plants, keeping them closely packed instead, so that the stiffer ones support the more delicate ones. There are a few plants which can be a trial, like the thalictrums. *Thalictrum delavayi*, in particular, does sometimes need staking because it is very tall and is easily blown over. I try to plant it in among low shrubs and other stouter plants that help to hold it upright. I must admit I rarely enjoy looking at staked plants. If you visit some botanical gardens at the end of April, you will see the piles of pea-stakes ready to go into the borders, but the border planting begins to look acceptable only when the brushwood is lost among the new season's growth.

PLANT FAMILY ATTRIBUTES

There are surprisingly large differences of height within certain families of plant (which are, after all, very similar to our own families, with brothers, sisters and cousins, and close relatives and far-flung ones. The distant relatives may well have the same great-grandmother, but the similarities are far less marked). It is much the same with plants. Take persicarias, for example. Some of them, like *Persicaria affinis* and *P. vacciniifolium*, make spreading carpets across the ground, and then, at the other end of the scale, there is *P. amplexicaulis*, making a bushy plant a good 1.2m/4ft high and across.

I find people occasionally fail to appreciate the wide differences there are in one family, and when buying plants may well not look them up. Then, to their chagrin, the plant that they bought for edging a border turns out to be a striking architectural feature instead. It is important to make sure that if the plant you originally wanted is not available, you pick one that has similar features. Simply because it bears the name *Campanula*, say, is not enough. There are several kinds, both dwarf edging ones and tall

All cultivars and selections of *Persicaria amplexicaulis*, flowering from July onwards, are easy and reliable perennials and are excellent attractors of pollinating insects.

ones like the statuesque *C. lactiflora*, standing at about l.5-2m/5-6ft high with huge heads of typical powder-blue bell-shaped flowers. Some of the low-growing campanulas, like *Campanula carpatica* var. *turbinata* and *C. glomerat*a var. *alba* 'Schneekrone', with its spike of white bells in midsummer, are useful for ground cover.

Take also the gentian family. Most people think of gentians as low mats on the ground with beautiful dark blue bells, but *Gentiana lutea* is strikingly different: a dramatic foliage plant, standing 90cm-1.2m/3-4ft tall, carrying stiff spires of yellow blooms and the only similarity with its low-growing relatives is the bell shape of the flowers. I try in my catalogue, as do most nurseries, to describe the plants carefully, but people sometimes neglect to read the entries properly. Coloured photographs in books and magazines, while delightful, can also be misleading since

Although Beth and her husband, Andrew, kept many records of the plants, there are some that we still remain unsure of. Looking back towards the golden larch is one such plant. A delightfully scented, deciduous azalea, it is, we are led to believe, *Rhododendron occidentale.*

they frequently fail to give any indication of the actual size of the plant, especially in close-up.

One of the other dangers you have to guard against when buying plants in a nursery is impulse. You may be so overcome by the beauty of a particular plant that you do not stop to think about its needs: where it will grow, whether you have the right situation for it or how long the flowers last. If it is very short-flowering, no matter how exquisite, you might be better off with something less spectacular with a longer flowering season.

It is always worth creating different levels in the planting, and one way is to grow climbers over trees, particularly where there are no supporting walls (see page 165). I have a *Clematis viticella* climbing up a pale pink cherry, *Prunus* 'Shirofugen', with flowers that do not last long, so that the clematis will flower throughout summer when the cherry has finished. I learned to do this from Christopher Lloyd at Great Dixter, where it is practised very successfully.

One of many imposing clumps of hosta to be found throughout the garden, *Hosta fortunei* 'Spinners' is one of the best variegated selections. The pale-pink plumes of *Astilbe × arendsii* 'Venus' and Bowles's golden sedge, *Carex elata* 'Aurea', complete this early-summer view.

SPACING THE PLANTS

Where possible I try to plant in groups rather than to dot plants about singly. But you can go overboard on the uniform grouping of plants as carefully calculated groups can look too stiff and formal. Once the planting is established, I like to see plants run into one another a little or seed themselves. I do not always plant in defined groups of three or five, but may drop one or two of the plants further away, just as if they had seeded themselves. Even if I do not do that, nature will often take a hand and do it for me, which looks much more natural and more attractive.

Even in large borders, it is important to make the best use of the space, and you can do this by putting plants closer together than the books often advise, provided they grow and flower at different times. Many people make the mistake of planting everything the same distance apart, but successful spacing has less to do with how much room the plant needs and rather more with what you are planting next to it. In certain cases, if you have plants that are growing at the same pace and flowering at the same time, you should not squash them close together, but you can certainly put the spring bulbs very close to the summer-flowering perennials.

Different plants often use different strata of the soil. I have planted dog's tooth violets, *Erythronium dens-canis*, very close to the hostas, but they have finished, both flowers and leaves, by the time the hostas have made their leafy clumps, and their roots are much shallower. When you are planting, do not think about the space as just an area across the surface of the soil, but also of the area in depth beneath the surface, rather like a sugar cube. Different plants use different layers and some will send their roots deep down, whilst others will sit lightly on the surface. Understanding this comes from observation and experience, but sometimes it comes accidentally, too, when

This closely planted group of astilbe, daylilies and a lone *Miscanthus sinensis* 'Morning Light' still allows space for the odd plant to run through or self-seed.

'Even in large borders, it is important to make the best use of the space, and you can do this by putting plants closer together than the books often advise, provided they grow and flower at different times.'

101

unconsidered plants seed close together and surprise you by how compatible they turn out be.

Thoughtful use of space allows plants to decorate the same area over a long period. In a small area, I have *Ajuga reptans* 'Atropurpurea' with our native *Fritillaria meleagris,* with its chequered bells of smoky plum, growing through it but mixed among them are the crimson flag lilies, *Hesperantha coccinea,* which have scarcely broken the surface of the soil in spring but will flower much later in the year, in October or November. Take another example: clumps of the little purple early-spring-flowering dog's tooth violet can be found meshed into clumps of autumn-flowering, dwarf-growing Michaelmas daisies and in other places they will have pushed their way through low-growing astilbes.

THE PLANTS THEMSELVES

Although they normally prefer part-shade, there are several hostas that tolerate open conditions, provided the soil does not dry out. There are some, such as *Hosta fortunei* var. *albopicta* f. *aurea* that scorch if you put them in sun, but there are a few others, including *Hosta undulata* var. *albomarginata,* with broad creamy margins to its rich green leaves and the large blue-grey-leaved *H. sieboldiana,* which make fine features along the front of an open border.

There are several different species of astrantia, including *Astrantia major* and *A. maxima,* that grow well in this situation. The variegated form of *A. major,* 'Sunningdale Variegated', has outstandingly beautiful leaves in spring and early summer. The flowers, quivering clusters of stamens with broad-petalled bracts surrounding them, stand about 90cm/3ft high and are attractive in a quiet way. Their chief attribute is that they flower right through the summer, with the added bonus that they press very well for

dried flower pictures, as the stamens spread out prettily like the spokes of a wheel.

I like to use violas and violettas among the edging plants, but not cultivated pansies with flowers as large as the palm of your hand. I grow the small-flowered carpeting ones which, to my mind, look prettier and daintier. *Viola cornuta*, the little horned viola with deep lavender-coloured flowers only 2.5cm/1in across, grows wild in the Pyrenees, and I have seen it on the same slope with *Thalictrum flavum* subsp. *glaucum* and *Persicaria bistorta* 'Superba', all of which enjoy damp conditions.

Leading off from the main grassed Open Walk, narrow paths connect to the long Shady Walk. Here the plants are shade- or part-shade lovers. With the soil too dry for large-leaved hostas, bergenias take over their role. *Bergenia* 'Beethoven', the flowers of which open white but quickly turn pink, is a particular favourite.

COLOUR IN THE BORDER

People often ask me about planning colour schemes for a border. In practice, I rarely think in terms of colour alone, being equally occupied with form. If I plant a colour that jars, I remove it. But, oddly enough, it rarely happens. I suspect this is because I select plants for the situation and in nature plants that grow in the same conditions tend to go well together. Take the scarlets – the very hard reds – that are a difficult colour to incorporate into a planting scheme. They could be planted in the Mediterranean Garden, where they will be softened by the grey-leaved plants – picture the scarlet flowers of *Anemone × fulgens* with the grey foliage of *Euphorbia characias* subsp. *wulfenii* in the background. Those plants would grow together in the wild and their colours offset one another – around the shores of the Mediterranean, for example, bright plants grow naturally in the grey stony landscape.

There are just a few red-flowered plants that require damp soil. In one of the sunny beds with moisture-holding soil, I have a large group of a euphorbia from the Himalayas, *E. griffithii* 'Fireglow'. Unlike the luminous green heads of other euphorbias, the flower bracts of this plant are very like the colour of tomato skins, a beautiful orange-red; this colour is enhanced by dark coral stems and leaves in the form called *E. g.* 'Dixter'. *Euphorbia g.* 'Fireglow' is at its best from June onwards, and flowers for weeks on end. If it spreads further than you intend it to, you can just put your spade through the wandering shoots and remove those you do not want. But in a poor gravelly soil this particular euphorbia would fail miserably.

A combination that pleases me in late spring is when the low-growing *Geum × borisii*, with its intense orange-red flowers, repeats the colour of the *Euphorbia griffithii* 'Fireglow' flowers, seen farther away along the border, while both are enhanced by the many shades of yellow or bronze

The bank on which the house stands is prone to become dry. A fine pineapple broom, *Argyrocytisus battandieri*, does well in these conditions, and the seat is a favourite place to enjoy the broom's delicious scent on a warm summer's day.

of the unfolding buds on trees and shrubs, creating a warm haze in the background. At that time of year there is no sight of any pink or mauve flowers to spoil the analogous colour scheme.

There are white flowers in this part of the border, such as some of the Michaelmas daisies nearby. In the wild, Michaelmas daisies usually grow in damp conditions. I have seen them right across America, on both the East and West coasts, growing wild – weedy little plants with washed-out colours and small flowers. They seed themselves like groundsel. Once, in Massachusetts, I was walking in a boggy area among tall reedy grasses and rushes, and saw the big purple flowers of another form of aster, growing with its feet almost in water. Many of the kinds we grow in Great Britain are hybrids – selected forms of all these many different cousins of daisies – but those that have over-large flowers and weak stems do not appeal to me.

I like to think of colour as much in terms of shadows as of true flower colour. It is the contrast between light and shadow in the foliage that is exciting – it gives the garden more atmosphere than if it had just been planned on flower colour alone, which is disappointingly one-dimensional. The dark purples of the foliage of *Ajuga* and *Viola riviniana* Purpurea Group make good deep shadows among the blue anemones in the spring and form a very charming combination with *Euphorbia amygdaloides* var. *robbiae* in a shadier part of the garden. *Ophiopogon planiscapus* 'Kokuryū', a Japanese grass-like plant with almost black leaves, makes a marvellous contrast or 'shadow' with another Japanese grass, *Hakonechloa macra* 'Aureola', which has leaves like yellow-striped ribbons; or I might have a *Carex buchananii* shooting up behind it like a fountain. This is a bronze colour with no green in it at all, which many people dislike, but its stems look charming when they catch the light.

'In practice, I rarely think in terms of colour alone, being equally occupied with form. If I plant a colour that jars, I remove it. But, oddly enough, it rarely happens. I suspect this is because I select plants for the situation and in nature plants that grow in the same conditions tend to go well together.'

Anemone × fulgens, with its bright scarlet flowers, is a plant that combines well with the glaucous grey-green foliage of *Euphorbia characias* subsp. *wulfenii*.

DESIGN STRATEGY

I think it is a good idea when planning a new border to make a list of the plants you will use, even if you do not make an actual plan. I like to have a list of the plants that I know will grow well and look good together. This will include: the taller plants that are going to the back of the border (or the middle if it is an island bed); the less dramatic plants that will be needed to set around them to show up the star performers, and some bulky ones like hostas, bergenias or epimediums to act as buffer zones to calm a piece of planting or hold it securely together. I always start with my lists and then I go and look in what I call my 'pets' corner' where I keep the plants that I have brought back from my travels and from which I select ones suitable for the bed I am planning. I look through them all and may add others – from the nursery or from other parts of the garden – whose shape, form and foliage complement each other. I will need a tall grass, perhaps, or an *Actaea* or an *Aconitum* to make a vertical. I will also need something bulky like the persicarias – *Persicaria amplexicaulis,* for example, which is wonderful in the latter part of the year – and then the shorter plants and the mound plants and so on. It is the shapes of the plants that I think of first, but I will also consider the pink flowers of some of the cranesbills and the shrimp-pink or flame-coloured tapers of various persicarias, and then I might decide it would be attractive to put in some purple-leaved ajugas to add a deeper tone, but not necessarily a contrast of colour.

If you concentrate on colour alone, unless you take things out and replace the flowers once they are over with something else – which is very labour intensive, costly and terribly artificial – the garden lacks other values. What I enjoy most in my garden is the contrast of leaf and form, and, of course, the promise always of the flowers to come. If you go along a border and see everything flowering at

the same time, you get the sickening feeling, 'What is going to be here in three weeks' time?' Of course, in my garden things do have to be cut down, but there is usually something coming up to take their place, or there is something so dramatic in the way of a foliage plant that you failed to notice. You do not need have to have flower colour all the time. A few well-placed and jewel-like flower colours, among foliage that keeps its form, can successfully illuminate the scene.

The Open Walks pass through sunny borders on either side. In spring, a fine cultivar of the marsh spurge, *Euphorbia palustris* 'Walenburg's Glorie', hugs the damper soil by the pond side. On the right-hand side, which is not as moist, the maturing foliage of hostas, astilbes and grasses holds the promise to come later on in the year.

The Shade Gardens

When Beth wrote this chapter, she had yet to create the Woodland Garden (see pages 152-169), where there is much denser shade. Here she talks about planting for shade in general and her experience of it in the shadier areas around the garden, but particularly along the Shady Walk beneath the mature oak trees.

SOMETIMES PEOPLE who have a yew under which nothing grows come to me and ask, 'What can I plant in the shade of this tree?' The simple answer is, 'Don't try. Put down a mulch of some kind – peat, leafmould or pulverized bark, and leave it at that.' There is very little light under such a dense tree and – more importantly – little rainfall through it. Lack of both light and moisture prevent almost anything from growing in these conditions. If, on the other hand, you have a tree whose canopy is less dense – 'lighter' trees, such as pines or silver birches, or even a mature oak with glancing sunshine coming through its canopy most of the time – the shade will be dappled and some rain will get through, unless there is very little rainfall in your part of the country, in which case your soil will be dry. If you have a very low rainfall, then the plants you can grow under a birch are very different from those that would grow there if you had twice the rainfall. You have to make a judgement

Beneath a swamp cypress, *Taxodium distichum*, the soil can become quite dry in summer, especially on the surface. Astrantias are adaptable and tolerant of such conditions: *Astrantia* 'Roma' in the foreground is a long-flowering selection, combining well with *Hosta sieboldiana* 'Frances Williams' on the right and the tall blue flower spires of *Aconitum* 'Stainless Steel' behind.

about the amount of light and shade, and the amount of moisture to determine what (if anything) you can grow successfully in the prevailing conditions.

What kind of shade?

There are really two types of shade: the shade cast by trees and shrubs and that cast by buildings. Near a building, plants may not get direct sunlight but they do get some light at all times. Plants in a north-facing border that has a high wall behind it will have better light than those under a tree which makes an umbrella over them, so beneath that wall you could have more flowering plants (which

OPPOSITE The garden forget-me-not, *Myosotis sylvatica*, threads itself between emerging perennials during late spring, contrasting well with the lime-green variegation of *Hosta* 'Gold Standard' and the fern behind. Leading the eye up to the trees is the deep pink-flowered *Weigela florida* 'Foliis Purpureis' with the wonderfully scented *Choisya* × *dewitteana* 'Aztec Pearl'.

Planting plan for border in dry shade
This is for a border measuring 7m/22ft wide by 2.5m/8ft deep. It is backed with Christmas box (*Sarcococca*) and Japanese anemones (*Anemone* × *hybrida*).

KEY

1 *Anemone* × *hybrida*
  'Honorine Jobert' (×6)
2 *Anemone nemorosa* (×11)
3 *Digitalis lutea* (×3)
4 *Brunnera macrophylla* (×5)
5 *Dicentra formosa* 'Langtrees' (×5)
6 *Dryopteris filix-mas* (×1)
7 *Epimedium* × *perralchicum*
  'Fröhnleiten' (×3)
8 *Erythronium dens-canis* (×9)
9 *Geranium macrorrhizum* (×5)
10 *Helleborus foetidus* (×3)
11 *Liriope muscari* (×3)

12 *Melica uniflora* f. *albida* (×3)
13 *Milium effusum* 'Aureum' (×3)
14 *Polygonatum* × *hybridum* (×3)
15 *Polystichum setiferum*
  (Divisilobum Group) 'Dahlem' (×1)
16 *Pulmonaria* (×3)
17 *Sarcococca* (×1)
18 *Tiarella cordifolia* (×5)

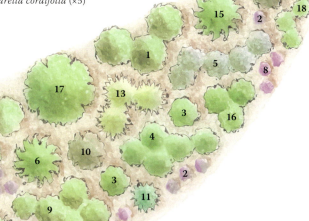

need light to flower as the denser the shade, the fewer the flowers). Lilies thrive in partial shade, but they would not do well under a dense tree canopy because there is never enough direct light.

There are few plants – attractive ones – that will grow in what must be called dry shade. By that I do not mean bone-dry shade, but shade that becomes dry in midsummer, when the leaf canopy is fairly dense and only a little rainfall gets through – plus the roots of the tree are going to consume a great deal of what little comes anyway – so the plants will have to hang on. You are not going to be able to have magnificent foliage and pretty flowers throughout the year in such conditions. You have to plant what will survive in that habitat. In particular, you have to grow plants that will make use of the moisture in the spring and are adapted to survive during the summer when the shade is at its most dense and the rainfall at its lowest. Plants like dwarf periwinkles, ivy and even cyclamens will stand amazingly dry situations.

If you have less dense shade, so water can get through, and regular rainfall, so the soil stays moist, then you have a much wider range of woodland plants to choose from, such as those that come from areas like the North American and Japanese woodlands, where they certainly have heavier rainfall than us. If you live in the west of England, Wales or Scotland, where you may have anything ranging from around 100-150cm/40-60in of rainfall a year, the plants you can grow in shade are in much greater variety.

In perpetually cool and wet conditions, many choice peat-loving plants can be grown, among them rhododendrons, delicate ferns, and the famous blue poppy of the Himalayas, *Meconopsis*. Anything I can grow in East Anglia most people could grow in sun, provided there is enough moisture during the growing season. But a few plants, such as *Actaea simplex* 'White Pearl', will be prone to scorching

Although now listed as an invasive species, *Rhododendron ponticum* produces attractive flowers which Beth preferred to those of other showier cultivars. Below it, a tapestry of ground-covering perennials – pulmonarias, tellimas and hostas – is in full growth.

in direct sunlight even when they have their roots firmly in wet soil. Most of the plants that grow well under my trees and shrubs are spring-flowering – they use the light before the leaf canopy comes. Shade gardens generally flower between March and June. The rest of the year the area will be predominantly foliage.

At the time of writing, the main areas of shade in my own garden are those where I have added to the existing trees –

mainly ancient oaks – for example on the west boundary, which comprises several fine old oaks to which we have added a whole mixture of evergreen and deciduous shrubs, making a long shady walk. Even here the shade is variable, and some parts of the border get full morning sun, but by midsummer, when the trees are in full leaf, there will be areas that become very shady all day. This provides an ideal place to grow big-leaved plants like hostas and ferns among carpets of creepy-crawly tiarellas, blue and white *Phlox stolonifera*, coloured-leaved forms of *Ajuga* and other low, carpeting foliage plants that clothe the ground and create interesting patterns of shape, texture and colour until well into the autumn.

Elsewhere in the garden I tend to create large island beds, generally long lozenge shapes, and all of them have a sunny side and a cooler, shadier side. According to what I need, I exploit one side or the other (as described in the Reservoir Garden on page 138). I plant my 'spine' of trees

Looking back up the path without a flower in sight. The bamboo, *Fargesia nitida*, has since flowered and died, and has been replaced with another bamboo, *Fargesia scabrida*. Taking centre stage is a heavily pruned *Acer negundo* 'Flamingo' (see also page 130) with *Hosta* 'Gold Standard', making a splash of light at its feet.

The European meadow rue, *Thalictrum aquilegiifolium*, is an occasional self-seeder almost anywhere but welcome because it is never invasively so. Its fluffy, candy-floss-like heads sit atop head-high dark stems rising from a sea of attractive foliage below.

'If you give the plant every chance and prepare the soil well, it will repay you by flourishing and reproducing itself. People are often disappointed that their plants do not grow as well as they expect and it is usually as a result of not choosing the right situation, and of not preparing the soil adequately.'

and shrubs slightly off centre. One bed where the soil is not good enough to grow delicate woodland plants might perhaps have a narrow shady side and so I will use the tougher, shade-loving plants there, and I exploit the open sunny side, giving it the wider space, backed by trees and shrubs. Elsewhere, where the soil is better quality and more retentive, it allows me to grow more interesting shade-loving plants. All the time I am thinking about my twin aims: to create a harmonious collection of plants and to use the soil, and the rain that falls on it, to best advantage.

THE SMALL SHADE GARDEN

Areas of shade occur in many different parts of the garden. One area here beneath a large oak and holly has many small choice things in it. It has many plants that could be

115

translated into a much smaller garden – beneath an apple tree, perhaps, rather than an oak. When I first planted this part of the garden, I had no help, nor had I learned about the value of using a good layer of mulch (either peat, leaf-mould or crushed bark) to reduce the problem of weeding. I concentrated on using ground-cover plants; some of the best are the small-leaved periwinkles. *Vinca minor* 'Variegata' makes an attractive carpet of green and cream leaves, while others have blue, purple or white flowers, and there are double-flowered forms in blue and purple. Originally, I made the mistake of putting dwarf periwinkles and cyclamens together, but the periwinkles over-ran the cyclamens. Cyclamens will eventually make ground cover from autumn until late spring. They seed themselves about, each one with a different marbled pattern on the leaves. The vincas are now kept well away and are often used around the base of shrubs. I have *Vinca minor* 'Bowles's Blue' around the base of *Hamamelis mollis*, making total cover beneath this wide spreading shrub, where it would be both laborious and boring to creep on hands and knees picking out regular crops of weeds. I never plant *Vinca major* – it is too invasive for most gardens – it is better suited as pheasant cover in a wood.

EARLY FLOWERS

In a shady area where the soil is not particularly good, vigorous plants like our native bluebell, *Hyacinthoides non-scripta*, *Arum italicum* susbsp. *italicum* 'Marmoratum', the white-flowered foxglove, *Digitalis purpurea* f. *albiflora*, and even some of the cranesbills, such as *Geranium macrorrhizum*, can battle it out together. The first flowers often appear in January when the buds of *Narcissus minor* 'Cedric Morris' (brought home from Spain by the late Sir Cedric many years ago) begin to open. In mild winters we can find plants like the white form of the wild primrose,

Primula vulgaris flowers in late winter and is an early harbinger of spring.

Primula vulgaris var. *alba,* in flower in January, as well as *Helleborus argutifolius.* Although the latter comes from the Mediterranean area, it is hardy in free-draining soil, producing shrub-like mounds of handsome, grey-green veined leaves with more cup-shaped green flowers than I have ever cared to count clustered at the top of stems about 60cm/2ft tall. *Helleborus foetidus,* our native hellebore, opens its first flowers in this semi-shaded area any time from January onwards. Both of these hellebores remain handsome for months, even when setting their seed.

On either side of the wide grass paths, tough ground-cover plants can be invaluable in areas of denser shade cast by evergreen trees. Hardy *Geranium endressii* on the right and *Epimedium* × *perralchicum* 'Fröhnleiten' on the left are ideal choices. (As shade from trees increases, grass pathways can become problematic to maintain.)

Among the first flowers to appear under an oak or apple tree in part-shade could be cyclamens. They are lovely whether in flower or not, because their variegated leaves are so attractive. I have a form of *Cyclamen coum* with round, totally silver leaves, like a ten-pence piece. The difference between *Cyclamen coum* and *C. hederifolium* is that the former has almost round leaves while the latter has ivy-shaped ones.

Other plants that flower in early March are the erythroniums. The dog's-tooth violet (*Erythronium denscanis*) is not in the least like a violet. Its mauve lily-like flowers look much more like cyclamens when their pointed petals reflex in the warmth of early sunshine. They are followed by *Erythronium* 'Pagoda' and *E. californicum* 'White Beauty', two hybrids of American erythroniums which are taller than *E. dens-canis* and have yellow and cream flowers. I plant drifts of them under the trees and shrubs. Visitors sometimes mistake them for small lilies. Most erythroniums have beautiful shiny leaves, richly mottled like snakeskin.

The last of my snowdrops are out at the end of March. I have an unusually large one that appeared about 25 years ago. It is scented and has two flowers to a bulb. The Royal Horticultural Society think it is a form of *Galanthus plicatus* subsp. *byzantinus*. Also out then is *Hepatica transsilvanica* – a large rich blue flower that I found in an old garden. I use a lot of *Pachyphragma macrophyllum* for both cover and effect beneath the shade of shrubs. It is an underrated plant which slowly spreads, making bold ground cover with its large, round, shiny leaves, contrasting so well here with *Euphorbia amygdaloides* var. *robbiae* behind it. When the snowdrops have gone, the pachyphragma's white flowers stand out like lately fallen patches of snow.

I think you need to make a setting for small plants. Most of the plants in this little area of the garden are species

First appearing from dormant tubers in August, the flowers of the ivy-leaved cyclamen, *Cyclamen hederifolium,* last for weeks. Its ivy-like marbled foliage unfurls to remain a feature until it begins its summer dormancy.

OPPOSITE Many blue-leaved hostas were given to Beth by the plantsman, Eric Smith. One of his best was *Hosta* (Tardiana Group) 'Halcyon', growing here alongside the understated green spikes of *Tellima grandiflora.* Touches of colour from self-seeding forget-me-nots and the orange-flowered Welsh poppy, *Papaver cambricum,* behind help to enliven the scene.

plants – that is, plants either as they were when found growing wild or perhaps as the first hybrids to retain their original character.

LATER FLOWERINGS

How heart-warming it is, early in the year, to find promise of what is to come. Lilies I planted as single bulbs the year before now come up with three or four noses. If you give the plant every chance and prepare the soil well, it will repay you by flourishing and reproducing itself. People are often disappointed that their plants do not grow as well as they expect and it is usually as a result of not choosing the right situation, and of not preparing the soil adequately.

A good mat-forming plant is *Waldsteinia ternata*, with glossy, evergreen, strawberry-shaped leaves. In spring, each plant will be edged with sprays of bright yellow saucer-shaped flowers. There are two kinds of leaf – large and small – on the same plant. Planted among *Waldsteinia* is *Arisaema candidissimum*, which does not appear at all until mid-June but when it does it is worth the fright that it may not reappear. The flowers come first, emerging with their leaves folded around them like a cigar. An almost reptilian head of the arum-like flower then unfolds; the hooded spathe is white with pink vertical stripes, and gradually the plant unfolds its three-part leaves, each one rather like a huge clover leaf, sometimes more than a foot across. The plant does not grow very tall, but makes an overlapping mound, perhaps 30-45cm/12-18in tall, of dramatic outspread leaves. It is an essential impact plant beside the small fussy leaves of *Waldsteinia* and the leaves of the variegated London pride, *Saxifraga* × *urbium* 'Aureopunctata', nearby. From midsummer onwards, the three together make an interesting design without any flowers. The arisaema leaves later fade to a honey colour before they disappear.

'You have to grow plants that will make use of the moisture in the spring and are adapted to survive during the summer when the shade is at its most dense and the rainfall at its lowest.'

Recent years have seen an increase in the range of *paniculata* cultivars of hydrangea, with *Hydrangea p.* 'Limelight' one of the most outstanding.

THE SHADE GARDEN IN WINTER

In winter there are still clumps of grasses remaining, which we do not like to cut down too soon. *Chasmanthium latifolium* is an American grass that makes a graceful outline here, and beyond it is Bowles's golden grass, *Milium effusum* 'Aureum', just beginning to make new shoots of bright yellow leaves. By early spring, they will look like patches of sunlight falling between the bare branches. This is one of the few ornamental grasses I use which is invasive owing to seeding, but since it seeds true it is easy to recognize and remove, or plant elsewhere.

Creating a winter carpet is a little plant from American woodlands, *Tiarella cordifolia*, or foam flower, so called because of the multitudes of tiny fluffy white flower-spikes

On the clay bank, under the shade of a *Magnolia × soulangeana* and a surrounding canopy of trees, the slender white flower spikes of the bugbane, *Actaea matsumurae* 'Elstead Variety', reliably light up the border during early autumn.

that appear in April. Threaded among it is *Omphalodes cappadocica*, a veronica-like flower with its small, clear-blue sprays, and a really choice plant for cool positions. Ajugas do very well under trees and between other plants. Small bulbous plants come up through them and then die down, leaving the interest of a carpeting plant remaining. However, in winter itself, although many of the plants are not in flower, there is still a lot to enjoy. A lively patch of foliage is made by the variegated form of London pride – *Saxifraga × urbium* 'Aureopunctata'. It flowers in May with sprays of delicate pink flowers but in winter the fresh rosettes of dark green leaves, speckled with gold, can still be enjoyed.

I prefer not to see large expanses of bare ground even in winter. I like as far as possible to cover the soil all year round, but there are some plants that disappear totally. If you have a proportion of plants which remain in winter, it helps to keep the garden alive and if you can retain a few seed-heads or attractive grasses they also help to create little scenes. You can, if you search around, find plants to provide total ground cover throughout the year. Places like public parks might well find it an advantage but as I am a collector, I like to mix deciduous and evergreen plants. I do not mind having a few bare spaces here and there – it is all part of the change into winter – but I find they look much more attractive if the soil is protected with a mulch.

FAVOURITE PLANTS FOR SHADE

Epimediums are very good plants for shady places. There are many varieties, all with pretty shield-shaped leaves held on thin wiry stems, creating an overlapping effect which makes me think of the German roof tiles that look like fish scales. Before the new leaves appear in early spring and the flower stems begin to push through the old leaf stems, we cut away the old leaves. The flowers are like tiny columbines,

OPPOSITE Tolerant of part-sun or shade, so long as it is cool and damp, *Rodgersia pinnata* 'Superba' is valued for its horse-chestnut-like foliage, let alone the added attraction of its rose-red flowers and following seed-heads.

BELOW One of the most useful plants to give height in any shady border, including those in dry shade, is Solomon's seal, *Polygonatum × hybridum*. Growing to almost a metre tall by the time it flowers in May, its foliage creates wonderful textural contrast with fresh new fern fronds.

in either creamy-yellow or pink. Sometimes visitors say to me, 'Mine have never flowered'. They might think that is so because the flowers are practically hidden among the last year's leaves. If you cut these down, you will see the little flower-buds appearing low down, followed later by a filmy cloud of tiny pastel-coloured flowers. When the new leaves unfold, many of them are suffused with brick-red or coral-pink over very pale green. Then, as the plant matures, the bright marbled effect fades to green and forms part of the cool carpet of the shady garden. But in autumn the warm colours return and the green leaves become burnished with bronze and coral tints.

I also have many different dicentras in this part of the garden: one with ferny greyish leaves, others with bright green leaves, and some with flowers like Dutchman's breeches rather than the lady's locket of the plant's common name. Dicentras are nearly all in shades of rosy pink and white. Lady's locket itself, *Dicentra spectabilis* (now *Lamprocapnos spectabilis*), is quite a grand plant and does not run about like the smaller edging forms.

Where you have more space and are not afraid of something being a little invasive, *Euphorbia amygdaloides* var. *robbiae* makes a good all-year-round plant. It forms large handsome rosettes of dark-green leathery leaves and from the centre of each rosette there unfolds, in spring, a slowly expanding head of typical luminous-green spring flowers. The flowerheads can remain all summer and in some gardens they fade to soft coppery shades. It spreads itself by underground runners and is one of the few euphorbias that tolerates shade so makes a good plant in a big garden, in a shrubbery, or under mature trees. If you have a small garden you might have to say a firm 'No' to it, but it is something I recommend to anyone looking for plants that show well in winter. It has good leaves for arrangements indoors and strong form in the garden.

The burnished autumn tints of *Epimedium* × *rubrum* turn from summer's glossy green. This old foliage is removed in late winter to allow the deep-pink flowers and fresh, bronze-red tinted foliage to emerge in spring.

OPPOSITE This damp hollow is full of horse-chestnut-shaped foliage of *Rodgersia podophylla* vying for space with the shuttlecock fern, *Matteuccia struthiopteris*. The mauve flowers of *Rhododendron ponticum* subtly enhance the scene. The acid soil and light shade afforded to a venerable specimen of *Stewartia pseudocamellia* encourages it to produce its exquisite white camellia-like flowers at the height of summer. (It has needed the aid of a prop for many years.)

Ferns flourish in cool shade. In East Anglia I am unable to grow some of the ferns from the redwood forests along the west coast of Oregon, where the rainfall is 150-250cm/60-100in and where *Polystichum munitum* grows as tall as me. Gardens with wet climates are perfect for many ferns, which must have a moist atmosphere as well as damp leaf-mould soil. Gardens exposed to drying winds are more limited in the number of ferns they can grow well but some ferns are tough and will grow almost anywhere. Perhaps the best is the male fern, *Dryopteris filix-mas,* but even that does not appreciate being put into a hot sunny border. It tolerates surprisingly dry shade and I have seen it growing well in the rooty bottom of a hedge. It is a handsome fern, though not among the most choice ('choice' often means more difficult.) I think the polystichums are more elegant. Several forms of the soft shield fern, *Polystichum setiferum* Acutilobum Group, are both daintier and more elegant, and not difficult to grow in cool soil when sheltered from wind as well as sun. A good form of our native fern is *Polypodium × mantoniae* 'Cornubiense', an evergreen fern, pretty to use in winter flower arrangements with *Skimmia* berries and snowdrops, if your rooms are not overheated. The species, *Polypodium vulgare*, has more simple leaves, not so intricately cut. The hart's-tongue fern, *Asplenium scolopendrium*, becomes rather tatty by the end of winter but I relish its strong contrast of form among either finely cut or rounded leaves.

Most people's eyes glaze over when I recommend ivies for poor shaded soil, such as an impossibly dry piece of ground beneath a dense tree. I myself have a practically bone-dry place beneath a great holly. Certainly, the nearer you get to the trunk of a mature yew or a holly, the more difficult it is going to be to grow anything; mulching may be the best option. Under my holly, I have found dwarf periwinkles and various forms of common ivy, *Hedera helix*, to be the only

The Lenten rose, *Helleborus × hybridus,* comes in many shades from cream and pink through to the darkest maroon. The dark-flowered selections are usually the most popular, but Beth particularly loved the delicacy afforded by the green-shaded, white-flowered ones.

OPPOSITE A perfect example of Beth's 'green tapestry', here a woven carpet of foliage including silvery pulmonarias, ajugas, hardy geraniums, hostas and ferns. The lovely, arching plumes of *Miscanthus sinensis* 'Yaku-jima' on the left create a counterpoint to the pink-flowered variegated *Phlox paniculata* 'Norah Leigh' alongside it.

plants I can establish in such conditions. Ivies seem to grow in the driest places and there are so many different kinds with really attractive leaves, different in shape and form, as well as those with patterns or different variegations. I had a long bare bank of clay at one end of the long shady border, which I have completely buried beneath shawls of different forms of ivy. It was such raw clay that even the native weeds could not establish themselves there. I dug sloping holes in the clay (so they would not fill with water), put a spadeful of compost into each hole and then firmed in the little plants. In a comparatively short time, the bank became covered with green, eventually smothering the clay beneath. Now other shade-loving plants are colonizing among the trails of ivy. *Euphorbia amygdaloides* var. *robbiae*, *Iris foetidissima* and *E. a.* 'Purpurea', the red-tinged form of our native euphorbia, are all adding interest and contrast of form.

There is not an enormous range of plants or bushes that will remain evergreen and tolerate hard winters. I am grateful for one ivy which I have that grows as a shrub. It is called *Hedera helix* f. *poetarum* 'Poetica Arborea' and it slowly forms a bush of only flowering shoots – there are no long running trails, nor will there ever be, because it was propagated originally from a mature fruiting branch. Every winter it is loaded with clusters of fruit. In the normal English ivy, these turn black, but ours turn to soft orange in spring. I also have a Portugal laurel, *Prunus lusitanica*, planted close to the bole of the great oak and, for a slim vertical, there is an upright yew, but this bush ivy makes a contrasting rounded shape which is very useful.

There are various forms of violas which retain carpets of leaves in winter, including blue- and white-flowered forms of *Viola cornuta* along the edge of the border. The leaves of ajugas may be slightly damaged by frost but they make a decorative contribution, including the pink-washed form, *Ajuga reptans* 'Burgundy Glow', while the variegated form makes a pattern of cream and green. A mossy saxifrage with finely cut leaves makes good contrast. Just peeping through the soil at about the same time is *Viola septentrionalis*, which produces large white unscented flowers. You can easily find the clumps before the leaves appear because the rhizome-like shoots lie practically on the surface.

Small evergreen shrubs well suited to small gardens are the various forms of Christmas box, *Sarcococca*. They like

Wallich's wood fern, *Dryopteris wallichiana*, and *Hosta sieboldiana* 'Frances Williams' take centre stage here along the long Shady Walk, with *Hydrangea aspera* Villosa Group flowering in late summer.

shade and make small neat bushes of glossy, pointed leaves. In January, if the weather is not too severe, you can pick little sprigs of tiny sweet-scented white flowers even from quite young plants.

At the end of the bed is a large bush of the evergreen *Viburnum davidii*. It spreads out across the path like a great bulwark where the garden changes as the land rises up to an exposed gravel bank. Here, if you stand among one specific group of plants (all being plants that like cool,

shady conditions) and, looking towards the higher level of the Mediterranean Garden (where the plants enjoy sun in gravel soil) you can see from a distance the change in leaf types – the drought-loving grey plants like *Artemisia* are on the open slope, contrasting with the group planted in shade. Walking into the sunshine in summer, it feels several degrees warmer, away from the shade.

THE NORTH-FACING CLAY BANK

The bank of heavy clay soil between the reservoir and the southern end of the long Shady Walk grows epimediums well. For contrast I grow the spider-like Japanese plant with black strap-shaped leaves called *Ophiopogon planiscapus* 'Kokuryū' (syn. *O. p.* 'Nigrescens'). In winter, we can find clusters of shining dark purple berries among the black leaves: the birds do not appear to eat them. The berries are preceded in late summer by sprays of little pink flowers.

The large, rounded blue-green leaves of *Hosta sieboldiana* contrast strikingly underneath the delicate, filigree-like purple leaves of the Japanese maple, *Acer palmatum* 'Atropurpureum', and silvery leaves of the taller, rounded variegated *Acer negundo* 'Flamingo' behind. It is pruned hard each spring to induce a proliferation of fresh new growth, although reverted green-leaved shoots have to be removed later.

Hellebores are the spring theme along this cool border, as many forms of *Helleborus × hybridus* are at their best from February to April and they come in many shades of plum, rose and smoky purple, while others are pure white or green- and bronze-shadowed. Most of them are are derived from species that grow in thickets or on the edges of woodland round the Black Sea below the Caucasus mountains. Many are heavily speckled inside with maroon. Some forms are now being selected to hold up their heads to face you rather than drooping like lampshades, but I admire their modesty and rather like having to bend to look at them.

Bergenias grow here, as they will almost anywhere. They are very adaptable plants and I find their large leathery leaves equally useful in the dry garden as full-stop plants where a hosta would not survive so well. Bergenias make more lasting features than hostas since they are evergreen.

A lovely dark-coloured form of the Lenten rose, *Helleborus × hybridus*, contrasts well with an underplanting of wild primroses, *Primula vulgaris*.

THE LONG SHADY WALK

In this part of the garden, where the shade is cast by a row of oaks, I have more room to grow bigger and perhaps coarser plants than I have in the small shade garden beneath the great oak and holly. It is the ideal place for many different kinds of *Pulmonaria* – *P. saccharata* has the largest leaves, handsomely spotted. *Pulmonaria rubra* has coral-red flowers which never turn blue, followed by large rosettes of velvety light-green leaves.

Half-way along the long Shady Walk, an old hawthorn tree was decapitated, the roots treated so that it would not grow again and the trunk then used as a support for ivy. Now *Hedera colchica* 'Sulphur Heart', a large-leaved ivy with irregular yellow centres to the leaves, forms a tall column with a rather dark holly as a good backdrop. By making use in this way of unwanted stumps, quick vertical interest can be obtained while waiting for newly planted

'Small evergreen shrubs well suited to small gardens are the various forms of Christmas box, Sarcococca. They like shade and make small neat bushes of glossy pointed leaves. In January, if the weather is not too severe, you can pick little sprigs of tiny sweet-scented white flowers even from quite young plants.'

131

trees to achieve height. From January onwards, there will be a succession of snowdrops along this gently curving border. There are a few rhododendrons along the boundary bank but this is not rhododendron country. If I could grow them easily, I am sure I would be tempted to grow more, especially the wild unimproved species, which I much prefer. Many of those I have are forms of *Rhododendron ponticum*, valued primarily for their evergreen leaves and their wind resistance. If you are not so troubled by desiccating winds as we are here, then you can grow many more beautiful ones.

There is room in this part of the garden for some of the more rampant ground-cover plants. One of the loveliest, in spring and early summer, is an American phlox, *Phlox stolonifera*. Above the prostrate rosettes of light green stand heads of soft blue or white flowers.

Viola riviniana Purpurea Group is one of my favourite ground-cover plants; modest, with its small dark-purple leaves and light-purple flowers, it comes true from seed, and spreads adventitiously, running round hostas and other heavy clumps. It has no scent. Only *Viola odorata* is scented, with purple, white or pink flowers, but unfortunately I find it more difficult to grow here than the other violets. Its leaves are only too often attacked by aphids or some pest that causes them to roll up in an unsightly fashion.

Invaluable as ground cover in large shrubberies are *Trachystemon orientale* and *Pachysandra terminalis*, but both are very invasive plants. *Helleborus foetidus* and *Tanacetum parthenium* 'Aureum' provide shade and cover around the leaves of a special dwarf narcissus in summer. There will also be shade from the oak overhead, all of which is helping to keep away the dreaded narcissus fly that lays its eggs in the neck of the bulb.

Another handsome but rampant scrambler is *Rubus tricolor*. I mostly use it as ground cover either under trees

Taking over as snowdrops fade, *Pachyphragma macrophyllum* produces short, showy heads of chalk-white flowers. Fresh green foliage emerges shortly afterwards, creating ideal ground cover throughout the summer.

or down a bank, but I have also seen it grown up a fence. It is a relative of the bramble, but why it is called 'tricolor' I cannot think as it seems to me to have only two colours. It makes trails of long, lax stems covered with soft copper-coloured bristles. Simple shining leaves eventually make really extensive ground cover in shade, often scrambling over birch roots.

Because there is so much work to be done, we do not always notice what is happening and do not cut back in time something that is becoming too invasive. An example of this is an attractive yellow-leaved ivy that has taken over too much ground at one end of the long Shady Walk and there are erythroniums underneath which could be choked. Certainly, the silver-leaved *Lamium maculatum* is being squeezed out, so time must be taken to sort out all these invaders.

The late-spring pale-pink flowers of *Deutzia × hybrida* 'Mont Rose' set off by the fresh green foliage of the running shuttlecock fern, *Matteuccia struthiopteris*. A winter-long feature of the garden at their feet is *Arum italicum* subsp. *italicum* 'Marmoratum' with its dark glossy green spear-shaped, wavy-edged leaves, clearly veined with ivory.

The Reservoir Garden

Since Beth wrote The Green Tapestry, *this area of the garden has been remodelled, initially by Beth and more recently by her head gardener, Åsa Gregers-Warg, who describes at the end of the chapter what has subsequently been done.*

THIS PART of the garden is an open area of large informal borders with wide grassy walks. Although the soil here can dry out after a long period without rain, it is not as poor as in the Mediterranean Garden. We added a layer of clay to the original gravel soil when we dredged the reservoir and spread it, when dry, like caked face powder over the gravel. Trees and shrubs have done well in the centres of these beds, their strong roots able to cope with the stiff surface clay, while a regular straw mulch is improving the top soil. But I had to remove some of the clay from the wider borders around the shrubs, replace it with gravelly soil and then fork both soils together before adding more grit, compost and old farmyard manure to make an acceptable soil for herbaceous plants.

The established Judas tree, *Cercis siliquastrum*, adds a sense of maturity to the new planting, while many bulbs, such as *Allium* 'Purple Rain', provide colour in spring and early summer. Repetition of colour, or form, helps to give the planting cohesion.

Whereas on the original gravel we had been restricted in our choice of plants, we are now able to grow, among others, some of the old border chrysanthemums, such as *Chrysanthemum* 'Anastasia' and *C.* 'Emperor of China'. The latter, an old hybrid chrysanthemum reintroduced by Graham Stuart Thomas, flowers in late autumn.

Some of the hardy geraniums (cranesbills) that do not like very gravelly soil also flourish here. One of them, *Geranium wallichianum* 'Buxton's Variety', is a treasure, producing royal-blue flowers, white-eyed and appealing, for weeks on end from late summer until the first frosts. Along the border edges I planted the dwarf mountain forms of *Phlox*, *P. douglasii* and *P. serrulata*, which do well here, but not the tall border phloxes – they need a moister soil.

'I always design my island beds with a spine of trees and shrubs. Sometimes the spine goes roughly through the middle of the bed, at others it may be offset to leave more space on one side or the other to make better use of the sunny or the shady side.'

ABOVE The original Reservoir Garden, as it was in 2009, with much of Beth's planting based around low-maintenance evergreen shrubs, with little room for perennials. Only the Judas tree (far left) remains as an established feature of the new planting.

OPPOSITE In the revised planting today, the silver-grey colour of *Stachys byzantina*, lamb's ears, is repeated by the architectural foliage of *Cynara cardunculus* and *Poa labillardierei*, while forget-me-nots and alliums provide seasonal splashes of colour. *Iris* 'Benton Deirdre' is one of many irises bred by the late Sir Cedric Morris, who carefully selected them for their understated elegance.

THE ISLAND BEDS

Most of the beds in the Reservoir Garden are what are termed island beds, being surrounded by mown grass. I always design mine with a spine of trees and shrubs. Sometimes the spine goes roughly through the middle of the bed, at others it may be offset to leave more space on one side or the other to make better use of the sunny or the shady side, as I mentioned in the Shade Gardens (see page 115). Where I have a wide sunny side and a much narrower shady side, I consider the narrow side the 'minus' side because although it has seasonal interest it is not exciting all year round. You walk past it rather than stop to enjoy individual treasures. Bold clumps of bergenias, hellebores and carpeting plants like lamiums and *Geranium maculatum* keep the soil free of weeds. In some places, I feel there cannot be two borders of equal interest facing each other because we cannot absorb, let alone enjoy, too much at once. I think in some circumstances a quiet, unexciting piece of planting makes a necessary contribution to the design.

Several different veronicas grow around the edge of this part of the garden. There is understandable confusion in many gardeners' minds between veronicas and parahebes. Veronicas generally behave as herbaceous plants, while parahebes form semi-woody little bushes. Both make most attractive mounds or mats to edge the borders, their neat green leaves being completely buried beneath the wealth of tiny flowers in gentian-blue or white.

Potentillas do well in the sunny beds, among them *Potentilla* 'Miss Willmott' and *P. atrosanguinea*, which has flowers of the rich dark red you see when a fresh drop of blood oozes from a wound. A yellow one with an orange eye and silver strawberry-like leaves is called *Potentilla argyrophylla*. Kniphofias are planted for their interesting late summer and autumn flower spikes.

OPPOSITE TOP Grown for their attractive dark foliage, *Sambucus nigra* f. *porphyrophylla* 'Eva' and *Rosa glauca* need full sun to provide the best leaf colour. The white form of our native foxglove, *Digitalis purpurea* f. *albiflora*, was always favoured by Beth; any pink seedlings are removed to keep the strain pure.

OPPOSITE BOTTOM It is not difficult to see why *Eremurus* sometimes goes by the name of desert candle. Here, the burnt-orange spires of *E.* 'Cleopatra' glow as they catch the early summer evening light, surrounded by *Salvia verticillata* 'Purple Rain', the globular seed-heads of *Allium* 'Purple Rain' and silvery *Stachys byzantina*.

ABOVE Attractive seed-heads of *Agapanthus* are left to prolong the season of interest. It is well behaved here in the UK, but considered a noxious weed in other parts of the world. Always take care when introducing new plants into the garden.

THE SUN AND SHADE BEDS

I like to make a mixed planting of deciduous and evergreen trees and shrubs, so there is always something to look at in the garden in winter. If they are all deciduous, the garden has no form in those months and, if they are entirely evergreen, the overall impression is heavy and lumpen looking. Yellow-leaved shrubs offer a much-needed lightening effect among other darker-leaved ones, while the

This delightful hardy umbellifer, *Oenanthe pimpinelloides*, which carries clusters of tiny white flowers in summer, is allowed to self-seed among clumps of *Nepeta × faassenii* 'Purrsian Blue', a more compact catmint ideal for smaller gardens.

partial shade from trees overhead prevents leaf scorch on tender yellow-leaved forms.

On the sunny side of an island bed, *Onosma alborosea* is a plant adapted to sunny conditions, its leaves protected by a covering of bristly hairs. When not in flower, the rosettes of grey leaves make an interesting feature or foil for another plant in flower alongside. The flowers appear in spring from the centre of each rosette. Tightly rolled clusters or croziers of coral-pink buds open as white tubular flowers. It can look even better when allowed to droop like a shawl over the edge of a low wall or rock face.

Haplopappus coronopifolius makes cushions of finely cut evergreen foliage which continue to produce a succession of bright orange daisy flowers from midsummer until December. The bright green leaves make a good contrast with grey-leaved helianthemums nearby. Unalleviated grey foliage can look particularly flat and uninteresting. Helianthemums come in many varieties with green, grey or variegated leaves and with single flowers in many shades from white to crimson and cream to orange. They are likely to be damaged by very cold winters but, even in cold gardens or heavy soils, this problem can be lessened if attention is paid to the drainage.

Walking round the Reservoir Garden in winter, the eye is caught by long-lasting designs created with foliage alone. *Libertia ixioides*, with its dense tufts of narrow leaves, stained orange, harmonizes pleasantly with spreading carpets of golden-leaved thymes. But I do not always place plants the first time in a way that pleases me, even though I am planting all the time.

The year begins with drifts of a fine snowdrop, *Galanthus caucasicus*, quickly followed by small-flowered daffodils, including the species *Narcissus minor*, *N. pallida* and the hybrid, *N.* 'W. P. Milner'. Providing lush foliage in the early spring are the shining leaf clusters of *Colchicum speciosum*

In autumn and winter *Calamagrostis × acutiflora* 'Karl Foerster' makes an outstanding vertical, its bleached columns standing firm without support or damage. It partners well with the distinctive seed-heads of *Phlomis russeliana*, providing structure until being cut down in early spring.

'Unalleviated grey foliage can look particularly flat and uninteresting. Helianthemums come in many varieties with green, grey or variegated leaves and with single flowers in many shades from white to crimson and cream to orange.'

(which produces purple goblet-shaped flowers in autumn) and clumps of *Iris foetidissima*. These are followed by a range of fritillaries. There are many species of these strangely attractive bulbs which grow in all kinds of conditions throughout the temperate climates of the world. The best known include the crown imperial fritillary, *Fritillaria imperialis*, and the snakeshead fritillary, *F. meleagris*.

There are groups of *Anemone blanda* 'Bridesmaid' whose pure white flowers stand out like brilliant patches of snow in the cold bareness of early spring. I also use the smaller herbaceous plants to edge the beds, including *Geranium tuberosum*, which produces a delightful airy mass of tiny pink-and-white flowers standing about 30cm/12in high in early summer.

To encourage new healthy foliage and a second flush of bloom, *Knautia macedonica*, *Salvia verticillata* 'Purple Rain' and *Geranium* 'Orion' are cut back hard, straight after flowering. *Nepeta*, *Pulmonaria*, *Alchemilla mollis* and several other perennials receive the same treatment elsewhere in the garden.

THE NEW RESERVOIR GARDEN

Beth recognized when she wrote *The Green Tapestry* that the planting here still had a long way to go. As she said, 'It is a bit like a teenager, this part of the garden, with plenty of future promise but not quite yet mature. At the moment I feel it is lacking in character.'

Situated on a gentle south-facing slope, overlooking the reservoir, this area forms a natural link between the Water Garden, with its moisture loving plants, and the Woodland Garden. As Beth described in the earlier part of this chapter, she tried to improve the gravel soil in the 1970s by adding a layer of clay dug out from the reservoir. Unfortunately, the two layers were never mixed thoroughly, resulting in large areas being covered in a thick layer of heavy clay – wet and sticky all winter and hard as concrete in summer.

Many of the herbaceous perennials in Beth's original planting scheme struggled with the difficult soil and slowly dwindled. Over time, the tapestry effect she had aimed at was lost and the beds became predominantly filled with shrubs, deciduous and evergreen, interspersed with a few perennials and grasses. Only tough, vigorous ground cover, such as bergenias and *Geranium endressii*, thrived, forming carpets beneath the shrubs. Although still providing some interest, the Reservoir Garden had become more of a transition area rather than somewhere visitors chose to linger. Four decades after it was first planted, the Reservoir Garden was in need of major rejuvenation. The only sensible approach was to remove all the plants and start again. At the time, it was a daunting task to tackle a project of this size knowing it was never going to be a quick fix, as there were plenty of persistent weeds to eradicate before we could begin to improve the heavy soil. Removing and replacing all of the soil was never really an option – not only would it not sit right with Beth's ethos, it would also be far too costly.

Euphorbia margalidiana flowers almost continuously throughout the year. Nestled between clumps of *Thalictrum* and *Amsonia* 'Ernst Pagels', this spurge quickly forms a giant dome. *Amsonia*, on the other hand, has a reputation for being somewhat slow to establish, though 'Ernst Pagels' is well worth the wait, with its pale blue, star-shaped flowers in summer and excellent autumn colour.

Remodelling the Reservoir Garden

Work began in autumn 2015 by clearing the original planting, which had been there for nearly forty years. A few key plants were left to add maturity and provide structure to the new scheme. A fine Judas tree, *Cercis siliquastrum*, is a centre piece at the lower end of the new planting, while two New Zealand flax, *Phormium tenax*, make dramatic clumps of sword-shape leaves. Once cleared, the entire area (approx. 1000m²) was carefully dug over by hand to remove remaining roots, unwanted bulbs and perennial weeds.

To help break up the heavy clay, we knew we would need to add plenty of organic matter. Good-quality farmyard manure is difficult to come by these days, so instead we settled on using spent mushroom compost, with the added benefit of it being weed-free. In total, 150 tonnes were spread across the surface and ploughed in. To cover the empty ground over the summer *Phacelia tanacetifolia* was used as a green manure. Being vigorous and fast-growing, it blooms within six to eight weeks of sowing, producing an abundance of pollen and nectar enjoyed by bees and hoverflies. Dug into the ground while still green, before it has a chance to set seed (unless you are happy for it to self-seed), it improves both fertility and soil structure.

Where initially there had been three island beds with wide sweeping grass paths between, the layout was remodelled, keeping a main path for ease of maintenance, while introducing a new series of narrow, meandering paths taking the visitors in, amongst and up close to the plants. The old turf was replaced with a hard-wearing, permeable path, top-dressed with self-binding aggregate (CEDEC).

Redesigning our borders is always an organic process. Working in the same way Beth did, there is no detailed design on paper from which to work – only a rough idea and a list of suitable plants. Colourwise, the planting scheme is a soft mixture of yellows, blues, mauves and

In late spring the Judas tree's bare branches are covered in clusters of rose-pink, pea-like flowers over several weeks. Forget-me-nots make great gap-fillers, but care must be taken so that emerging perennials, especially the weaker growers, are not going to be smothered.

pinks but, above all, the emphasis is on Beth's preference for contrasting shape, texture and form, as well as subtle variations in foliage colour.

Starting with a blank canvas gave us the opportunity to introduce a mixture of old, reliable favourites combined with new acquaintances, many of which would struggle with the wet soil in the Water Garden or shrivel up in the dry Gravel Garden. Just as a chef would try new recipes before including them on a restaurant menu, we are keen to trial any new plants we acquire before introducing them to our nursery: *Nepeta* 'Blue Dragon', characterized by a strong upright habit and large violet-blue flowers, turned

Renovation of this area began in autumn 2015 by clearing the original planting.

Once cleared, the entire area was forked over to remove roots, unwanted bulbs and perennial weeds, before plenty of organic matter was added to improve the soil, enabling a greater range of plants to be grown.

A few key plants were left from the original planting. The fine Judas tree, *Cercis siliquastrum*, provides the centrepiece at the lower end of the new planting.

out to be very rampant and needs reducing every year. *Verbena macdougalii* 'Lavender Spires', a superb sterile vervain with branching habit and deep lavender flowers over a long period, appears to be more tolerant of heavier soil than *V. bonariensis. Amsonia* 'Ernst Pagels' was slow to establish but now looks splendid next to a clump of *Iris* 'Benton Menace' (one of many Sir Cedric Morris-bred irises that we grow). Nearby an impressively big *Euphorbia margalidiana* blooms from April onwards while, across the path, another specimen at half its size appears less happy, perhaps being more exposed to cold winds. *Agastache* 'Blue Boa' appears to be tougher and more long-lived than other agastaches we have grown. It makes a perfect companion to *Echinacea, Eryngium planum* 'Blaukappe' and *Pimpinella major* 'Rosea' as they mingle alongside the main path. Camassias, alliums and tapered spires of *Eremurus*, the foxtail lily, add drama to the borders in early summer while ornamental grasses add movement and late-season

Striking, elegant spires of *Eremurus* 'White Beauty Favourite', the foxtail lily or desert candle, add drama to the summer borders, while also making a strong, vertical accent. They combine beautifully with the white globes of *Allium stipitatum* 'Mount Everest'. They are planted together with perennials that can fill the empty gaps as the untidy foliage dies back.

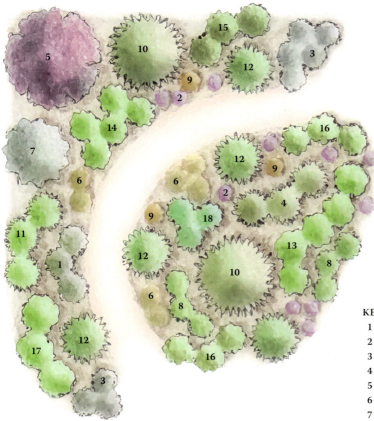

Planting plan for improved soil in full sun
This part of the garden comprises several different-sized beds, divided by a series of paths. This planting plan is for a curved border and an island bed, over an area approx. 4.5m/14ft by 5m/16ft.

KEY

1 *Achillea* (×3)
2 *Allium* 'Purple Rain' (×11)
3 *Anaphalis* (×8)
4 *Calamagrostis* (×3)
5 *Cotinus coggygria* (×1)
6 *Crocosmia* (×7)
7 *Cynara cardunculus* (×1)
8 *Eryngium* (×6)
9 *Fritillaria imperialis* (×3)
10 *Miscanthus* (×2)
11 *Panicum* (×3)
12 *Pennisetum alopecuroides* 'Black Beauty' (×4)
13 *Phlomis russeliana* (×5)
14 *Phlox paniculata* (×5)
15 *Pimpinella major* 'Rosea' (×3)
16 *Salvia nemorosa/S. × sylvestris* (×6)
17 *Sanguisorba* (×3)
18 *Thalictrum* (×3)

interest. Tall and elegant, *Stipa pseudoichu* is best planted rising out of a void so its silvery arching plumes can be fully appreciated. *Miscanthus sinensis* 'Dronning Ingrid' has become a firm favourite, flowering earlier in the year than many other miscanthus varieties while also providing invaluable winter structure.

Two recent dry summers with scorching temperatures sometimes above 30°C/86°F, coupled with prolonged spells of drought (in the height of summer in 2018 there was a 50-day period without a single drop of rain), has already made us reconsider some of the plant choices. Inevitably the planting will continue to evolve over the years to come.

Maintenance

To help supress annual weeds and retain moisture, we have been using a mulch made out of green waste, and in autumn fallen leaves are spread directly over the soil, carefully avoiding plants such as bearded irises, as their rhizomes prefer to sit on the surface and bake in the sun.

Seed-heads are left over the winter for as long as they look attractive. One of the benefits of not having too many early spring bulbs is that we can wait until quite late to cut down all the perennials whereas in other parts of the

Many herbaceous plants retreat during autumn, but ornamental grasses, such as *Miscanthus sinensis*, and attractive seed-heads continue to provide colour and interest throughout winter. In mild spells, perennials, especially those protected by the Judas tree (seen earlier in summer on page 144), may continue to bloom intermittently.

garden everything has to be cut down around Christmas to prevent trampling on bulbs as they are starting to emerge.

'Editing' the borders is an ongoing process. Self-seeders are welcome but need to be managed or they quickly become a nuisance. *Erigeron annuus*, the tall fleabane, produces a mass of pretty, small white daisies but easily smothers more delicate neighbours, especially those emerging later in the season. The combination of fertile soil and open ground (with many empty gaps still to be filled) has meant we spend a lot of time weeding out seedlings. The pale-yellow scabious, *Scabiosa columbaria* subsp. *ochroleuca*, produced an astounding number of seedlings in its first year here. As our nursery relies on the garden for seed and cutting materials, we need to take care that the true forms are not diluted by seedlings different from the parents. *Salvia verticillata* 'Purple Rain' and the distinctly paler *S. v.* 'Hannay's Blue' are grown only a metres apart so must not be allowed to mingle or cuttings may be taken from the wrong plant.

The new Reservoir Garden was officially opened on Beth's 94th birthday on 27th June 2017. Having spent a couple of years working on the project, discussing the different stages with Beth (who at this time was more or less housebound and only ventured outside occasionally) it was rewarding to be able to share this moment with her. I am so pleased she was able to enjoy the finished result and give it her approval.

OVERLEAF Autumn's first frost settles on the new Reservoir Garden. Planted in spring 2017, many of the plants quickly established in the freshly improved soil. Here, large clumps of *Pennisetum alopecuroides* 'Black Beauty' sit comfortably amongst various seed-heads and ground cover edging the meandering paths, allowing visitors a close-up view. Though the pennisetum performed well and looked stunning in its first year, it has since struggled during recent summers so may have to be replaced with a more drought-tolerant alternative.

149

The Woodland Garden

Since Beth wrote The Green Tapestry, *a wild, wooded area of about one hectare beyond the Reservoir Garden has been been turned into a new Woodland Garden. Its planning and creation is described here by David Ward.*

THE CATALYST for Beth's Woodland Garden was the storm that raged through the south-east of England on the night of 15th-16th October 1987. It is interesting to note that there are very few references in *The Green Tapestry* to the Great Storm, as it became known. Beth and her husband, Andrew, had agreed that this area, which they knew as Badger's Wood (although the badgers had long departed), would remain untouched and become a haven for native flora and fauna.

It was not until a good two years after the storm that Beth felt ready to turn her mind to the practicalities of how to tackle the opportunity presented to her by Nature. Further inspiration came from a visit in 1988 to the woodland garden at Castle Howard in Yorkshire after which Andrew capitulated to her long-held desire to create a woodland garden beneath the shady canopy of spindly oaks.

Work began in the autumn of 1989 with Beth selecting which trees, mainly oak with a few ash and birch, that she wished to keep; all the others were removed. Once the

This emerging tapestry of spring foliage indicates the moisture provided by the half-hidden small ditch. The pleated, hosta-like foliage of *Veratrum californicum* contrasts well with clumps of Bowles's golden sedge, *Carex elata* 'Aurea'. Blue forget-me-nots are allowed to self-seed, their sky-blue flowers adding another note to the predominantly yellow and green palette while a paperbark maple, *Acer griseum*, draws the eye up from ground level.

route of the paths and the actual beds was roughly decided, it was time to concentrate on the dry and sandy soil. It was decided to run water pipes down to this area, as the level of shade and the low rainfall meant that irrigation would be needed. Compost and well-rotted manure were added as the soil was prepared for planting the following spring.

PLANTING

This was a large area to plant and although we had earmarked many of our nursery stock plants for it, it was clear that we needed to establish an understorey of shrubs beneath the tall oaks, which would then create the microclimate and protection from the desiccating winds so needed by many woodland plants. A visit to the Savill Garden at Windsor Great Park, where we were shown around by John Bond, then Keeper of the Gardens, was an inspiration to Beth, and we came away with a van full of unusual and interesting shrubs to add to those Beth already had in mind.

During the clearing and preparation, it became clear that the prevailing south-westerlies whistled through from the rise of surrounding farmland, made worse by the neighbouring farmer's grubbing up of the apple orchard which had acted as a windbreak. Beth quickly planted a new barrier of tough, hardy evergreen shrubs including cotoneaster, hollies, laurel, bamboos and even *Rhododendron ponticum*, which she had a soft spot for.

As usual, Beth followed no paper plan as she began planting. A spine of shrubs, both evergreen and deciduous, would fill the centre of each bed providing shade and shelter for the harmonious combinations of herbaceous plants, ferns and grasses she had in her mind's eye, or which she thoughtfully scribbled onto a piece of cardboard (where once we dreaded them, we now treasure Beth's carboard lists of jobs to do). Among choice evergreens acquired from the Savill Garden and elsewhere were several viburnums,

Highlighting the understorey planting in the Woodland Garden is this fine specimen of coral-bark maple, *Acer palmatum* 'Sango-kaku'. Many herbaceous plants display good autumn colour, one of the best, seen here, being Solomon's seal, *Polygonatum × hybridum*.

variegated hollies, *Mahonia*, *Pieris* and *Skimmia* which, in particular, Beth had used widely around other shady areas of the garden, appreciating both their ease of growth and their broad evergreen form. In particular, the flowers of the delicately scented *Skimmia × confusa* 'Kew Green' had become a favourite for her winter flower arrangements. Although small (not even as much as a metre high), there are two forms of winter box, *Sarcococca hookeriana* var. *digyna* and *S. confusa*, which also scent the air for several yards during the winter months.

Careful to prevent too much additional shade or cover being cast, we chose to plant the evergreen shrubs sparingly and many deciduous shrubs were used. The cornelian cherry, *Cornus mas*, makes a large broad feature, providing a delightful frame of bare branches smothered in tiny puffs of pale-yellow flowers during February, creating a charming picture with snowdrops at its base. Later, in April, *Amelanchier lamarckii*, the Juneberry, flowers with cherry-like blossoms held against burnished new growth. It is a sight for a week and then fades into the background until its autumn blaze of colour. Other prominent shrubs that shed their leaves include flowering currants, the bare branches of which Beth would pick when laden with buds, to open in the warmth of the house. May-flowering *Deutzia* feature prominently to provide late colour as the Woodland Garden moves into the calm of summer.

Beth's enthusiasm for a woodland garden was fuelled by her desire to grow and enjoy as many plants as possible and although the great oaks around the garden created shade, many of the borders were quite narrow and the scope

A simple bench creates a resting place, surrounded by garlic-scented wild ramsons, *Allium ursinum*. This native plant, widely used as a culinary herb, is a survivor from the original wild wood.

OPPOSITE *Gunnera tinctoria* and *Matteuccia struthiopteris*, the shuttlecock fern, thrive in damp conditions near the small ditch, in contrast to the main part of the wood which is much drier.

therefore limited. Here, with two acres of virgin ground, Beth dreamed of swathes of herbaceous plants and bulbs that would provide a long season of interest.

SEASONAL FEATURES

The natural cycle of a woodland garden, or indeed any area in constant shade, is for many of the plants to emerge quickly and flower before it becomes too shady. Think of our woodlands in spring, full of bluebells, wood anemones, celandines and so forth, all rushing to take advantage of the available light and moisture before the overhead canopy comes into full leaf. From then on, we rely more on foliage and form to provide the interest, so for these conditions you need ferns, grasses, hosta and heuchera, to name a few.

The year can both start and end with snowdrops, as over the years we have amassed a sizable collection and through constant division and replanting 'in the green' we are able to display bold clumps of many. We hoped eventually to

'Beneath the canopy of newly fledged oak leaves, still bright yellowish-green, the whole wood floor is heaving with life in every shape and form...'

RIGHT This summer scene is dominated by the loose spires of *Veratrum californicum*, a wet meadow plant from North America. Hidden amongst summer foliage, the spring-fed ditch keeps the soil moist enough to support a wealth of foliage, including hostas, ferns and grasses, which would struggle in other parts of the wood.

BELOW *Galanthus elwesii* 'Mrs Macnamara' is one of the first snowdrops to show, coming into flower as the New Year starts.

create a mass planting of snowdrops, looking principally for good 'doers', with a few more unusual, if slightly less showy, forms. Perhaps it is the darker days, but the turn of the year sees *Galanthus elwesii* 'Mrs Macnamara' stand out, whiter than white, in full flower during the early part of January to be followed by large drifts of *G.* 'James Backhouse', a snowdrop that on closer inspection can display aberrant or misshapen petals. January also sees us searching for the

first buttercup-like flowers of winter aconites. Beth was always keen to spot these delightful plants, in a mild season in January, later if cold. It has taken many years for them to establish themselves, but now they seed around freely.

The main flush of snowdrops can be seen throughout February. Whenever asked to choose a favourite, Beth would always say, 'How could one choose? It's like asking which is your favourite child.' But, that said, she could always be prompted to pick a few, such as *Galanthus* 'Hippolyta', the neatest of the doubles we grow, although one needs to get down low to appreciate the true symmetry of the inner, green-stained petticoats.

Among the many plants passed to Beth by Sir Cedric Morris came several snowdrops, many of which were of the *Galanthus elwesii* type, distinguished by their broader, grey-green leaves. One such form stood out and was eventually named *Galanthus elwesii* 'Cedric's Prolific', due in part to its willingness to increase – it is a valuable mid-season snowdrop. Another snowdrop that may originally have come from Cedric is a form of *Galanthus plicatus*. It was eventually named after Beth, but alas the stock has 'seeded out' or cross-pollinated and the patches we now

BELOW The ditch remains relatively moist well into summer, but its shallow sloping upper side can dry out. Here, as in many parts of the wood, tougher ground cover, such as *Geranium endressii* and *Dicentra formosa*, are particularly useful.

have contain a mixture of seedlings. The original form is a fine plant, with large globular flowers and two flower stems per bulb, which extends its flowering well into March.

Following on from the snowdrops in March are the daffodils, although the first flowers of one special little narcissus always appear around Christmas time. *Narcissus minor* 'Cedric Morris' was found in the wild in Spain by Basil Leng, a friend of Cedric's, and given to Beth by him. It is a perfect miniature daffodil, untroubled by winter, and amazingly lasts way into February. We annually chop the bulbs up (a technique called 'chipping') to propagate as many as possible. The reliable *Narcissus* 'February Gold' is in full flower by March and is followed by the later white daffodils, such as *Narcissus* 'Jenny' or *N.* 'Thalia'.

'Towards the end of March, as the early yellow daffodils, including the little Narcissus minor, *are fading, sprinklings of primroses take their place. Is any flower lovelier or more appealing in a natural setting?'*

ABOVE *Narcissus* 'February Gold' seldom lives up to its name but it is the dominant daffodil throughout March, its swept-back petals affording a more naturalistic look than the classic form. The wood is a haven for wildlife and a refuge for this fine cock pheasant.

Hellebores have always been a favourite, and many forms of the Lenten rose, *Helleborus × hybridus*, were selected by Beth, either from our stock beds or from plants which were purchased for sale in the nursery. Looking at their best as the snowdrops finish, the lush leafy stems are already over a foot high and full of bud and flower. Beth preferred the single varieties, although she appreciated the complicated beauty of many recently introduced doubles.

The Woodland Garden is the natural home to many shade-loving plants and, as spring progresses, the plants emerge rapidly. Amongst patches of blue wood anemones, *Anemone nemorosa* 'Robinsoniana', can be found clumps of erythroniums, and we have a particularly fine form of the European *Erythronium dens-canis*, with heavily marbled leaves and all-too-fleeting, reflexed pink flowers. Some choice treasures can be found tucked away. Returning from one of her annual trips to the German nursery of Countess von Stein Zeppelin, Beth had bought back many treasures, one of which was a tiny root of a dark-leaved form of *Polygonatum × hybridum* 'Betburg'. Years of propagation have built up sufficient stock to sell.

As summer progresses, the overhead canopy becomes denser, blocking light out from reaching the woodland floor. Foliage comes to the fore, contributing greatly to the interplay of texture and form. Ferns play an important part during any season, many being evergreen, the gardeners only tidying them up come the spring. Amongst the toughest is our own native male fern, *Dryopteris filix-mas*. Surviving almost anywhere if given shade and some moisture, it can rival many more of its luxuriant foreign cousins. *Dryopteris wallichiana*, from Asia and South America, is late to emerge but looks stunning with its almost black midribs to each frond. Soft shield ferns, *Polystichum*, are used widely, of which both the upright *Polystichum setiferum* (Divisilobum Group) 'Dahlem' and the more horizontally

growing *P. s.* (Divisilobum Group) 'Herrenhausen' are easy to grow. *Asplenium scolopendrium*, the hart's-tongue fern, is an ideal evergreen fern for dry shade. No finer hardy fern can be grown than *Adiantum venustum*. Resembling the indoor maidenhair fern, this will slowly colonize a favourable spot with lace-like overlapping fronds, pale bronze as they emerge, gradually maturing to acid green and finally ageing to rusty brown to last through the winter. Several grasses are shade tolerant and although the range is limited, as grasses do tend to be sun lovers, they are an invaluable addition. Perhaps the most striking and easy to

The cycle of a woodland is for the plants to flower before the overhead canopy reduces both light and moisture. Many snowdrops start flowering well before the New Year but it is not until January that the show really begins. *Galanthus* 'James Backhouse', with its long, often misshapen flowers, is one of the best early-season snowdrops; many others soon follow.

grow is *Milium effusum* 'Aureum', Bowles's golden grass, and the cheeriest of bright yellow in the spring. Much better behaved is the golden form of Japanese hakone grass, *Hakonechloa macra* 'Aureola', which makes soft clumps of ribbon-like foliage vividly variegated gold and buff and is a superb companion for blue hostas. A few flowering verticals can be found in the form of the European goat's beard, *Aruncus dioicus*, or the North American bowman's root, *Gillenia trifoliata*.

The woodland floor is home to many ground-cover plants, and one stand-out performer is certainly *Geranium macrorrhizum*, creating dense carpets of apple-green scallop-edged leaves, many of which turn fiery red and yellow during autumn while others remain green throughout the winter. April and May is their time to flower, in shades of pink, and even the 'white' *Geranium macrorrhizum* 'Album' has the palest of pink flowers.

Narrow paths meander through the woodland. The planting was always designed to be dense, with many evergreen ground-cover plants carpeting the woodland floor. Just a few weeks earlier, this scene was one of snowdrops and early daffodils.

A recently introduced pure white form, *G. m.* 'Glacier', looks promising, although maybe not so vigorous. These geraniums are easily kept in check, with woody rooting stems quickly removed.

A feature of woods and forests the world over is for some plants to clamber up the trees and race rapidly towards the light, and many of the trees in the Woodland Garden were soon paired up with a suitable climber. Although slow at first, several specimens of the climbing hydrangea, *Hydrangea anomala* subsp. *petiolaris,* have crept up, and now their ladder-like framework displays their lacy flowers high up in the canopy. Honeysuckles generally have disappointed, while a vigorous form of *Clematis montana* flowers well high up.

Generally, the garden is too dry to grow roses to perfection – a heavier soil would be preferable, such as that in and around the new Reservoir Garden. But the vigorous climbers seem able to cope and several now grow high into selected hosts. Beth chose certain trees with space and

With many of the trees supporting a climber, this oak, on the edge of the woodland, gives the rambling rose, *Rosa* 'Paul's Himalayan Musk', the chance to reach the light. A vigorous Rambler, it flowers profusely, scenting the air for anyone choosing to rest on the bench beneath it.

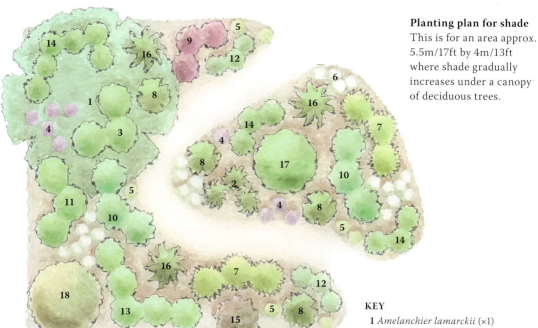

Planting plan for shade
This is for an area approx. 5.5m/17ft by 4m/13ft where shade gradually increases under a canopy of deciduous trees.

KEY
1 *Amelanchier lamarckii* (×1)
2 *Asplenium scolopendrium* (×3)
3 *Buglossoides purpurocaerulea* (×3)
4 *Cyclamen* (×9)
5 *Eranthis* (×7)
6 *Galanthus* (drift)
7 *Hakonechloa macra* 'Aureola' (×6)
8 *Helleborus* × *hybridus* (×4)
9 *Heuchera* (×3)
10 *Hosta* (×6)
11 *Kirengoshoma palmata* (×3)
12 *Lamium maculatum* (×6)
13 *Lamprocapnos spectabilis* (×5)
14 *Pachyphragma macrophyllum* (×9)
15 *Persicaria microcephala* 'Red Dragon' (×1)
16 *Polystichum setiferum* Acutilobum Group (×3)
17 *Skimmia japonica* (×1)
18 *Spiraea japonica* 'Goldflame' (×1)

light for the climbers to reach for. An old reel of cotton-coated telegraph wire was used to guide the plants up into the lower branches. *Rosa filipes* 'Kiftsgate', *R.* 'Bobbie James' and *R.* 'Paul's Himalayan Musk' were chosen, scenting the warm summer air along the winding pathways.

Autumn in the Woodland Garden starts quietly with both pink and white Japanese anemones spreading through the light woodland soil. Healthy clumps of *Kirengeshoma palmata* stand among ferns and yellowing hostas with maple-like leaves over which hang their waxy flowers of butter-yellow. Soon, colchicums, with their goblet-like naked flowers, spring up to make bold drifts of pink (where not too drawn by shade) among the ground cover. Always the last to flower is perhaps the loveliest, *Colchicum speciosum* 'Album', which brings its pure white to autumn as snowdrops do to spring.

With so many shrubs, berries and autumn colour abound. The edge of the woodland sees fine forms of mountain ash, the Chinese *Sorbus pseudohupehensis* with pink berries – better in some years than others – lasting well into the winter. The white-berried *Sorbus glabriuscula*, the glabrous mountain ash, sits above a group of *Cornus sanguinea* 'Midwinter Fire' – a fine sight on a sunny winter's day. Spindle bushes, *Euonymus* in variety, both fruit and show glorious autumn foliage colour. The April flowering Juneberries, *Amelanchier lamarckii*, once again deserve a mention as they rapidly colour and drop within days. Female forms of *Skimmia japonica* can be seen laden with berries well into the winter months.

MANAGEMENT

The management of the Woodland Garden, as with other areas of the garden under large trees and ever-expanding shrubs, has been an ongoing learning process. Existing trees are monitored, and action is taken where needed. Recently two large ash trees, which were constantly shedding dead branches and generally looking poorly, were removed. This really opened this area up and one or two of the shrubs, used to dappled shade all their lives, suddenly had to cope with a lot more sun.

With so many leaves falling each year, we soon learned that the best thing to do was to leave them where they fell. Leaves are moved off the paths with a leaf blower and we make sure that a relatively shallow layer remains on the plants at the front of the beds, where the smaller, more choice plants are likely to be. The paths and walkways in the Woodland Garden, which have to stand up to constant and concentrated footfall, have always been of bare soil topped either with bark or a slightly more binding soil. A light dressing of stone chips helps, once trodden in.

As envisaged, irrigation is needed when the wood gets dry, although this is constantly reviewed and has been considerably reduced in recent years. Another of Beth's

Dormant in the earlier part of summer, late August and September sees the first of the colchicums to flower. *Colchicum* 'The Giant' lives up to its name with large pinkish-purple naked flowers. The large glossy-green foliage follows in the spring.

167

phrases was 'to use the secateurs, not the hosepipe'. In other words, during dry spells, think about pruning or cutting the plants back as a means of reducing the plants' water requirement. In practice, we now cut back swathes of ground cover such as vincas, *Symphytum* and hardy geraniums, removing all moisture-sapping top growth. It is beneficial for the plants too, encouraging them to clothe themselves in young, tidier foliage.

Although, in the main, the woodland is dry, there is an area into which drainage water has been piped down from higher land and, to make best use of this valuable resource, a shallow-sided ditch was created. This provided enough moisture to include a slightly different range of plants such as hostas, rodgersias and large-leaved ligularias. Damp-loving ferns, such as the sensitive fern, *Onoclea sensibilis,* and the shuttlecock fern, *Matteuccia struthiopteris,* run through the planting. A striking feature here is *Veratrum californicum*, with its pleated, hosta-like leaves and imposing spikes of loose creamy-white flowers during summer. Also, again perhaps being a little too keen to cover the ground, we planted a variegated selection of the giant Japanese butterbur, *Petasites japonicus* var. *giganteus* 'Nishiki-buki', which soon became far too comfortable, as its spear-like underground shoots rapidly started to colonize the light woodland soil.

Perhaps our biggest concern, and certainly one of the most time-consuming tasks, has been trying to control the now rampant *Arum italicum* subsp. *italicum* 'Marmoratum', a plant we once treasured and still value in its true form in winter flower arrangements. The marbled leaves show considerable variation and seem to hybridize, forming monster plants. It is a bulbous plant, so is difficult to locate during the summer, and best tackled when in growth. But it is all too easy for the small bulbils which drop off the main bulb to be missed and almost impossible

At the woodland edge, a suckering stand of cut-leaved stag's horn sumac, *Rhus typhina* 'Dissecta', makes a fiery splash of colour in early autumn. Further to the right, a smoke bush, *Cotinus coggygria*, adds to the display but in a different shade.

to get out intact from amongst tree and shrub roots. The red berries too are a problem, consumed by birds and passing through them as they roost in the trees at night, so the seed then germinates where it falls. The gardeners now painstakingly remove all the flowers during the summer, so no berries develop.

ADDITIONS AND AFTERTHOUGHTS

A recent extension to the bottom of the Woodland Garden has been to open a walkway and allow visitors access to a peaceful, shaded grassy walk adjacent to our neighbouring farmer's reservoir. This area has now been sympathetically and quietly transformed into our Reflection Garden.

Veratrum album, seen earlier as a foliage plant, here in full flower during late summer.

Simple oak posts are available for plaques in memory of loved ones, who might have appreciated such a place. Unfortunately, we have no control over the water or what our neighbour chooses to do. The reservoirs were first dug out in the 1950s and expanded in the mid-1970s. They were created to provide irrigation for the surrounding acres of orchards but, over the years, many dry summers have seen water drawn to the point where the reservoirs are emptied down to a muddy hole.

Now the orchards have long gone, so it depends on what crops are planted as to how much water is used; cereal crops are not irrigated but potatoes are. Noisy pumps are

The Reflection Garden has been created as a haven of tranquillity for those seeking a quiet space for contemplation (above left), either in memory of their loved ones (above and left) or for themselves. A visitor's shadow, caught on the tree trunk (left), adds an atmospheric twist.

used to extract the water, which is not ideal, but we realize that livelihoods have to be made.

As already mentioned, it was 1989 when the wood first started to be cleared and the whole project spanned several years, with the public only being allowed access the Woodland Garden in around 1993. Unbeknown to Beth at the time was that land was soon to become available to allow the creation of a new car park, which enabled the transformation of the old one into the Gravel Garden. Consequently, work on the Woodland Garden was put on hold during the winter of 1991/92 while all efforts were diverted to working on the Gravel Garden, the new car parking area, and some land for additional stock beds.

Having spent the best part of ten years observing her plants in minute detail, Beth eventually put pen to paper to write a book about her experiences. *The Woodland Garden* was published in 2002, with a revised edition, *Beth Chatto's Shade Garden*, published in 2017.

The view of the neighbouring farmer's reservoir from the Reflection Garden. Whilst snowfall is a rare event here, the effect when it first settles is magical, defining the bare branches of surrounding woodland trees.

The Scree Garden

This relatively small part of the garden (often referred to by Beth as her Mediterranean Garden) is close to the house, situated on its south-west facing side. Beth's experience of the growing conditions here, and the planting suited to them, informed her choices when it came to creating the new Gravel Garden. Over the years it has been largely redesigned and replanted, and is now referred to as the Scree Garden. David Ward introduces the reasons for the change at the end of Beth's description of this part of the garden and summarizes the development that has recently taken place but is still a work in progress.

IT IS HARD looking at this part of the garden today to imagine what it was like thirty years ago. Very little grew on it, as the soil was so poor and dry that even the native weeds curled up and died in the long weeks of drought. The land here – around the south-west facing side of the house – consisted of almost pure gravel, with scarcely any dark humus soil on top, so we knew that we would have problems in most dry summers. In 1960 we moved into the newly built house and I sat on a southfacing slope in the sun, dug my hand into the warm bank and brought out white sand – it ran through my fingers like sand in an egg-timer. Although I thought we understood something about

The planting choice near the steps leading down from the Scree Garden to the Water Garden below demonstrates that the soil is dry and sandy at this level. *Phlomis italica* sprawls over the low retaining wall with, in the foreground, Cedric Morris's self-seeding annual poppy, *Papaver rhoeas* Mother of Pearl Group. Beyond, the similarly self-sown spires of *Verbascum bombyciferum* add to the Mediterranean feel.

Even evergreens have their seasonal highlights: rising from the silvery mats of lamb's ears, *Stachys byzantina* 'Cotton Boll', are their stiff stems of velvety, bobble-like flowers while the flowerheads of the waxy-leaved spurge, *Euphorbia characias* subsp. *wulfenii*, benefit from the warmth of the house walls.

drought-resistant plants, having always lived in this part of the country where it is particularly dry, I knew this was going to be drier than anything we had ever had before. Our first garden in Colchester had been based on chalky boulder clay, which is more retentive and so does not dry out quite so quickly.

To start with, I collected all the leafmould I could find around the place, which was not much, and then I bought mushroom compost which was a great help (it contains a fairly high proportion of chalk, so you must be careful where you put it if you wish to grow lime-hating plants like rhododendrons, certain primulas, and other plants from damp woodland conditions). I began with the premise that I would have a problem with drought however much organic matter I used because of the very low rainfall and because the soil was so free draining. I knew that even if I managed to improve the texture of the soil with organic matter that would hold some moisture for a while, the planting had to depend largely on species adapted by nature to drought. I thought immediately of grey-leaved foliage plants like *Cerastium*, silver filigree-leaved artemisias, bush sages and handsome waxy-leaved euphorbias, all from sunny, stony areas around the Mediterranean. Hence my two names for this part of the garden: the Dry Garden, because of the basic conditions, and the Mediterranean Garden, because many of the plants I have chosen come from countries in that region.

One of the things I like best about this part of the garden is its permanence – most of the foliage remains all year round. On well-drained gravel soil these plants tend to grow tough and wiry, as they are on a starvation diet. Some of them would not survive the winter in much wetter parts of the country. If their leaves are lying on cold, soggy soil, they will rot. In areas of high rainfall some plants, cistuses for example, will grow rampantly in summer and make too

A close-up of the tightly packed lime-green flowerheads of *Euphorbia characias* subsp. *wulfenii,* which make such a dramatic display in flower from March till May and a handsome evergreen foliage plant thereafter. Flowering stems are removed before they go to seed in early summer.

much soft growth. They are then much more likely to be affected by frost in winter. Cistuses are not the hardiest of shrubs, and their flowers last only a day, but they have such a wonderful, butterfly-like charm that I would not like to be without them. They also make a substantial contribution to the garden in winter, with their evergreen leaves. I do not often lose them here but when I planted them lower down the slope towards the water garden, on moister, richer soil (which I did when I first came here), I did. With many drought-loving plants, it is the combination of alternate wetting and freezing that kills them. They will survive surprisingly low temperatures if they remain dry.

The foliage of plants from hotter parts of the world has evolved to cope with drought: in some, a coating protects the leaf by preventing excessive evaporation. The 'grey' plants have green leaves covered with a tightly pressed mat of white wool or silky hairs (with the same result as if we were to put on a blouse to stop getting sunburnt). Some of the euphorbias have what we call a glaucous leaf, a green leaf covered with a light coating of wax which gives it a greyish-blue sheen and stops it scorching. Many plants with small, finely cut or dissected leaves – rosemary and thyme, for example – are protected by aromatic oils. Still another way that plants protect themselves is to make thick 'swollen' leaves: plants like stonecrops, sedums and houseleeks, *Sempervivum*, store water, when it is available, in their fat, juicy foliage.

A totally grey garden can be uninteresting, and if you are not careful, it may look like an ash heap, so I try to use plants that can add touches of vivid greens, such as *Santolina rosmarinifolia* subsp. *rosmarinifolia* with its moss-green, cypress-like leaves. Candytuft, *Iberis sempervirens*, makes a mound of rich dark-green leaves smothered in spring with dazzling white flower-heads. There are a few yellow-greens that I introduce for contrast,

Rock roses, like the low-growing *Cistus parviflorus* here, thrive in the warm, free-draining soil in this part of the garden, as does the prolifically seeding *Papaver somniferum*, that has popped up. Flowering in June, cistus are pruned shortly after flowering and quickly make new growth, keeping them bushy and within bounds.

like the golden-leaved wild marjoram, *Origanum vulgare* 'Aureum', with small scented leaves. The true marjoram is a typical Mediterranean plant seen along the roadsides in southern France. As a gardener creating a picture, you sometimes need plants that are not utterly natural, like the golden-leaved forms. One of the brightest is golden lemon balm, *Melissa officinalis* 'All Gold'. It overwinters as basal rosettes and then, in spring, bright yellow leafy shoots emerge and grow to about 45cm/18in tall. Like some other yellow-leaved plants, it needs protection from direct sunlight. There are also several forms of golden thyme here, such as *Thymus vulgaris* 'Golden King' and *T. pulegioides* 'Bertram Anderson'.

Over the years the shape of this small Mediterranean Garden has changed as I have been able to afford to buy more compost and materials to make raised beds. Some of the beds are raised to different levels, which I think adds interest and variety to the design of the garden. If you have

The redesign of the original Mediterranean Garden involved the creation of raised beds, constructed from old, broken-up council paving, which was laid and cemented into low retaining walls. These beds now contain a colourful selection of smaller plants that were unsuited to the scale of the Gravel Garden. In late summer the scarlet *Zauschneria californica* is particularly prominent.

a flat garden, and a small one in particular, you can change and improve it out of all recognition by making raised beds. They need only be raised knee-high or so, or perhaps even less – just 15cm/6in will sometimes do. If you can acquire enough soil and add well-made compost or old farmyard manure and grit to improve the quality and create the required depth, it is very helpful.

Along the west-facing wall which separates the garden from the nursery there is now a raised bed about 45cm/18in high. There, in the original border of poor sandy soil, even the native weeds curled up and died, and the sedums and sempervivums shrank to their innermost rosettes as the soil sometimes felt warm enough to poach an egg on during some of the summers we have had. To start with, we raised the surface by adding a mixture of improved soil, grit and compost. A peat bed would be totally unsuitable and impossible to maintain in such a dry situation. Good drainage was provided because none of these plants would tolerate too much wet at their roots.

When the bed was finally planted, it was mulched with grit. This helps to keep weeds down, but – and this is most important – it makes nice dry collars for plants to rest on, so they will not rot off at the neck. Many of the plants here originate from rock-slides or gritty scree areas. When you see them growing wild in the mountains, it is only too easy to be misled. Your back and your nose may well be scorching, and the rocks so hot that you cannot bear to sit on them, but you see these lovely little cushion plants studding the ground and you think, 'That would look lovely in my East Anglian garden.' Not a bit of it. Although the plants are hot on the surface, underneath they are being fed by melting snow from perhaps 300m/1,000ft away, which is trickling down the mountain slope.

I am not attempting to grow such plants, which are the delight of alpine enthusiasts, but what I am able to grow

Barely knee-high, these raised beds with low walls are an ideal solution for smaller gardens or those with less than ideal soil conditions. Filled with a free-draining soil, they look best with low-growing, creeping plants to soften the edges like the blue-grey waxy-leaved *Euphorbia myrsinites*.

OPPOSITE A late-summer planting combination. From the bottom of the photograph: pale-pink *Gypsophila* 'Rosenschleier' with *Hylotelephium telephium* (Atropurpureum Group) 'Karfunkelstein' behind. Essential for contrast of form is the large-leaved *Bergenia pacumbis* spilling over the wall and the blue-flowered shrubs, *Caryopteris* × *clandonensis* 'Heavenly Blue' and *C.* × *c.* 'Worcester Gold'. Above them is the rapidly growing *Salix udensis* 'Golden Sunshine'.

'The foliage of plants from hotter parts of the world has evolved to cope with drought: in some, a coating protects the leaf by preventing excessive evaporation. The 'grey' plants have green leaves covered with a tightly pressed mat of white wool or silky hairs (with the same result as if we were to put on a blouse to stop getting sunburnt).'

An early-summer scene from the original planting in the Mediterranean Garden with its fine Judas tree, *Cercis siliquastrum.* (Unfortunately, high winds eventually damaged the tree beyond repair and it was removed, prompting replanting of the entire bed.) Here, in May, among the shrubby mounds of *Ballota* and euphorbias is the bulbous *Allium karataviense*, its tennis-ball-sized flowers lasting well into summer before turning into attractive seed-heads.

are plants that generally thrive in the mountains around the Mediterranean – ones such as dianthus, sedums and sempervivums – that will endure drier conditions and spend the summer sitting on parched stony soil.

When all the flowers have gone, and some of the foliage too, there is still enough shape to make you feel that the garden is furnished in winter. More than any other part, the Dry Garden remains interesting all year round. It is a never-ending pleasure making patterns with leaves, regardless of the flowers. In the drier parts of the garden, even in November when there is not a flower in sight, there is still plenty of colour from the foliage with silver and grey, grey-blue and glaucous green. Bronze tangles of shrubby potentillas add warmth. Just as interesting as leaf colour, however, are its many forms and textures, from very feathery leaves to large simpler ones, which provide contrast. If the overall planting design is fussy, made with only tiny leaves like those of thyme and lavender, it will lack any real impact.

In the summer, the Mediterranean Garden is wonderfully scented. Why the Lord decided to put perfume into these leaves, goodness knows, but I think aromatic oils are a way of conserving moisture and keeping the leaf active in very dry conditions. There are thymes here which smell of caraway seeds or of lemon. Even in winter there is still the odd scented leaf on the lemon verbena, *Aloysia citriodora*, under the south wall of the house and the lemon balm, *Melissa officinalis*, at its feet, is also scented.

THE SUBSEQUENT REPLANTING AND CREATION OF THE SCREE GARDEN

Thirty years on again, this part of the garden has undergone substantial revision and replanting, which started in Beth's lifetime but continues very much on her original principles and using the plants she loved most.

OPPOSITE In mid-summer, the pea-like yellow flowers of the dwarf shrub, *Genista* 'Lydia', guide visitors around the prickly-leaved *Yucca nobilis* near the steps leading down from the Scree Garden to the cool tranquillity of the Water Garden beyond.

This narrow, somewhat impractical stepped path connecting the upper Scree Garden with the lower Water Garden was often referred to by Beth as the 'goat path'. A fine 'full-stop' plant, *Stipa gigantea*, the aptly named golden oat grass, hints at the dry soil towards the top.

By the mid-1990s it was clear that after over thirty-five years the original Mediterranean Garden needed an overhaul and the proposed building of a new tearoom necessitated moving Beth's old wooden greenhouse. This, along with the realization that the open-plan design of the new Gravel Garden was not the place for smaller, choice plants, provided the impetus for change.

Once the greenhouse was relocated (in 1997), the plants Beth wanted to keep were dug out and put aside and the original rectangular beds and bulb-laden soil removed. An area of roughly 30m/100ft long by 17m/60ft wide was laid bare, providing a blank canvas on which to paint a fresh scene. The only feature we left was the lovely old Judas tree, *Cercis siliquastrum*.

We created a series of five raised beds with interlocking oval shapes, to encourage visitors to walk around. Once completed (in 1999), these beds were filled with a free-draining soil, ready to be planted, and the paths between finished with a top dressing of gravel. Flat, creeping plants were chosen, along with strong verticals and small bushy plants, with low sprawling plants to soften the edging wall, providing both flower and foliage interest. Many plants that had struggled to gain a foothold in the Gravel Garden

'Just as interesting as leaf colour are its many forms and textures, from very feathery leaves to large simpler ones, which provide contrast. If the overall design is fussy, made with only tiny leaves like those of thyme and lavender, it has no impact.'

Planting plan for a raised bed in full sun
This plan for a raised island bed measures approximately 5.5m/17ft wide by 3.5m/11ft deep and has a tapestry of mainly low-growing plants.

KEY
 1 *Allium tuberosum* (×3)
 2 *Anemone × pavonina* (×7)
 3 *Armeria* (×3)
 4 *Dianthus* (×1)
 5 *Erigeron karvinskianus* (×3)
 6 *Erodium* (×3)
 7 *Eryngium bourgatii* (×3)
 8 *Euonymus japonicus* 'Micophyllus Pulchellus' (×1)
 9 *Euphorbia rigida* (×3)
10 *Gypsophila repens* (×5)
11 *Libertia perigrinans* (×5)
12 *Limonium bellidifolium* (×3)
13 *Phyla nodiflora* (×5)
14 *Pulsatilla vulgaris* (×3)
15 *Sedum spurium* (×5)
16 *Sempervivum* (×24)
17 *Thymus* (×5)
18 *Tulipa linifolia* Batalinii Group (drifts)

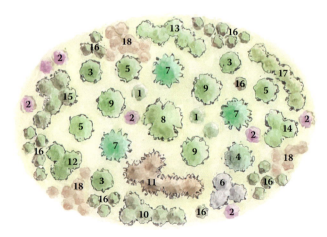

have found their natural home here. But some of the most successful have been plants Beth originally grew here, like thymes, sedums and sempervivums, while new verticals, such as *Salvia* (syn. *Perovskia)* 'Blue Spire' and *Libertia ixioides,* have become established. The lovely old Judas tree succumbed to wind damage and was removed in 2016.

With the aim of creating Beth's much-loved mosaic of intricate foliage and shape – the 'green tapestry' from which the original book drew its name – the planting rapidly established itself and matured in the fresh soil. Where once Beth would have spent her evenings watering, the redesign has meant that beds now seldom need to be watered. This part of the garden is still a work in progress, as invariably some plants will thrive whilst others may falter.

The recently planted scree bed originally dominated by the Judas tree, *Cercis siliquastrum,* is now full of interesting new plants as well as some old favourites. Beth's original greenhouse behind the bed is still the only heated space available and is home during the winter months to the succulent and pelargonium collection that furnishes the summer container display (see pages 192-193).

Other Areas of Interest

PREVIOUS CHAPTERS in this book cover the areas of the gardens in terms of the history and practice of the design and perennial planting, based on Beth's own observations in *The Green Tapestry*, but with some updating to cover the thirty years since that book was written. Planting has been constantly revised and, in some cases, entirely new areas of the garden have been created, like the Woodland Garden. These are the areas open to visitors.

But worthy of note is the development of the nursery itself, which has grown in importance over the years, sustaining both the ethos of the gardens and the gardens themselves, Beth's special container garden and the wilder area used by the Education Trust.

OPPOSITE Seating outside the Visitor Information Centre. May sees the wisteria in full bloom and scenting the air as visitors walk out into the Gravel Garden to begin their journey around the gardens during one of its peak periods of interest.

LEFT This inviting, almost secretive, little pathway gives our gardeners access to the nursery stock beds and the garden in front of the Willow Room (the hub for activities promoted by the Beth Chatto Education Trust).

THE NURSERY AND STOCK BEDS

In the early days, as Beth travelled the country giving talks and demonstrations, she soon realized that the plants she was taking with her were not widely grown so they were difficult for the general public to buy. That gave her the idea to start a business. The embryonic nursery, adjacent to the house, grew and frames were built and stock beds planted. In 1967 the business was registered as Unusual Plants. Word spread and visitor numbers increased gradually as the nursery expanded to cope with demand. This steady approach exploded ten years on when Beth began both exhibiting at the Chelsea Flower Show and writing books about her garden experiences and her treasured plants.

There are few places where a garden and nursery have developed over the years, as hers did, hand-in-hand, each needing the other in order to progress. Many established gardens have a nursery added at a much later date, or vice-versa, with a nursery creating a show garden to display the plants it sells. Beth was very much a nursery woman, as well as a plantswoman, and many of her self-taught techniques are still practised at the nursery today.

The nursery has always catered for the retail market, providing visitors with the opportunity to obtain plants

ABOVE The nursery propagates and produces the majority of the plants it sells on site, with a range of around 2,000 different types that are sold through the nursery or via mail order.

LEFT AND OPPOSITE Whilst the nursery uses plants in the garden for collecting seed and for cuttings, the stock beds (left) are needed for those plants that have to be dug up and divided. The Stock Bed walk takes visitors out to view many of these plants, including the hylotelephiums (sedums) and salvias seen here (opposite).

LEFT Stock beds of hostas, which are divided when dormant during the winter months. (As rabbits have always been a problem, certain areas are fenced to protect those plants susceptible to them.)

they have seen growing in the gardens or displayed at shows, either by direct sales or via mail order. Plants have been sent by post for almost as long as the nursery has been in existence, and the growth of the internet and online ordering has driven this side of the business to the fore.

The garden was, and still is, a vital source of propagation material, be it for collecting seed or taking cuttings, but for some plants (and there are many) the only means of making more of them is by division. To avoid digging plants from the garden, stock beds have been created close by and visitors are now encouraged to view these areas with a recently created Stock Bed walk, which takes visitors past the Willow Room (see pages 194-5).

These days, technology plays an increasing role in everyone's lives and it has been an enormous help in the nursery's day-to-day running. A real-time stock control system linked to the website means that control of numbers, as well as scheduling when, and in what quantity, plants should be produced, all helps, not to mention individual labels for all plants – a far cry from the days when customers were given a clip board, pencil, and blank labels to use!

The nursery now produces in the region of 200,000 plants, covering almost 2,000 different types, the majority of which are propagated and grown on site. With an eye to the environment, the plants are grown free from pesticides, and weeds are controlled by topping the pots with a mini-bark pot topper. In 2018, the nursery moved over to using peat-free compost for potting, along with taupe-coloured pots that are more easily recycled than the traditional black pots. The business is constantly searching for ways to reduce its environmental footprint, in line with Beth's sustainable ethos of planting.

ABOVE Opposite the Willow Room, stock beds of grasses such as silvery *Miscanthus* and pencil-thin *Molinia* show a range of autumn colour and form. The grasses are dug and divided in the spring. The handsome oak, one of many splendid ones in the gardens, is always last to shed its leaves.

POTS AND CONTAINERS

While the garden has always been planted up on a permanent basis, using mostly hardy perennials and some shrubs but little in the way of successional planting, the use of half-hardy plants has been still been a constant feature. Each year, usually in late May or early June, a special 'pot' compost is made and the pots planted up. The pot displays are mainly concentrated around the house and the adjacent tearoom/garden entrance area. These include Beth's ever-present collection of succulents, which are moved out from the greenhouse during the frost-free months and displayed invitingly en masse. This collection has been increased over the years and has always sat well with our dry East Anglian summers.

Mixed groupings of more thirsty half-hardy plants have always been assembled close to the house, for ease of watering. The raised patio overlooking the garden ponds has seen many creative displays over the years, although the shade of a dense *Magnolia × soulangeana* has affected the plants chosen. The courtyard area, overlooked by the kitchen, has often had a small succulent display or, in some years, just one shapely container suffices.

More recently a selection of pelargoniums has become a collection, providing both a splash of colour and some wonderful leaf textures and fragrant scents, including those of rose or lemon.

Cuttings are taken during late summer and by November all the mother plants are cut back and moved inside, many into Beth's original 'Pratten' greenhouse, to provide further cuttings, which in their turn will become the display plants the following year.

OPPOSITE TOP On the other side of the wall from the Scree Garden is the summer home for the succulent collection. All are moved back into the heated greenhouse by late October.

OPPOSITE BOTTOM Heavy shade is cast by a fine *Magnolia × soulangeana*, so the chosen container plants at its base are those whose foliage is their main feature, such as begonias and hostas.

ABOVE A bright and cheery collection of pelargoniums displayed in the sunny courtyard area.

The Willow Room (see also page 87) overlooks the tranquil surroundings of the Pump Pond, where kingfishers can often be heard and seen. It is used for classes and courses by the Beth Chatto Education Trust, which also organizes wider events, such as an annual lecture, held close by at the University of Essex. Speakers have included gardening *illuminati* like Dan Pearson, Alan Titchmarsh and Christine Walkden.

THE WILLOW ROOM

Beth was passionate about working in harmony with the natural world. She believed that the key to creating a healthier planet lay in better education and it was her wish that the garden would somehow play a role in achieving this. In 2016 the Beth Chatto Education Trust was set up to transmit her passion for plants, along with the need for an ecological approach, to all age groups. The Trust is run independently of the gardens and the business.

Many of the courses take place in our education building, the Willow Room, which provides a well-equipped and comfortable indoor space for various educational events. For outdoor activities there is a dedicated, safe enclosed area, known as the wild corner, at the far end of the stock beds. It has a large pond, created in a glade of mixed trees that Beth planted many years ago. Importantly, this quiet area is well away from visitors to the gardens.

As a charity, we are continuously building an extensive programme for both children and adults. And although it has only been running for a relatively short time, the feedback from the courses, workshops and events has been rewardingly positive. These include school visits and holiday activities, RHS qualification courses and a large number of plant and gardening workshops, as well as artistic and well-being courses. In short, they cover anything that enhances the enjoyment, understanding and interest in plants, gardens and the environment as a whole.

Beth was a strong and determined plantswoman, who made a real difference in the world. Our aim is to continue that tradition to help others who wish to do the same.

Plant Directory

THE FOLLOWING is an updated cultivation guide to some of the perennials (in Latin name order of the genus to which each belongs) that Beth either grew or would want to have grown. There are many other perennials we could have included, some of which we sell in the nursery today, but we have tried to provide a mixture of the more familar and useful perennials together with some of Beth's own particular favourites.

The plant hardiness zones at the end of each entry relate to the zones in common use in North America. They are a general guide to the annual average minimum temperatures that the plant in question will withstand. However, hardiness ratings are far from an exact science. Many factors play a part in the plant's ability to withstand cold including the chill factor of the wind, whether the plant was turgid when the first frosts arrived and whether the soil is free draining or not. The rating serves only as a general guide to the plants that should grow in a particular area and it would be unwise to try to grow any plant that is obviously outside the temperature range for your area.

Note: *The nomenclature of plants is a constantly evolving science. While every effort has made to include recent changes, it may not have been possible to include them all.*

Plant Hardiness Zones (USDA system)

Zone	C°	F°
1	below -46°	below -50°
2	-46° to -40°	-50° to -40°
3	-40° to -34°	-40° to -30°
4	-34° to -28°	-30° to -20°
5	-28° to -22°	-20° to -10°
6	-22° to -16°	-10° to 0°
7	-16° to -12°	0° to 10°
8	-12° to -6°	10° to 20°
9	-6° to -1°	20° to 30°
10	-1° to -4	30° to 40

OPPOSITE **Cyclamen hederifolium**

ACANTHUS

A. mollis

This imposing plant has large, deeply cut, glossy green leaves which make a feature all the year round unless winters are exceptionally hard. Tall flower stems carry curiously hooded purple and white flowers in late summer. It needs sun and good drainage. Up to 1.5m/5ft. ZONE 7.

ACHILLEA

A. filipendulina 'Gold Plate'

Well known, with its tall, stiff stems bearing flat heads of tiny yellow flowers. Dries excellently, retaining its colour. Flowers midsummer. For full sun and needs good drainage. 90cm/3ft. ZONE 3.

A. millefolium 'Lansdorferglut'

Free-flowering cultivar with feathery foliage and flat heads of deep pink flowers which fade through various shades to a dull cream. Flowers from early to late summer. 75cm/2½ft. ZONE 3

A. 'Moonshine'

Valued for its flat heads of pale clear yellow flowers, held on branching stems above beautiful silvery grey foliage. Good to cut and dries well, retaining colour. Flowers in midsummer and again often in autumn. It needs well-drained soil in sun. 60cm/2ft. ZONE 6.

ACORUS

A. calamus 'Argenteostriatus'

Handsome, sword-like leaves boldly variegated cream and green with rose-pink bases in spring. Deliciously spicy scent when crushed in the hand. Flowers of no merit. Needs damp soil or shallow water. 90cm/3ft. ZONE 3.

ACTAEA

A. rubra

From the woods of north-east America. Does better if grown in part shade, when it becomes the most showy of this genus, with large clusters of smallish berries, jade green in July, gradually turning scarlet and lasting until early autumn. 75cm/2½ft. ZONE 3.

A. simplex (Atropurpurea Group) 'Brunette'

Selection with purple-black foliage and stems, and sweetly scented small white flowers in late autumn. Needs moist, retentive soil in sun or part shade. 1 .8m/6ft. ZONE 3

A. s. 'White Pearl'

For a cool shady place, not dry. A most elegant plant in autumn. Branching stems carry long snowy-white bottlebrushes which become lime-green seed-heads. 1.2m/4ft. ZONE 3.

TOP *Achillea filipendulina* 'Gold Plate'
ABOVE *Actaea rubra*
LEFT *Acanthus mollis*

ADIANTUM

A. pedatum

A hardy, unusually shaped fern with handsome divided fans of bright green rounded leaflets held on shining purplish-black wiry stems. 30-38cm/12-15in. ZONE 3.

AGAPANTHUS

The following forms are both hardy in well-drained but well-fed soil and sun. All flower throughout August, pick well and make good green or dried seed-heads in September. In very cold situations a winter mulch is needed for protection.

A. 'Ardernei Hybrid'

Large well-shaped heads of white flowers with rose/purple flecks on petal tips. Black dot-like anthers. 90cm/3ft. ZONE 7.

A. campanulatus var. *albidus*

From clumps of strap-shaped leaves appear smooth bare stems carrying round heads of close-set white, trumpet-shaped flowers. 60cm/2ft. ZONE 7.

A. 'Evening Star'

Purple-stained stems with dark buds opening to pale/dark blue flowers. 60cm/2ft. ZONE 7.

A. 'Windlebrooke'

Outstanding deep indigo buds and dark blue flowers. 60cm/2ft. ZONE 7.

AJUGA

A native woodland plant. Prefers sun or part-shade and retentive soil.

A. reptans 'Atropurpurea'

Deep purple highly polished leaves and spikes of deep blue flowers. 25cm/10in. ZONE 3.

A. r. 'Burgundy Glow'

Beautiful foliage suffused rose and magenta, regularly edged with cream. Vivid carpet all winter. Flowers blue. 10cm/4in. ZONE 4.

ALCHEMILLA

Alchemillas thrive in sun or part-shade and retentive soil.

A. mollis

Invaluable in the garden and for picking. Forms a mound of velvety

ABOVE *Ajuga reptans* 'Atropurpurea'

ABOVE *Agapanthus* 'Windlebrooke'
LEFT *Agapanthus* 'Ardernei Hybrid'

rounded leaves. When their serrated edges are full of dewdrops, each leaf looks like a beaded shawl. For weeks in midsummer the long sprays of frothing lime-green starry flowers are a delight. 45cm/1½ft. ZONE 3.

ALLIUM
(see also NECTAROSCORDUM)

A. ampeloprasum
The wild leek's tall, strong stems carry large spherical buds that burst open in midsummer to form dense heads of small pink flowers. 1.5-1.8m/5-6ft. ZONE 4.

A. atropurpureum
Upturned clusters of dark purple flowers in June. 60cm/2ft. ZONE 4.

A. carinatum subsp. pulchellum
In July and August this dainty allium sends up a number of slender stems from which dangle masses of dusty-lilac bells. 38cm/15in. ZONE 4.

A. cristophii
This plant, both strong and delicate, has amazing globular flower-heads the size of small footballs in late spring to early summer. Each flower-head is composed of many metallic-looking little lilac stars. It dries particularly well, the delicate spoke-like stems retaining their purple colour. 60cm/2ft. ZONE 4.

A. flavum
This small plant is distinguished by its tight little clumps of almost blue foliage set off by heads of small lemon-yellow bells in mid- to late summer. 23cm/9in. ZONE 4.

A. hollandicum
Has flower-heads the size of small oranges, packed with deep-lilac flowers in May, carried on tall slender stems. 90cm-1.2m/3-4ft. ZONE 4.

A. karataviense
In early spring the leaves emerge tightly rolled, showing their maroon edges. They open broad and curving, the dark pewter-green setting off the pale beige-pink flower-head, large as a tennis ball, between them. The fleshy seed capsules dry into translucent petals. 15cm/6in. ZONE 6.

A. lusitanicum
In late summer cool lilac heads are held above flat vigorous clumps of swirling grey-green leaves. 15cm/6in. ZONE 5.

A. nigrum
Found wild in S. E. Europe. It has densely packed flattish heads of purple flowers but it varies in depth of colour. 90cm/3ft. ZONE 5.

A. oreophilum
This short-stemmed allium looks best on the edges of dry sunny borders. In midsummer it produces small clustered heads of large deep-rose-pink flowers, which dry into sun-bleached seed-heads. 10cm/4in. ZONE 6.

A. 'Purple Rain'
Has a huge flower globe up to 15cm/6in in diameter in early summer. Loved by bees and butterflies. Well-drained soil in sun. 60cm/2ft. ZONE 4.

A. sphaerocephalon
The small bulbs divide freely to produce a mass of slender bare stems topped with small plum-shaped heads of purple flowers in late summer. 45cm/1½ft. ZONE 4.

LEFT *Alchemilla mollis*
BELOW *Allium* **'Purple Rain'**
BOTTOM *Allium sphaerocephalon*

ALSTROEMERIA

A. ligtu hybrids
Tall stems carry large heads of many small lily-like flowers, exquisitely veined in shades of pink to apricot. July to August. 75cm/2½ft. ZONE 7.

A. psittacina
From Brazil. Narrow lily-shaped flowers, dark crimson with bright green tips, streaked with black. Needs warm well-drained site. Flowers from July onwards. First crop makes handsome seed-pods. 90cm/3ft. ZONE 7.

ANAPHALIS

A. triplinervis 'Sommerschnee'
Makes slowly spreading clumps of felt-grey foliage topped with clusters of pearly-white everlasting daisies in late summer. Hang them to dry for winter flower arranging. Plant in sun in retentive soil. 25cm/10in. ZONE 3.

ANEMONE

A. × *hybrida* 'Honorine Jobert'
Unsurpassed old variety. Pure white flowers with yellow stamens carried on branching stems. Flowers for weeks on end in autumn. 1.2m/4ft. ZONE 5.

A. magellanica
Neat clumps of dark green, finely cut leaves are a setting for cool lemon-yellow flowers in spring, followed by large, woolly seed-heads. This needs sun and good drainage. 30-38cm/12-15in. ZONE 5.

A. nemorosa 'Robinsoniana'
A lovely blue form of the wild wood anemone. In spring, nodding buds, stained purplish-rose, open to the sun breathtaking flowers filled with yellow stamens. Best in retentive leaf-mould soil, in part shade. 10cm/4in. ZONES 4-5.

A. pavonina
Tuberous perennial with divided basal leaves. Cup-shaped red, blue or purple

flowers, often with a white central zone in spring. 40cm/16in. ZONES 4-5.

A. tomentosa
One of the best Japanese anemones. Pale pink flowers, dark on reverse, are earlier than hybrids. 1.2m/4ft. ZONE 4.

ANGELICA

A. archangelica
A great plant valued for both its architectural effect and its delicate flavour. In its second year there rises from the broad divided leaves a stout branching stem ending in wide heads of cow parsley-like flowers in late summer. The green seed-heads are most decorative. The young hollow stems can be preserved in sugar. Unfortunately, it is biennial, but it is well worth while carefully placing a few seedlings for the following year. Grows in damp retentive soil in sun or part shade. 2-2.5m/6-8ft. ZONE 6.

TOP LEFT **Anemone tomentosa**
TOP RIGHT **Alstroemeria ligtu** hybrids
ABOVE **Angelica archangelica**

ANTHEMIS

All forms of *A. tinctoria* need to be replanted occasionally in refreshed and retentive soil to retain vigorous, free-flowering clumps, and all need full sun.

A. tinctoria 'E. C. Buxton'

Above a low neat mound of ferny green leaves, thin stiff stems carry creamy-yellow daisies endlessly throughout the summer. 50cm/20in. ZONE 3.

A. t. 'Wargrave Variety'

Much admired for its cool lemon-yellow flowers; looks well with *Euphorbia griffithii* 'Fireglow'. 75cm/2½ft. ZONE 3.

ANTHRISCUS

A. sylvestris 'Ravenswing'

Irresistible form of Queen Anne's lace. Dark brownish leaves which contrast with creamy white lacy flowers from early summer for several weeks. Easy in sun or shade. Grows true from seed. 75cm/3½ft. ZONE 6.

ARMERIA

A.maritima 'Dusseldorfer Stolz'

Short grassy mounds studded with a show of large light-red flowers in midsummer. 15cm/6in. ZONE 3.

ARTEMISIA

With their beautiful, highly aromatic silver foliage these plants are invaluable as ground cover or background plants in the hot, dry garden where there is plenty of sun and good drainage. In all artemisias the foliage is valued more than the flowers, which are insignificant.

A. abrotanum

Also known as southernwood or lad's love. Plant this deliciously aromatic plant beside a path or sitting area. It makes a shrubby plant densely set with whorls of leathery sage-green foliage, a lovely contrast for salvias or cistuses.

Spring pruning keeps it well shaped. 75cm/2½ft. ZONE 5.

A. dracunculus

The true French tarragon. Narrow green foliage adds very distinctive flavour to salads, chicken and fish dishes. 60cm/2ft. ZONE 4.

A. pontica

Forms a miniature forest of stiff, upright stems clothed in finely cut silver-grey scented foliage. Excellent feature and ground cover in dry sunny places. Spreads by underground stems. 45cm/1½ft. ZONE 5.

ARUM

A. italicum subsp. *italicum* 'Marmoratum'

These exotic leaves unroll from the leaf mould in late autumn, continuing to grow throughout the winter, bowing beneath bitter frost but standing undamaged immediately it thaws. By April they are the full height, dark-glossy green, spear-shaped and veined with ivory. In September appear stems of red berries. 38cm/15in. ZONE 4.

ARUNCUS

Aruncus are best in sun or half shade and retentive soil.

A. aethusifolius

Produces low clumps of fresh green leaves as finely cut as chervil but with more substance. A forest of wiry flower stems rises 30-35cm/12-14in

ABOVE *Anthemis tinctoria* 'E. C. Buxton'
BELOW *Arum italicum* subsp. *italicum* 'Marmoratum'

high, carrying tiny astilbe-like heads of small creamy-white flowers in June. By September they are still attractive, with barren heads tinted light chestnut and seed-bearing heads dark shining brown, while foliage develops pink and reddish autumn tints.
25-30cm/10-12in. ZONE 3.

A. dioicus
Also known as goat's beard. A superb plant. Forms large clumps of elegant light-green foliage above which rise great creamy plumes of tiny flowers in midsummer. It also has the benefit of interesting seed-heads. Needs rich soil. 1.2m/4ft. ZONE 3

ASPHODELINE
Both these plants are for sunny areas with good drainage.

A. liburnica
Comes into flower when *A. lutea* is already forming seed-heads. Similar, but much more delicately made; branched heads of much paler yellow flowers – effective in late summer. 90cm/3ft. ZONE 7.

A. lutea
Tall stems bear whorls of grey-blue grassy leaves. The strap-petalled, star-like flowers are bright yellow. The seed-pods that form after them are composed of a wand of bright green

cherries which eventually turn brown. 90cm/3ft. ZONE 6.

ASPHODELUS
A. albus
Seen everywhere around the Mediterranean on dry, stony soils, it thrives in sunny areas with good drainage. From fleshy roots it produces a huddle of long narrow leaves above which stand tall, smooth, strong branching stems topped with spires of long narrow buds which open in early summer to starry-white flowers, a soft brown vein running down the centre of each petal. 1.2m/4ft. ZONE 7.

ASPLENIUM
A. scolopendrium
The hart's tongue fern forms open clusters of long ribbon-shaped leaves. Tolerant of most conditions it will suffer in prolonged drought. There are many forms, which vary in height from about 30-60cm/1-2ft. ZONE 5.

ASTER
All prefer retentive soil, in sun.
A. amellus 'Veilchenkönigin'
An excellent old variety. Stiff dark stems carry open heads of intense violet well-shaped flowers in September and October. 38cm/15in. ZONE 4.

Drought-tolerant plants (small)
Allium (dwarf)
Anemone × fulgens
Anemone pavonina
Armeria
Calamintha
Carlina
Dianthus
Diascia
Erigeron karvinskianus
Eriophyllum
Euphorbia myrsinites
Festuca
Haplopappus
Origanum
Sedum (dwarf)
Stipa tenuissima
Teucrium × lucidrys
Thymus
Tulipa sprengeri
Zauschneria

A. × frikartii 'Mönch'
Without doubt the best Michaelmas daisy. Large bold flowers, rich lavender blue. Flowers from August until October. 75cm/3½ft. ZONE 4.

ASTILBE
All prefer retentive soil, in sun.
A. × arendsii 'Fanal'
Dark stems and leaves set off deep red spires of flower. 60cm/2ft. ZONE 4.
A. × arendsii 'Venus'
Plumes of pale pink flowers. 90cm/3ft. ZONE 4.
A. 'Bronce Elegans'
A beautiful dwarf hybrid. Green foliage darkened with bronze and arching sprays of tiny cream and salmon-pink flowers in summer. 30cm/1ft. ZONE 4.
A. chinensis var. pumila
Slowly spreads into a carpet of broadly

cut foliage. Slender spikes of rosy-mauve flowers from late summer to autumn. 30cm/1ft. ZONE 4.
A. c. var. taquetii 'Superba'
This unusual astilbe flowers in late summer. Tall stately stems carry dense spires of fluffy rosy-mauve flowers. 1.2m/4ft. ZONE 4.

ASTRANTIA
A. major 'Alba'
Looks like old-fashioned posies with many upturned heads, each made of green-tipped segments filled with quivering creamy centres from mid to late summer. 75cm/3½ft. ZONE 4.
A. m. Gill Richardson Group
Named after a fine plantswoman, this form is strong growing with deep wine-red flowers on robust stems. Needs good light to achieve best intensity of flower colour. 75cm/2½ft. ZONE 4.
A. m. 'Sunningdale Variegated'
Possibly the most beautiful foliage plant in spring with large, hand-shaped leaves elegantly marked with yellow and cream. Branching stems of white, pink-flushed, posy flowers during summer to autumn. 75cm/2½ft. ZONE 4.
A. maxima
Graceful branching stems topped with posy-like strawberry-pink broad petalled flowers with masses of pink stamens. 75cm/2½ft. ZONE 4.

LEFT *Aster × frikartii* **'Mönch'**
BELOW *Astilbe × arendsii* **'Fanal'**
BOTTOM *Astilbe × arendsii* **'Venus'**

ATHYRIUM
A. filix-femina
Slender and graceful, the lady fern comes in several different forms. They vary in height from tiny ones only a few inches tall to some with fronds up to 1.2m/4ft high. They all need retentive soil and shelter from drying winds. ZONE 4.
A. niponicum var. *pictum*
Delicate grey fronds, flushed with purple, held on purple-tinted stems. This fern needs a position sheltered from wind in moist leaf-mould. 15-23cm/6-9in. ZONE 4.

BALLOTA
B. pseudodictamnus
One of the loveliest greys. From a woody base spring long curving stems of round leaves clothed in grey-white felt. Tiny mauve flowers are buried in felty green bobbles held along the length of curving stems; very desirable to cut. The drier the conditions, the whiter the foliage becomes so good drainage is important. Grows best in full sun. 75cm/2½ft. ZONE 8.

BAPTISIA
B. australis
A superior lupin-like plant needing sun and deep retentive soil. Slim spires of rich blue flowers in summer followed by clusters of black swollen seed-pods on dark, stiffly upright stems. 90cm/3ft. ZONE 3.

BERGENIA
B. cordifolia 'Purpurea'
A superb plant, ideal for ground cover, with large rounded wavy leaves which frost burnishes to purplish-red. The flower stalks – the colour and thickness of rhubarb – support dangling sprays of vivid magenta flowers intermittently throughout summer. 45-60cm/1½-2ft. ZONE 4.
B. crassifolia 'Autumn Red'
Has smaller leaves than *B. cordifolia*. Fresh green in summer, flat and spoon-shaped, held upright in rosettes so that the richly carmine backs contrast with the polished green and bronze fronts in autumn. In May, soft-pink flowers make a fine display. 38cm/15in. ZONE 4.
HYBRIDS
B. 'Abendglocken'
Medium-sized, spoon-shaped leaves form good rosettes, assuming tints of bronzed enamel in late autumn/winter. 30cm/1ft. ZONE 6.

Drought-tolerant plants (medium/large)
Agapanthus
Allium (taller)
Alstroemeria ligtu
  hybrids
Artemisia
Asphodelus
Ballota
Cistus
Cynara
Echinops
Eryngium
Euphorbia characias
  subsp. *wulfenii*
Iris (bearded)
Lavandula
Linaria
Lychnis coronaria
Nectaroscordum siculum
  subsp. *bulgaricum*
Onopordum
Santolina
Stipa gigantea
Verbascum

ABOVE *Astrantia major* 'Alba'
LEFT *Ballota pseudodictamnus*

B. 'Abendglut'
Neat rosettes of crinkly edged rounded leaves turning maroon and plum-red in winter. Semi-double vivid rose-red flowers are produced in spring. 30cm/1ft. ZONE 6.

B. 'Admiral'
Leaves have bronze and crimson tints in winter and are erect, oval and weather-resistant. In spring, the cherry pink flowers are held on stems well above the foliage. 30cm/1ft. ZONE 4.

B. 'Ballawley'
Largest of all with shining fresh-green leaves all summer, bronzed and reddened by frost. It has branching heads of rose-red flowers on tall stems in spring, a few still appearing in the autumn. 60cm/2ft. ZONE 4.

B. 'Beethoven'
An Eric Smith hybrid. The large, dense clusters of white flowers, flushing pink as they mature, are held in coral-red calyces. Flowers in April. 30cm/1ft. ZONE 4.

B. 'Morgenröte'
Large rosettes of rounded leaves produce dense heads of cherry-pink flowers in spring and often an impressive second flowering later in the summer. 45cm/1½ft. ZONE 6.

B. 'Schneekönigin'
An interesting German hybrid. Extra large, pale shell-pink flowers in spring and leaves that remain green. 40cm/16in. ZONE 4.

B. 'Silberlicht'
In late spring this has large striking trusses of pure-white flowers which flush pink, either with age or from the weather conditions. 30cm/1ft. ZONE 6.

B. 'Sunningdale'
Vivid rose-pink flowers are held on bright coral stems. The foliage has good autumn and winter colour. 30-38cm/12-15in. ZONE6.

BETONICA
B. macrantha
Makes slowly spreading clumps of rich green scallop-edged leaves, while rosy-mauve funnel-shaped flowers in whorls are held on erect branching stems in June. A lovely plant for retentive soil and full sun. 60cm/2ft. ZONE 3.

BLECHNUM
B. chilense
A magnificent evergreen fern with huge arching leaves of dark matt green, it needs a cool, damp site in lime-free soil. It requires protection in winter in very cold climates. The roots are slowly invasive. 75-90cm/2½-3ft. ZONE 3.

BRUNNERA
B. macrophylla
In spring, long sprays of tiny forget-me-not-blue flowers are followed by robust clumps of basal leaves, each huge and heart-shaped, making good ground cover in shade or part shade and retentive soil. 45cm/1½ft. ZONE 3.

B. m. 'Hadspen Cream'
Large light-green leaves are bordered with primrose. 45cm/1½ft. ZONE 3.

B. m. 'Jack Frost'
Heart-shaped leaves are almost entirely silvered, with green veins and rim. 45cm/1½ft. ZONE 3.

Plants for shade (small and low-growing)
Ajuga
Aruncus aethusifolius
Cardamine
Corydalis
Dicentra
Epimedium
Geranium macrorrhizum
Lamium
Lysimachia nummularia
Omphalodes
Ophiopogon planiscapus
 'Nigrescens'
Pachysandra
Phlox stolonifera
Primula vulgaris
Pulmonaria
Tellima
Tiarella
Uvularia
Vinca
Waldsteinia

BELOW *Bergenia* 'Schneekönigin'

BUTOMUS
B. umbellatus
Grows in shallow water in bogs. Sheaves of stiff grassy leaves make fine verticals. Flower stems carry umbels of rose-pink flowers in midsummer. 1.2m/4ft. ZONE 6.

CALAMAGROSTIS
C. × *acutiflora* 'Karl Foerster'
An outstanding vertical especially in autumn and winter. Narrow flower panicles held bolt upright on needle-like stems form a slender column. They bleach straw colour, standing firm without support, throughout winter. 1.5m/4½ft. ZONE 5.
C. brachytricha
Needle-like flower stems carry pyramidal shaped flower-heads like elegant bottle-brushes. Grey-green with a touch of mauve when fresh, fading to buff. A fine, autumn flowering vertical. 1m/3ft. ZONE 6.

CALAMINTHA
C. grandiflora
Useful for the edge of a well-drained, sunny border, neat little bushes of fresh green foliage, dotted with rose-pink blossoms all summer. 25cm/10in. ZONE 6.

CALTHA
C. palustris 'Alba'
The lovely white variety of the marsh marigold. From early spring to midsummer. It grows in wet, boggy areas. 15cm/6in. ZONE 3.
C. palustris **var.** *radicans* **'Flore Pleno'**
The double marsh marigold, whose golden flowers come as early as the single form but last longer. Spring. 30cm/1ft. ZONE 3.

CAMASSIA
These are bulbous plants from the rich meadows of north-west America, valued vertical features in early summer, either in borders or naturalized. They need retentive soil and sun.
C. quamash
Has shorter stems of dark-blue flowers in May. 30cm/1ft. ZONE 5.
C. leicthlinii **subsp.** *suksdorfii* **'Electra'**
Produces extra large heads of lavender-blue flowers in early summer. 90cm/3ft. ZONE 6.

CAMPANULA
C. lactiflora
A splendid sight when the stout leafy stems are crowned with great heads of powder-blue bell flowers. Well placed among shrubs. Mid- and late summer. 1.5m/5ft. ZONE 7.
C. latifolia macrantha 'Alba'
A much-admired white form of the milky bellflower. 1.2m/4ft. ZONE 7.

LEFT *Calamagrostis* × *acutiflora* 'Karl Foerster'
BELOW *Campanula latifolia macrantha* 'Alba'

CARDAMINE

C. pentaphyllos

A spring delight for cool retentive soil in shade. Fine cut leaves and nodding flower stems unroll together, the flowers soft lilac, like large cuckoo flowers. 30-38cm/12-15in. ZONE 6.

CAREX

C. elata 'Aurea'

A lovely sight by the water's edge or in a sunny place in damp soil. This graceful sedge has bright golden grass-like foliage with pointed clusters of brown flowers held stiffly upright in June. 60cm/2ft. ZONE 5.

CARLINA

C. acaulis subsp. **simplex**

Makes a mound of very finely cut, prickly dark green leaves topped with dramatic thistle-like flowers on short stems (30cm/1ft). Each consists of a pale straw-coloured disc surrounded by 'silvered' petals. They open in late summer and dry in perfect shape. ZONE 7.

CENOLOPHIUM

C. denudatum

The Baltic parsley has a mound of finely cut leaves from which tall stems arise bearing flat green flower-heads in summer. 30cm/1ft. ZONE 6.

CENTAUREA see RHAPONTICUM

CHAEROPHYLLUM

C. hirsutum 'Roseum'

This lovely cow parsley is one of the joys of early summer. Over a base of feathery leaves stand branching stems, each holding a flat-topped head of tiny pink flowers. Does best in sun or part shade in good, retentive soil. 60cm/2ft. ZONE 3.

CHAMAENERION

C. angustifolium 'Album'

Also known as rosebay willowherb. Tall stems carry slender spires of pure-white flowers, enhanced by star-shaped green sepals. Spires of unopened buds above the open flowers, with rows of pale sterile seed-pods below, maintain

TOP **Chaerophyllum hirsutum** 'Roseum'
ABOVE **Carlina acaulis** subsp. **simplex**
LEFT **Carex elata** 'Aurea'

interesting form and colour for weeks in late summer. Slowly invasive. Does best in retentive soil and sun. 1-1.5m/3-5ft. ZONE 7.

CHRYSANTHEMUM

C. 'Clara Curtis'
One of the best late-summer-flowering plants, forming domes of blossom composed of single clear-pink daisy flowers. Divide it in spring every few years and plant in full sun, in fertile, well-drained retentive soil. 75cm/2½ft. ZONE 4.

C. 'Emperor of China'
This old hybrid has beautifully quilled petals, deep crimson in the centre but fading to silver-pink as the layers of petals unroll. By the end of flowering time in November the foliage becomes suffused and veined with rich crimson. Best in sun and retentive soil. 90-1.2m/3-4ft. ZONE 5.

CIRSIUM

C. rivulare 'Atropurpureum'
While not actually prickly, this handsome thistle has glowing ruby-red flowers that draw attention all summer and into autumn. 1.2m/4ft. ZONE 6.

CISTUS

All cistuses flower from July to August and require well-drained soil and sun.

C. × hybridus
Forms a medium-sized bush of light-green crinkled foliage. Flower-buds pink, opening to white cups. 1.2m/4ft. ZONE 8.

C. ladanifer
The dark-green slightly sticky foliage makes an excellent background all the year in the dry garden, but in midsummer, covered with huge white flowers splotched with purple, it commands admiration. 1.5m/5ft. ZONE 8.

C. × purpureus
Fresh green foliage all year, slightly crinkled, smothered in summer with large rich-pink flowers, each with a purple splash. 1.2m/4ft. ZONE 8.

COLCHICUM

C. speciosum 'Album'
In retentive soil and sun, this produces superb white flowers, rounded, like large wine goblets on pale-green stems, to be treasured. 15cm/6in. ZONE 6.

C. s. 'Atrorubens'
A rare wine-purple form with purple-stained stems. Plant in full sun. 15cm/6in. ZONE 6.

C. 'The Giant'
An autumn flowering bulb with large bold pale rosy-mauve flowers that stand up well to the weather. Increases freely. Best in full sun or part shade. 20cm/8in. ZONE 6.

ABOVE *Cirsium rivulare* **'Atropurpureum'**
BELOW *Colchicum* **'The Giant'**

CORYDALIS

C. cheilanthifolia

Attracts admiration with its soft mounds of finely dissected fern-like leaves. They are soft olive-green, complementing the long succession of light yellow flowers in early summer. 25-30cm/10-12in. ZONE 4.

C. solida

A fleeting delight in early spring. From bulbous roots this corydalis produces finely cut blue-grey leaves which are just right for the delicate heads of plum-purple flowers. Retentive soil in part-shade. 8-10cm/3-4in. ZONE 5.

C. solida subsp. *solida* 'Beth Evans'

A charming selection with fern-like foliage and the showiest sugar-pink flowers. Best in part shade. Foliage will die back by the end of spring. 15cm/6in. ZONE 6.

CRAMBE

C. cordifolia

From a mound of huge green leaves, bare branching stems soar skywards, carrying wide clouds of starry white flowers in July, like a giant gypsophila. Needs sun and retentive soil. 2m/6ft. ZONE 7.

CRINUM

C. × powellii

A bulbous plant. From the top of stout purplish stems tumble large trumpet-like rose-pink flowers for several weeks in late summer. Usually grown against a warm wall, it flourishes in sun and retentive soil in open ground, if well drained, fed and mulched in winter. Good in tubs. 1.2m/4ft. ZONE 8.

C. × p. 'Album'

Large, beautifully shaped pure-white trumpets. Both these crinums are deliciously scented. 1.2m/4ft. ZONE 8.

CROCOSMIA

C. × croscosmiiflora 'Honey Angels'

Soft creamy-yellow flowers, abundantly produced in late summer. It needs sun and good drainage. 60cm/2ft. ZONE 7.

C. 'Lucifer'

This imposing plant has stiff, pleated, blade-shaped leaves topped with large heads of brilliant flame-red flowers, from June to July. 1.2m/4ft. ZONE 7.

CYCLAMEN

C. coum

A variable species, some with green leaves, others with silver marbling

BELOW *Crocosmia* **'Lucifer'**
BOTTOM LEFT *Corydalis* **cheilanthifolia**
BOTTOM RIGHT *Cyclamen* **hederifolium**

on green. The leaves can be round or kidney shaped. From spring onwards the flowers, in shades from white to rich carmine, are produced. 5cm/2in. ZONE 4.

C. hederifolium
Also known as the ivy-leaved cyclamen. Attractive large leaves patterned with silver and with flowers in shades from white (*C. h.* 'Alba') to pink. Increases freely if left undisturbed. 10cm/4in. ZONE 4.

CYNARA
C. cardunculus
The cardoon is a magnificent feature plant with arching, boldly cut silver-grey leaves forming a great mound, above which stout stems carry large, thistle-shaped luminous-blue heads. 2m/6ft. ZONE 7.

DARMERA
D. peltata
In early spring tall, naked stems appear from thick, flattish rhizomes carrying flat heads of pale pink flowers. Scallop-edged, parasol-shaped leaves, up to 30cm/12in across, follow. For damp soil in sun. 60-90cm/2-3ft. ZONE 5.

DESCHAMPSIA
D. caespitosa 'Goldschleier'
This tufted hair-grass is one of the loveliest, either grouped among shrubs or rising alone above smaller plants. It forms dense tussocks of narrow, arching green leaves and by midsummer many tall flower stems tower above the foliage, carrying large airy plumes of tiny silver-green flowers. Gradually flowers and stems turn bright straw-yellow. Needs retentive soil in sun. 1.2m/4ft. ZONE 5.

DIANTHUS
The following pinks are valued as good ground-cover plants in sun and dry well-drained soil, making tidy close plants. There are many more available. Most flower in midsummer.

D. deltoides
The maiden pink. Abundant little starry flowers of carmine stand for weeks over solid mats of dark green foliage. Lovely with thymes. 20cm/8in. ZONE 3.

D. 'Mrs Sinkins'
The heavily scented old favourite pink, used for edging cottage garden paths, has double blooms of creamy-white. Midsummer. 23cm/9in. ZONE 5.

ABOVE LEFT **Darmera peltata**
ABOVE **Cynara cardunculus**

Plants for shade (medium/large)
Actaea
Anemone × hybrida
Angelica
Aruncus dioicus
Astrantia
Cenolophium denudatum
Digitalis
Hosta
Kirengeshoma
Lamprocapnos spectabilis
 (syn. *Dicentra spectabilis*)
Ligularia
Lysimachia
Maianthemum
Persicaria
Polygonatum × hybridum
Rheum
Rodgersia
Veratrum

DIASCIA

D. integerrima

Stiff stems with narrow grey leaves start to arch when bearing tapering heads of salmon pink flowers from summer to early autumn. 45cm/1½ft. ZONE 8.

D. 'Ruby Field'

This good form floats sprays of salmon-pink nemesia-like flowers over neat flat mats of small green leaves. Mid- to late summer. 15cm/6in. ZONE 7.

DICENTRA

D. formosa 'Langtrees'

Forms soft hummocks of deeply divided, almost blue leaves on pink stems, from which dangle small pink and cream flowers in spring and early summer. Likes cool conditions. 30cm/1ft. ZONE 4.

DIGITALIS

D. ferruginea

A gem. This perennial foxglove sends up tall flower stems bearing in midsummer close-set rounded buds which open to smallish short trumpets of coppery yellow, veined brown. Grows in sun or part shade provided it has good drainage. 90cm/3ft. ZONE 5.

D. lutea

Sends up tall spikes of small, slim, pale yellow flowers. 1.2m/4ft. ZONE 4.

D. parviflora

Small copper-coloured flowers on a short stout flower stem. 60cm/2ft. ZONE 5.

D. purpurea f. *albiflora*

A white-flowered form of the native foxglove. Best in part shade. 1.2m/4ft plus. ZONE 3.

DIPSACUS

D. fullonum

The native teasel. Prickly basal leaves followed by prickly stems of cone-shaped purple and white flowers in the second year. Can be dried. Loved by finches. 1.4m/5ft. ZONE 5.

D. inermis

A plant of coarse character (much liked by moths), its strong branches carry pin-cushion heads of tiny creamy flowers which, by autumn, become dome-shaped seed-heads. Needs retentive soil. 1.8m/6ft. ZONE 6.

DISPORUM

D. sessile 'Variegatum'

From a wandering starfish-shaped rootstock rise slender stems bearing pretty fresh green leaves, broadly

TOP *Dipsacus fullonum*
ABOVE *Diascia integerrima*
LEFT *Digitalis purpurea* f. *albiflora*

striped with cream. Creamy-white bell-shaped flowers dangle beneath the leaves in spring. It likes part shade and retentive soil. 30-38cm/12-15in. ZONE 4.

DRYOPTERIS
D. filix-mas
The male or buckler fern will tolerate almost any situation except very water-logged soil and is the only form that can stand quite dry shade. It unrolls elegant sheaves of typical light green fern-like fronds that deepen in colour. Although not truly evergreen, it lasts well into winter. 90cm-1.2m/3-4ft. ZONE 5.

ECHINACEA
E. purpurea
An imposing plant with fine dark foliage carried on stiff, branching stems that need no staking. Large broad-petalled flowers of rich mauve-crimson are enhanced by central cones which glisten orange-brown. Long flowering period from late summer. Plant in sun in retentive soil. 90cm/3ft. ZONE 3.

ECHINOPS
E. ritro 'Veitch's Blue'
Also known as globe thistle. Tall statuesque plant with shiny leathery leaves with sharp spiny tips. Round drumstick heads of hard blue flowers. Prefers hot sun and poor soil. 1.2m/4ft. ZONE 6.

EPIMEDIUM
Most valued and beautiful foliage plants that will put up with dry or part shade but making superb ground cover more quickly in rich damp retentive leaf-mould. Best cut down in early March to reveal the delicate sprays of tiny columbine-like flowers.
E. × rubrum
A splendid ground cover in shade and among shrubs. Elegant heart-shaped leaves on wiry stems emerge in soft tints of bronze-red, fading to light green, but assume vivid coral-red shades in autumn. Rose-pink flowers in spring. 23cm/9in. ZONE 4.
E. × youngianum 'Niveum'
Neat clumps of smaller foliage in soft shades of milk-chocolate in spring, over which float clouds of pure white starry flowers. A gem. 25cm/10in. ZONE 5.

ERANTHUS
E. hyemalis
Winter aconite. A cheery winter-flowering bulb, with bright yellow flowers above a ruff of bright green leaves during January/February. Takes a

BELOW *Eranthus hyemalis*
BOTTOM LEFT *Echinacea purpurea*
BOTTOM RIGHT *Echinops ritro* 'Veitch's Blue'

213

while to spread and must be allowed to seed to do so. 75cm/3in. ZONE 4.

EREMURUS

Also called foxtail lily, this spectacular perennial has straight, unbranched stems, crowded along their upper parts with small, star-shaped lily flowers. There are several species and hybrids, differing only in size and shades of white, pink and yellow. Perhaps the most spectacular is *E. robustus*. 2.5m/8ft. ZONE 5.

ERIGERON

E. 'Dimity'

Makes tidy clumps of evergreen leaves with a succession of pinkish-mauve daisies in midsummer. Ideal edge-of-border plants, which look lovely with ajugas. Best given sun and a retentive soil. 30cm/1ft. ZONE 7.

E. karvinskianus

The daintiest of daisies on wiry stems, opening white and fading to rose. Seeds freely into cracks and crevices in midsummer. 30cm/1ft. ZONE 7.

ERIOPHYLLUM

E. lanatum

Very useful ground cover in sun-parched but well-drained soil, it quickly makes large patches of silvery-white finely divided leaves, with a show of orange-yellow daisies from late spring to early summer. 15cm/6in. ZONE 7.

ERYNGIUM

E. agavifolium

Makes a spectacular foliage plant which forms large rosettes of broad, strap-shaped light-green leaves, sharply toothed, from which rise branched stems carrying cylindrical greenish-white heads. 1.5m/5ft. ZONE 6.

E. bourgatii

Individual basal leaves shown off against dry bare soil are deeply divided, crisply curled and prickle-edged with broad, silvered veins and scattered spots. Heads of blue-green flowers crown a distinctive plant in summer. 60cm/2ft. ZONE 6.

E. giganteum

Also known as Miss Willmott's ghost.

ABOVE *Erigeron karvinskianus*
BELOW LEFT *Eremurus hybrid*
BELOW CENTRE *Eryngium bourgatii*
BELOW RIGHT *Erythronium dens-canis*

Widely branching heads of metallic silvery green cones of flowers are surrounded by silvered blue-green bracts. Dries well. 75cm/2½ft. ZONE 6.

E. planum
Slender stems carry a large head of many thimble-sized cones surrounded by a spiny ruff. Stems and flowers dark blue. 90cm/3ft. ZONE 6.

E. tripartitum
Wiry, wide-spreading branching stems carry many cone-shaped heads surrounded by deeper blue spiny bracts in midsummer. 45cm/1½ft. ZONE 6.

E. variifolium
Forms a flat handsome rosette of green richly marbled leaves with heads of small spiky flowers in late summer. The small spiny leaves on the stems and the stiff flowers create a metallic effect. 45cm/1½ft. ZONE 6.

ERYTHRONIUM
All erythroniums do best in rich leafy retentive soil, in part shade.

E. californicum 'White Beauty'
Pale cream lily-shaped flowers reflex to show cream stamens with a ring of reddish stain at their base. Broad, wavy, shining leaves, slightly marbled. 25cm/10in. ZONE 3.

E. dens-canis
The matt, chocolate-blotched, oval leaves of the dog's-tooth violet are as attractive as the delicate rosy-mauve flowers whose petals reflex like cyclamens in spring sunshine. Forms bundles of ivory-white pointed corms in leaf-mould soil. 15cm/6in. ZONE 3.

EUPATORIUM
E. cannabinum 'Flore Pleno'
A beautiful form of hemp agrimony that graces the border for weeks in late summer and autumn. Tall leafy stems carrying clusters of rose-coloured flowers. 1.5m/5ft. ZONE 4.

E. purpureum subsp. maculatum 'Atropurpureum'
This form has darker stems and brighter rose-purple flowers on slightly shorter stems. 1.5m/5ft. ZONE 4.

EUPHORBIA
E. amygdaloides var. robbiae
Although it will grow in dry shade, this evergreen spurge is marvellous in good retentive soil. It is invasive, so unsuitable for very small gardens. Handsome dark-green rosettes carry showy heads of yellowish green flowers which open in spring and last through summer, turning bronze tinted in autumn. Useful as evergreen ground cover. 60-75cm/2-2½ft. ZONE 6.

E. characias subsp. wulfenii
A dramatic feature plant in the dry garden from the eastern

TOP *Eupatorium purpureum* subsp. *maculatum* 'Atropurpureum'

ABOVE LEFT/RIGHT *Euphorbia characias* subsp. *wulfenii*

215

Mediterranean. Handsome all the year round. Long, stiff stems clothed in blue-grey foliage form a large clump. From March to May each stem carries a huge head of lime-green flowers. Likes shelter from wind. *E. characias* subsp. *characias* is the Mediterranean form, a tougher plant whose dull green flowers have sinister-looking black eyes. These two subspecies are much interbred in gardens and often cannot be named with any certainty. 90cm-1.2m/3-4ft. ZONE 6.

E. cornigera

Handsome for weeks in midsummer. Begins with a closely packed small head of vivid lime-green flowers set off by white-veined leaves. Side branches appear, carrying more flowers until a large loose head is formed. Several stems arise from one rootstock. Needs rich retentive soil in part shade. 90cm/3ft. ZONE 6.

E. epithymoides

One of the best euphorbias, with neat mounds of brassy-yellow heads all through spring. The whole plant takes on coral tints in autumn. 38cm/15in. ZONE 5.

E. e. 'Major'

In spring this looks like a larger form of *E. epithymoides* but the foliage is more luxuriant. Late crop of flowers in autumn. 45cm/1½ft. ZONE 6.

E. griffithii 'Fireglow'

Has tomato-red flowers, light olive foliage with red veins and orange-brown stems. It will grow in full sun and likes retentive soil. The veins and backs of the young leaves are coral-red and the flowers a brilliant flame-red. It flowers from early to late summer. 90cm-1.2m/3-4ft. ZONE 5.

E. myrsinites

Prostrate stems radiate from a central point carrying wax-coated blue leaves and terminating in a large head of lime-green, apricot-tinged flowers in early spring. 15cm/6in. ZONE 5.

E. palustris

Its many leafy stems create a bushy shape up to several feet across. It is topped with wide flat heads of greenish-gold flowers for several weeks in spring and early summer. In the autumn the dying foliage sometimes turns brilliant shades of cream, orange and crimson. Needs moist soil. 90-1.2m/3-4ft. ZONE 6.

E. seguieriana

A superb plant. Following *E. epithymoides*, it blooms for three months, with exquisite lime-green flower-heads on many thin stems. The leaves are narrow and blue-grey. 45cm/1½ft. ZONE 7.

Plants for shade (bulbs, ferns and grasses)

BULBS

Arum
Colchicum
Erythronium
Fritillaria
Galanthus
Leucojum
Narcissus

FERNS

Adiantum
Asplenium
Athyrium
Dryopteris
Polypodium
Polystichum

GRASSES

Hakonechloa
Melica
Milium effusum
 'Aureum'

BELOW LEFT ***Euphorbia griffithii* 'Fireglow'**
BELOW CENTRE ***Euphorbia epithymoides***
BELOW RIGHT ***Euphorbia myrsinites***

E. sikkimensis

In February and March basal rosettes of ruby-red leaves appear. Quickly the stems become tall and willowy, and the leaves turn light green, with a white vein and red leaf-stalks, giving a fresh effect from the end of July into September. Flowering begins in early July and by August the blue-green seed-pods contrast with vivid lime-green collars. 1.2-1.5m/4-5ft. ZONE 6.

EURYBIA
E. divaricata (syn. *Aster divaricatus*)
Gertrude Jekyll showed us how to plant this among bergenias where its thin, shiny black stems, topped with frothy sprays of tiny, white, pink-flushed daisies, are supported by them. 60cm/2ft. ZONE 4.

FESTUCA
F. glauca 'Elijah Blue'
Looking wonderful in hot, dry weather, this strong form has needle-stiff, rolled leaves in vivid grey-blue. 25cm/10in. ZONE 5.

FOENICULUM
F. vulgare 'Purpureum'
The bronze fennel forms clumps of tall lush green stems covered with a cloud of bronzy-brown foliage. Yellow cow parsley-like flowers in late summer. Handsome throughout summer and autumn. Plant in well-drained sunny areas. 1.5m/5ft. ZONE 7.

FRITILLARIA
F. acmopetala
Greenish bells with dark brown markings dangle from tall graceful stems. This plant tends to produce many offspring which are slow in making flowering bulbs. For well-drained soil in a sunny position. 38cm/15in. ZONE 6.

ABOVE *Fritillaria imperialis*

F. camtschatcensis
This extraordinary fritillary likes a rich leaf-mould soil in sun or part shade. Its curious bulb looks rather like a spoonful of cooked rice squeezed into a round ball. The bulblets can be pulled apart and grown for several years before they make a flowering stem. The green glossy leaves are set in whorls around the stems. Several open pendant bells are produced in May, up to 3cm/1¼in long. They are deep black, smooth outside and heavily corrugated inside, where the colour is slightly lighter – a dark chocolate-maroon. 30-38cm/12-15in. ZONE 6.

F. imperialis
The crown imperial is one of the first bulbs to emerge in spring, producing a pungent scent in early March. The leaves are shiny and slightly twisted, spiralling around the thick stem and ending halfway up where the stem becomes purple. The stems are topped with plumes of narrow green leaves and drooping waxy orange bells – another form has yellow bells. If left to settle down, these plants will make grapefruit-sized bulbs. 1.2m/4ft. ZONE 5.

F. meleagris

Also known as the snake's head fritillary. It is easily grown provided the soil does not dry out during the growing season. The stems are lightly set with narrow blue-green leaves and carry tapering chequered bells with angular 'shoulders'. Flowers in April to May. 25cm/10in. ZONE 4.

F. persica

Spires of soft-purple bells with a grape-like bloom rise from clumps of leafy stems. The stems are not strong enough to support the blooms, but best allowed to lean against another plant rather than tied. Plant in a warm, well-drained site under a wall. 60cm/2ft. ZONE 6.

F. verticillata

Slender stems rise from a bulb set with whorls of narrow blue-green leaves, thinner towards the top of the stem where their tips become tendrils. The April flowers are open and bell-shaped, pale green with brown chequering inside. Each bulb produces several offsets. It has a reputation for shy flowering but once established on warm, well-drained, well-fed soil, will flower freely. 45cm/1½ft. ZONE 7.

GALANTHUS

In the wild there are a surprising number of different species of snowdrop. Because it has been cultivated for centuries, there are many garden hybrids and selected forms. Some require sharp eyes to spot the difference, but enthusiasts have ensured that many beautiful forms are preserved. Single forms may have larger flowers or green-tipped petals, while doubles have tightly packed petals. 10-20cm/4-8in. ZONE 4.

G. elwesii 'Cedric's Prolific'

This exceptional snowdrop came from Cedric Morris's garden. Large single flowers are held on long stems

supported by broad grey-green leaves up to 2.5cm/1in across. A vigorous grower, it quickly makes clumps of bulbs. 30cm/1ft. ZONE 4.

G. 'Hippolyta'

Rounded double flowers with green-tinged petticoats. Late season. 20cm/8in. ZONE 4.

G. 'James Backhouse'

Vigorous early snowdrop with distinctive elongated flowers. 30cm/12in. ZONE 4.

G. 'Lady Beatrix Stanley'

Large, well-shaped double flowers with long narrow sepals enclosing many layered, neat white petticoats, faintly edged green. Early flowering, It increases well. 20cm/8in. ZONE 4.

G. 'S. Arnott'

Has large cupped sepals, 5cm/2in across, that open up in winter sun to reveal the strong green arch to the top of the inner petals. It is scented and increases well. 25cm/10in. ZONE 4.

GALTONIA

G. candicans

An elegant plant, lovely to cut. Tall stems carry large wax-white bells, like

ABOVE LEFT *Fritillaria persica*

ABOVE RIGHT *Fritillaria meleagris*

a huge hyacinth. Plant the bulbs in spring. Flowers July until September. It needs sun and good drainage. 1.2m/4ft. ZONE 7.

G. princeps
Handsome, grey-green broad, strap-shaped leaves. Erect stems carry green waxy bells, earlier than *G. candicans*. 60cm/2ft. ZONE 7.

G. viridiflora
Flowers much later than the other two, with heads of wide-open pale green bells, remarkable in the garden or picked. September to October. 90cm/3ft. ZONE 7.

GAURA see OENOTHERA

GENTIANA
G. asclepiadea
The willow gentian produces many slender stems clothed with narrow glossy leaves and arched with its weight of true gentian-blue trumpets in early autumn. Does best in full sun and retentive soil. 60cm/2ft. ZONE 5.

GERANIUM
Commonly known as cranesbill, geraniums are among the most valuable of herbaceous plants, both to fill in between taller plants, or for the singular effects they create when in flower. Among my favourites are the following:

G. cinereum 'Ballerina'
This charming small cranesbill covers the ground with neat mounds of rounded, cut, greyish foliage. For weeks through summer, it produces large crinkled lilac flowers with heavy purple veining and dark centres. 15cm/6in. ZONE 6.

G. endressii
Makes mounds of light apple-green leaves with flowers in varying shades of pink, from June until late autumn. 38cm/15in. ZONE 3.

G. macrorrhizum
Flowers in May forming low weed-defeating carpets of scented leaves, some turning bright autumn colours while the rest remain green all winter.

Plants for dry shade
Arum
Brunnera
Cyclamen
Dicentra formosa
Digitalis
Dryopteris
Epimedium
Euphorbia amygdaloides
  var. *robbiae*
Geranium endressii
Geranium macrorrhizum
Helleborus foetidus
Lamium
Liriope
Melica
Pachysandra
Polygonatum
Polystichum
Symphytum
Tellima
Vinca

ABOVE **Galanthus 'Hippolyta'**
RIGHT **Galanthus 'James Backhouse'**

ABOVE *Geranium psilostemon*
LEFT *Geranium* Rozanne = **'Gerwat'**

Again, there are forms in several shades of pink, from almost white to reddish-purple. 30cm/12in. ZONE 5.

G. psilostemon
Forms large leafy plants with magenta-pink flowers with indigo eyes in June. 90cm/3ft. ZONE 6.

G. Rozanne = 'Gerwat'
Stops visitors in their tracks with its large violet-blue flowers with white centres from May onwards. 45cm/1½ft. ZONE 4.

G. sylvaticum 'Album'
Large mounds of soft divided leaves; pure white spring flowers. 60cm/2ft. ZONE 6.

GEUM
G. × borisii
Makes slowly spreading clumps of rich-green roundish, hairy leaves. The single flowers are an unusual shade of rich orange-red, very vivid against the bold foliage in early summer and sometimes again in late summer. Plant in retentive soil in sun. 30cm/1ft. ZONE 7.

GILLENIA
G. trifoliata
A graceful plant for semi-shade or full sun in cool retentive soil. Slender russet-coloured stems set with small trifoliate leaves carry sprays of narrow-petalled white flowers which float like moths at dusk in June. After flowering, reddish-brown calyces remain for weeks. 90cm/3ft. ZONE 4.

GLADIOLUS
G. papilio
Strangely seductive in late summer and autumn. Above narrow, grey-green blade-shaped leaves stand tall stems carrying downcast heads. The slender buds and backs of petals are shades of green, cream and slate-purple. Inside creamy hearts shelter blue anthers while the lower lip petal is feathered and marked with an 'eye' in purple and greenish yellow, like the wing of a butterfly. It increases freely. Needs sun and warm well-drained soil. 90cm/3ft. ZONE 8.

GLANDULARIA
G. corymbosa (syn. Verbena corymbosa)
Surprisingly likes moist, retentive soil, which it colonizes with tangles of low feathery shoots topped all summer with violet-blue clusters. Useful among *Trollius* or *Rudbeckia* or small bush willows. Flowers for weeks from midsummer. Full sun. 30cm/1ft. ZONE 8.

GLAUCIUM
G. corniculatum
Large rosettes of grey-blue heavily cut leaves; burnt-orange flowers in late summer and autumn are followed by long horn-like pods. Plant in sun in well-drained soil. 60cm/2ft. ZONE 7.

GLYCERIA
G. maxima var. variegata
A handsome plant for the waterside or heavy retentive soil. Broad, strap-like leaves striped with white and yellow are warmly shaded with pink in spring and autumn. 60cm/2ft. ZONE 5.

GUNNERA
G. magellanica
Usually astounds visitors seeing it for the first time since it is a low creeping plant with small round heavily-veined leaves hugging the soil to make weed-proof carpets in damp places. 10cm/4in. ZONE 6.

G. manicata
Grows in deep valleys in southern Brazil in rich alluvial soil. It produces the largest leaves in temperate gardens. The fruiting bodies on its flowering stems are more widely spaced and are long and flexible like fingers. The whole fruiting head is brownish-green to start with but its minute, round seed-capsules turn orange when ripe. 2.5m/8ft. ZONE 6 (if covered in winter).

GYPSOPHILA
G. dubia
Ground-hugging mats of green foliage on dark-red stems smothered with white flowers flushed pink. Flowers from May to June. 8cm/3in. ZONE 5.

ABOVE *Glaucium corniculatum*

ABOVE *Gillenia trifoliata*
RIGHT *Gunnera manicata*

221

FAR LEFT *Gypsophila paniculata*
LEFT *Hakonechloa macra* 'Aureola'
BELOW *Helleborus niger*
BOTTOM *Helleborus × hybridus*

G. paniculata

Traditional garden favourite with masses of tangled stems and clouds of tiny white flowers in midsummer. 1.2m/4ft. ZONE 4.

G. 'Rosenschleier'

A sight, later in summer or in autumn, with clouds of pale-pink double flowers. It also needs sun and good drainage. 30cm/12in. ZONE 3.

HAKONECHLOA

H. macra 'Aureola'

A grass that never fails to cause comment. It makes soft clumps of foliage about 30cm/12in high, each ribbon-like leaf vividly variegated gold and buff with touches of bronze. Needs retentive soil and cool conditions, but not dense shade. ZONE 7.

HAPLOPAPPUS

H. glutinosus

Forms a cushion of dark evergreen finely cut foliage studded with sun-loving orange daisy flowers, from August till first frosts. Looks beautiful hanging over a low wall or steps but must have good drainage. 15cm/6in. ZONE 6.

HELICTOTRICHON

H. sempervirens

Forms arching clumps of vivid grey-blue foliage and sends up oat-like

plumes of the same colour. Useful contrast in form among other grey-foliaged plants. Requires dry sunny conditions for the best colour. 1.2m/4ft. ZONE 5.

HELLEBORUS

H. argutifolius

One of my favourite plants. In summer the stems form compact mounds of veined grey-green leaves which fall apart in winter to make way for new shoots. In spring the large pale green flower cups turn upwards to fill the gap. If well fed, they will grow in full sun or part shade. 60-75cm/2-2½ft. ZONE 6.

H. foetidus

Although it has similar striking colouring, this species is quite different from *H. argutifolius*. Clusters of

FAR LEFT *Helleborus × hybridus* (double-flowered form)
LEFT *Helleborus argutifolius*

maroon-edged, palest-green thimble-sized bells dangle above small neat clumps of fan-shaped, finely divided holly-green leaves. It has a strange winter smell. 45cm/1½ft. ZONE 6.

H. guttatus
The name means 'spotted' or 'freckled' and there are forms with white or deep-pink flowers, heavily spotted inside with dark red. Some of the plum shades are peppered with very fine dark dust-like markings. 30-38cm/12-15in. ZONE 6.

H. × hybridus
Also known as Lenten roses. These produce the most sumptuous of late winter/early spring flowers. Their colours range from greenish-white through to soft plum and deep smoky-purple. The flower shapes also vary: from round prim cups to drooping ones, and with some that open large purple petals with pale cream stamens in startling contrast to dark purple 'petals'. They are easier to grow than the Christmas rose. They like cool conditions in semi-shade. Flower-buds appear at the end of January if the weather is not too severe and the flowers last into April. 45cm/1½ft. ZONE 4.

H. niger
The well-known Christmas rose, cultivated since Roman times. Although reputed to prefer heavy soil, it flourishes in my well-fed, well-drained, gravel-based soil on an open site. Rows of stock plants are crowded with blossoms in early March (never at Christmas). Several forms exist. We have one which flushes pink as the flowers mature. The leafy clumps stand about 30cm/1ft tall, the flower stems rarely so tall. Because we cut off the old leaves in winter, long before the buds emerge (to avoid damage by botrytis), they are not concealed. ZONE 4.

H. purpurascens
This has shorter stems than *H. × hybridus* with smaller, neatly cupped flowers in mid- or very dark purple, pale green inside. 30cm/1ft. ZONE 6.

H. viridis
This is a subtle plant with deciduous leaves and saucer-shaped flowers of a pea-green shade. 30cm/1ft. ZONE 7.

Plants for damp (not water-logged) soil in full sun/light shade
Astilbe
Caltha
Carex elata
Darmera
Eupatorium
Euphorbia palustris
Gunnera
Hemerocallis
Hosta
Iris sibirica
Ligularia
Lysimachia
Lythrum
Miscanthus
Onoclea sensibilis
Osmunda regalis
Persicaria
Primula bulleyana
Zantedeschia

FAR LEFT *Hemerocallis* 'Anzac'
LEFT *Hemerocallis* 'Pink Sundae'

HEMEROCALLIS

These daylilies are easy plants in any soil except the very driest. They thrive in sun or part shade. Their grassy clumps make good ground cover.

H. 'Anzac'

Large open-faced trumpets in guardsman's red with orange throats. 75cm/2½ft. ZONE 5.

H. dumortieri

The first daylily to make a fine show in early spring. Slender stems carry a wealth of perfumed rich yellow flowers from dark reddish buds. 60cm/2ft. ZONE 5.

H. lilioasphodelus

This lovely species has been grown since the 16th century. Perfect lily-shaped flowers of clear light yellow are very sweetly scented. They flower in early summer and look good among blue or pink cranesbills. 75cm/2½ft. ZONE 5.

H. 'Pink Sundae'

Softly ruffled pale apricot flowers with a paler zone on the centre of each petal. 90cm/3ft. ZONE 5

HESPERANTHA (syn. SCHIZOSTYLIS)

H. coccinea 'Major'

Makes spreading patches of grassy-leaved shoots that send up slender spires of slim buds. Throughout autumn and mild days in winter they open glistening, shallow cups, jewel-like and cherry-red. They need retentive soil and moisture all summer but also warmth and sun to encourage early flowering. 38cm/15in. ZONE 8.

H. c. 'Sunrise'

Large salmon-pink flowers open in October and continue into December. 38cm/15in. ZONE 8.

HEUCHERA

H. 'Plum Pudding'

Rounded, deeply scalloped leaves marbled with silver over a dark purple base. Insignificant white flowers. 45cm/1½ft. ZONE 5.

H. villosa 'Palace Purple'

Overlapping heart-shaped leaves, dark bronze red, with irregularly cut edges. Masses of wiry dark stems carry feathery heads of tiny white flowers followed by rosy-bronze seed-pods. Summer to autumn. For not too dry soil in sun or part shade. 45cm/1½ft. ZONE 5.

HOSTA

H. fortunei var. albopicta

A great garden favourite, it does best in deep moist soil in shade. The leaves alone will then be up to 23cm/9in long

Plants for retentive soil in sun (medium/large)

Achillea
Angelica
Anthemis tinctoria
Aster
Astrantia
Campanula
Chamaenerion
Chrysanthemum
Cirsium
Crocosmia
Dipsacus
Echinacea
Eupatorium
Euphorbia griffithii
Filipendula
Hemerocallis
Hesperantha
Inula
Iris pseudacorus
Kniphofia
Leucanthemum
Ligularia
Lychnis chalcedonica
Lysimachia
Lythrum
Macleaya
Miscanthus
Molinia
Morina
Persicaria
Rhaponticum
Rheum
Rudbeckia
Thalictrum
Trollius
Veronicastrum

and 15cm/6in across with a delicate, almost translucent texture. They are variegated when they first open with a yellow and cream centre and a border of dark green. The leaf becomes completely green by midsummer. 75cm/2½ft. ZONE 5.

H. f. var. albopicta f. aurea
Its delicate leaves are completely butter-yellow at first but turn light green by summer. 45cm/1½ft. ZONE 5.

H. f. 'Albomarginata'
The moderately large and heavily corrugated leaves are sage-green and ivory, and in rich soil will produce very dramatic variegations if sufficiently shaded. 75cm/2½ft. ZONE 5.

H. f. var. aureomarginata
Will take more light than most of the hostas, provided the soil is not too dry. The variegation lasts well into autumn. It quickly forms a good-sized clump. 60cm/2ft. ZONE 5.

H. 'Krossa Regal'
This is a large, grey-leaved plant. Handsome glaucous leaves on tall stems are lightly corrugated with parallel veins. Each tip tilts upwards so the wavy edges show a glimpse of pale grey-blue bloom on the underside. It produces spires of lilac flowers in mid- to late summer. 90cm-1.2m/3-4ft. ZONE 3.

H. plantaginea var. japonica
This rare plant is not the easiest to grow. It needs moisture and warmth well into the autumn. Then, in October, it produces very large, scented, lily-like flowers. The leaves are arching heart shapes of a glossy yellowish-green. 60cm/2ft. ZONE 3.

H. sieboldiana 'Frances Williams'
Broad, heavily quilted leaves with butter-yellow margins all summer. Sumptuous in part shade. 75cm/2½ft. ZONE 3.

H. s. var. elegans
This is a selected form with very large leaves in a deeper grey-blue tone, deeply veined and puckered. 75cm/2½ft. ZONE 3.

H. 'Spinners'
Makes large clumps of overlapping sage-green leaves broadly edged with cream, creating a strong focal point all summer. 60cm/2ft. ZONE 5.

H. (Tardiana Group) 'Halcyon'
In my garden this holds its blue colouring longer than other blue-leaved hostas. Fine heads of lilac-blue flowers are held on purplish stems in late summer. 30cm/1ft. ZONE 3.

BELOW *Heuchera* '**Plum Pudding**'
BOTTOM LEFT *Hosta sieboldiana* '**Frances Williams**'
BOTTOM RIGHT *Hosta* '**Spinners**'

H. 'Yellow Splash'
This hybrid has narrow, brightly variegated leaves, the vivid colouring lasting until the first autumn frosts. It tolerates open conditions better than some of the variegated ones. 30cm/1ft. ZONE 3.

HOUTTUYNIA
H. cordata 'Flore Pleno'
A distinctive plant for cool, retentive, moist soil or pond sides, it grows in either sun or shade. Elegant heart-shaped leaves shaded with purple are strongly orange scented, while the pure white double flowers are borne in cone-like clusters. Midsummer. 45cm/1½ft. ZONE 5.

HUMULUS
H. lupulus 'Aureus'
The attractive yellow-leaved hop. It colours best in full sun or part shade on not-too-dry retentive soil. ZONE 3

HYLOTELEPHIUM
H. 'Herbstfreude' (syn. Sedum 'Autumn Joy')
Produces early rosettes of fleshy grey-green leaves. Similarly coloured waxy buds open to rich pink starry flowers, deepening to brick red before developing warm brown seed-heads. Flower from late summer and is much loved by bees. Needs sun and good drainage. 75cm/2½ft. ZONE 4.
H. spectabile 'Brilliant'
Large flat heads of bright mauve-pink flowers, humming with bees, in late summer. 45cm/1½ft. ZONE 3.

INULA
I. magnifica
Truly magnificent where there is room to show it off from top to bottom and where it will not be tattered by strong winds. Rough-textured leaves, not unlike dock leaves but far larger, arching and wavy-edged, ascend stout stems in diminishing size to wide branching heads of large fine-rayed yellow daisies. Splendid in rough grass in retentive soil or by the waterside in full sun. Late summer to early autumn. 2-2.5m/6-8ft. ZONE 4.

IRIS
Although some iris, such as *Iris kaempferi*, do need moisture and sometimes several inches of water (as does *I. laevigata*), others thrive in dry conditions, in either sun or shade. There are many different species and varieties. The following are just a very brief selectionn.
I. 'Benton Arundel'
Given to us by the late Sir Cedric Morris at his garden, Benton End, in

TOP LEFT **Hosta 'Yellow Splash'**
TOP RIGHT **Humulus lupulus 'Aureus'**
ABOVE **Inula magnifica**
LEFT **Hylotelephium spectabile 'Brilliant'**

Suffolk. This is a pale version of *I.* 'Kent Pride', with flowers of dusky gold and brownish yellow in early summer. 90cm/3ft. ZONE 5.

I. 'Black Swan'
A tall Bearded iris, with upright silk-textured standards of translucent purple contrasting with broad, black-velvet falls. Looks particularly sumptuous among grey and silver plants. 90cm/3ft. ZONE 6.

I. pallida subsp. *pallida*
Worth growing for its beautiful foliage alone. Fans of broad-bladed grey leaves make a good accent all summer and well into autumn. Scented flowers with silk-textured, crinkly petals in pale lavender-blue are a bonus in late spring to early summer. 90cm/3ft. ZONE 6.

I. p. 'Argentea Variegata'
The boldly striped blue-green and white leaves keep their colour right through the growing season, and are more eye-catching than most flowers. Its own flowers, in June, are light blue. It needs a well-drained sunny border. 45cm/1½ft. ZONE 4.

I. pseudacorus 'Variegata'
A striking variegated form of the yellow flag. It grows wild in marshy ground or shallow water but will also grow in rich retentive soil. The yellow flowers have distinct brown markings. 90cm/3ft. ZONE 5.

I. 'Sibirica Alba'
A graceful iris, with branching stems of pure white flowers, it will thrive by the waterside or in good ordinary soil. It flowers from June to July. 75cm/2½ft. ZONE 4.

KIRENGESHOMA
K. palmata
Needs humus-fed, lime-free soil in semi-shade. From late summer to autumn, heavy clusters of fat swelling buds open to shuttlecock-shaped, waxy flowers about 5cm/2in long in pale butter-yellow. Irregularly cut maple-like leaves clothe dark purple stems which bow under the weight of flowers. Needs shelter from wind. 90cm/3ft. ZONE 5.

KNAUTIA
K. macedonica
Very free-flowering over a long period; dainty curving stems and branches full of crimson pincushions. Late summer to autumn. Retentive soil and sun. 60cm/2ft. ZONE 8.

LEFT *Iris* 'Black Swan'
BELOW *Iris* 'Benton Arundel'
BOTTOM *Iris pallida* subsp. *pallida*

KNIPHOFIA

K. 'Green Jade'

Forms a medium-sized plant with delicate jade-green flowers. Late summer to autumn. 1.2m/4ft. ZONES 7–8.

K. 'Ice Queen'

One of the palest hybrids with green-tipped buds opening to palest creamy yellow. There will never be a pure white poker, but this comes closest so far. 80-90cm/2-3ft. ZONES 7-8.

K. 'Little Maid'

Has neat, narrow foliage topped by slender stems closely set with tubular flowers extending more than halfway down the stem. Green in bud, flowers open ivory-white, produced for weeks in autumn. 60cm/2ft. ZONE 6.

K. rooperi

An impressive landscape species. Strong stems carry large chunky heads of brilliant orange and yellow flowers above broad arching foliage. From late summer to autumn. 1.2m/4ft. ZONE 6.

LAMIUM

L. maculatum 'Beacon Silver'

Makes very good cover in cool soil and part shade. Leaves totally silvered apart from narrow green edging. Has dark pink-lipped flowers in late spring. 10cm/4in. ZONE 3.

L. m. 'Pink Pewter'

Silvery leaves with crinkled green edges and pale pink flowers. 20cm/8in. ZONE 3.

L. m. 'White Nancy'

Another silver-leaved form that has ivory-white flowers in early summer. 20cm/8in. ZONE 3.

LAMPROCAPNOS

L. spectabilis (syn. Dicentra spectabilis)

Also known as bleeding heart or lady's locket. Needs rich, deep retentive soil in shade or part shade to produce tall stems drooping with the delicate rose and white lockets. Flowers early summer. 60cm/2ft. ZONE 5.

L. s. 'Alba'

Above delicately cut green leaves arch green stems bowed with beautiful ivory-white, heart-shaped lockets. Flowers for weeks in late spring and early summer. 75cm/2½ft. ZONE 5.

L. s. 'Gold Heart'

Different from the species, being clump forming, with golden yellow leaves. 60cm/2ft. ZONE 5.

Plants for retentive soil in sun (small and low-growing)

Alchemilla mollis
Aruncus aethusifolius
Astilbe
Carex
Geranium
Geum
Houttuynia
Persicaria affinis
Potentilla alba
Primula denticulata
Prunella
Stokesia laevis
Trachystemon
Trifolium
Viola
Waldsteinia

LEFT **Lamium maculatum 'Pink Pewter'**
BELOW **Lamprocapnos spectabilis 'Gold Heart'**

LATHYRUS

L. latifolius 'White Pearl'
A perennial pea producing sprays of pure white scentless but beautifully formed flowers. I let it scramble through old-fashioned roses and pick it for weeks in midsummer to put in little mixed bowls. It needs full sun and retentive soil. Up to 1.2m/4ft. ZONE 5.

L. vernus f. roseus
Forms a bushy little plant with many stems bearing neat divided leaves. In April it is covered with tiny rose-pink pea flowers. For sun or semi-shade in not-too-dry retentive soil. 30cm/1ft. ZONE 5.

LAVANDULA

L. angustifolia 'Rosea'
Spikes of dusty-pink flowers in June to July over compact bushes of narrow grey-green leaves. For sunny well-drained areas. 38-60cm/15in-2ft. ZONE 5.

L. pedunculata subsp. pedunculata
This is distinguished by much longer 'flags' or 'ears' of rose-pink. It survives successfully in this garden in well-drained soil. 38cm/15in. ZONE 8.

L. stoechas
A compact little bush covered in mid- to late summer with curious knobbly flower-heads which carry two kinds of flowers. The fertile flowers arranged in vertical rows are small and very

dark purple blue. Above them, to entice pollinating insects, is a 'flag' of large wavy bracts in a lighter shade of purple. It needs very well-drained soil. 38cm/15in. ZONE 8.

LEUCANTHEMELLA

L. serotina
A beautiful fresh feature for the end of the season in grass, among shrubs or in a big border. Strong clumps of stiff, leafy stems carry sprays of green-eyed chalk-white daisies. They turn to face the sun throughout October. Good to pick. 2m/6ft. ZONE 3.

LEUCOJUM

L. aestivum 'Gravetye Giant'
Graceful heads of white bell-shaped flowers above bold clumps of narrow strap-shaped leaves. Flowers in April. Does well in stiff, heavy soil by the water's edge. 60cm/2ft. ZONE 4.

LIBERTIA

L. chilensis
Beautiful species with tall spikes of large three-petalled flowers in pure white. Safer in a warm border in well-drained but not bone-dry soil. 75cm/2½ft. ZONE 8.

ABOVE *Leucojum aestivum* 'Gravetye Giant'
BELOW *Lavandula pedunculata* subsp. *pedunculata*

L. peregrinans

Fan-shaped clumps of stiff, very narrow leaves with wide, orange-stained veins. White flowers. Increases by running stolons. 45cm/1½ft. ZONE 8.

LIGULARIA

L. dentata 'Desdemona'

For moist, retentive soil and full sun. Has large heart-shaped leaves, bronze-purple above with bright magenta backs; big, branching heads of orange-rayed flowers appear in late summer. 1.2m/4ft. ZONE 3.

L. 'The Rocket'

Forms a fine mound of large round leaves with serrated edges. Tall, almost black stems standing well above the leaves carry long cylindrical spires of small bright yellow flowers, making a distinguished vertical feature in damp soil in late summer. 1.5m/5ft. ZONE 3.

LILIUM

L. martagon

Also known as Turk's cap lily. Tall stems are crowded with soft pinkish-purple flowers in midsummer. It needs full sun or part shade and a deep soil. There is also a white variety, *L.m.* var. *album*. 1-1.2m/3-4ft. ZONE 3.

L. speciosum

The flowers, produced in August and September, vary in colour from white to deep rose pink. Does best in rich soil. 1.2-1.5m/4-5ft. ZONE 4.

LINARIA

L. purpurea 'Canon Went'

A tall, delicate toadflax, carrying spires of tiny pale pink flowers throughout the summer. For sunny areas with good drainage. 75cm/2½ft. ZONE 7.

L. triornithophora

This means 'bearing three birds' – its buds look like tiny budgerigars. It has purple or occasionally pink flowers

all summer long until the first frosts. Needs sun and soil with good drainage. 90cm/3ft. ZONE 7.

LIRIOPE

L. muscari

Makes neat clumps of arching, dark, slender evergreen leaves. Spikes of small, bell-like purplish-blue flowers in autumn. 30cm/1ft. ZONE 6.

LOBELIA

L. cardinalis 'Queen Victoria'

A startling plant for damp, retentive soil and sun, best covered in mulch in late autumn until last frosts of spring have gone, which can damage emerging shoots. Beetroot-red leaves combine with brilliant scarlet flowers. 75cm/2½ft. ZONE 3.

LYCHNIS

L. chalcedonica

Called Maltese or Jerusalem cross, this has been known since the Crusades. The cross-shaped, brilliant scarlet flowers are arranged in dense flat heads on tall stiff stems, making a sharp accent in midsummer. Needs full sun in retentive soil. 90cm/3ft. ZONE 4.

BELOW *Ligularia* **'The Rocket'**
BOTTOM *Lilium speciosum* var. *album*

L. coronaria
Handsome clumps of downy grey leaves send up wide branching stems bearing deep burgundy campion-like flowers. Midsummer. 75cm/2½ft. ZONE 3.

L. 'Hill Grounds'
A hybrid between *L. flos-jovis* and *L. coronaria*, with grey foliage and bright magenta sterile flowers from late spring to autumn, if regularly dead-headed. 1m/3ft. ZONE 4.

LYSICHITON
These make superb bog-garden plants but need time to establish into flowering plants. Their large leaves make an impressive architectural feature.

L. camtschatcensis
From Siberia and Japan. This is a pure white-flowered species. 90cm/3ft. ZONE 5.

L. × hortensis
A cross between the two species in this genus (*L. americanus* and *L. camschatcensis*) with magnificent cream flowers in spring and huge leaves during summer. Does not seed, unlike its yellow American parent. Slow to propagate from division. 1.8m/6ft. ZONE 5.

LYSIMACHIA
L. ciliata
Emerges through the soil in spring with clusters of soft milk-chocolate brown leaves whose colour is only slightly diluted green as the stems elongate to carry a spire of delicately hung yellow flowers which last for weeks in mid- to late summer. Creeping rootstock in rich to damp soil in sun. 75cm/2½ft. ZONE 4.

L. nummularia 'Aurea'
Delightful ground cover in cool retentive soil and part shade, this creeping Jenny has bright gold foliage and shallow saucer-shaped yellow flowers in midsummer. 5cm/2in. ZONE 3.

L. punctata
Can be seen anywhere from ditch sides to seemingly dry front gardens, but for semi-wild planting it needs sun and damp retentive soil – it can then be

Plants for clay soil
Acanthus
Alchemilla
Anemone × hybrida
Darmera
Epimedium
Eupatorium
Euphorbia amygdaloides
 var. *robbiae*
Hemerocallis
Hosta
Inula
Kniphofia
Miscanthus
Molinia
Persicaria
Petasites
Rheum
Rodgersia
Sasa
Symphytum
Trachystemon

TOP LEFT *Lychnis* **'Hill Grounds'**
LEFT *Lysimachia punctata*
BELOW *Lysichiton × hortensis*

invasive. Spires of bright yellow flowers mid- to late summer. 90cm/3ft. ZONE 4.

LYTHRUM
L. salicaria 'Robert'
Makes a fine feature plant with branching spikes of small rose-pink flowers. Will grow in any good retentive soil, including the bog garden, but needs sun. Late summer to autumn. 1.2m/4ft. ZONE 3.

MACLEAYA
M. microcarpa 'Kelway's Coral Plume'
A statuesque plant for full sun and retentive soil. A running rootstock throws up tall strong stems. Large, rounded, deeply indented leaves are grey-green above, grey-white beneath. Long plumes of pale apricot buds open to cream fluffy flowers from late summer to autumn. 2m/6ft. ZONE 3.

MAIANTHEMUM
M. racemosum
Related to Solomon's seal and similar arching foliage, but instead of bells it has a tapering head of massed fluffy creamy-white flowers, sweetly scented. Late spring. Likes cool retentive soil and part shade. 75cm/2½ft. ZONE 3.

MALVA
M. moschata f. *alba*
Covered in silky, saucer-shaped white flowers, this pretty mallow causes comment for weeks in summer. Seeds itself usefully. Best in sun and well-drained soil. 45cm/1½ft. ZONE 3.

MATTEUCCIA
M. struthiopteris
The ostrich plume fern is perhaps the most beautiful for damp, even boggy, places sheltered from drying winds which brown the delicate fronds. Tightly rolled buds unfold from the top of short stems to form pale green shuttlecocks of exquisite lacy design. It is invasive, but easily controlled. 90cm/3ft. ZONE 3.

MELICA
M. uniflora f. *albida*
Above clumps of soft green foliage float sprays of dainty white buds. Tolerates dry shade. 60cm/2ft. ZONE 3.

MELIANTHUS.
M. major
Most sumptuous foliage plant from South Africa, but not reliably hardy although has survived here for many year in well drained soil with a winter mulch. Large grey-green leaves,

BELOW LEFT *Lythrum salicaria* 'Robert'
BELOW *Matteuccia struthiopteris*

deeply cut and tooth-edged, on thick, branching stems. A deep maroon flower spike may emerge. 1.2m/4ft or more. ZONE 9.

MELISSA

M. officinalis 'All Gold'
Has entirely rich-yellow matt-textured leaves from beginning of season to end. Good drainage and partial shade prevents leaf scorch. Insignificant flowers. 60cm/2ft. ZONE 4.

MILIUM

M. effusum 'Aureum'
Known as Bowles's golden grass. Non-running clumps of soft foliage, bright yellow in spring and early summer. Many fine stems support a cloud of tiny golden flowers and bead-like seeds. For part shade in leaf-mould soil. 60cm/2ft. ZONE 4.

MISCANTHUS

M. 'Purpurascens'
Shorter than some other forms, by late summer the upper surface of the leaves shows warm brown, enhanced by the shining pink central vein. Narrow pinkish-brown flower-heads appear in October, when the whole plant becomes suffused with shades of red, orange and buff. 1.2m/4ft. ZONE 4.

M. sinensis 'Gracillimus'
Forms a clump like a slender bamboo. Very narrow leaves, curling gracefully as they lengthen, are topped by plume-like inflorescences in autumn. 2m plus/6ft plus. ZONE 5.

M. s. 'Malepartus'
Imposing columns of arching, broad, silver-veined leaves and mahogany-red feathery plumes that fade to buff. 2m/6ft. ZONE 5.

M. s. 'Silbefeder'
A columnar feature plant, the tall stems are swathed from top to bottom

LEFT *Melianthus major*
BELOW *Miscanthus sinensis* 'Malepartus'

in narrow ribbon-like leaves and carry upright slender shuttlecocks of feathery plumes in silver-pinky-beige to stand among autumn flowers. 2m plus/6ft plus. ZONE 4.

M. s. 'Variegatus'
Quite distinct with its strap-shaped leaves, strongly variegated green and white, which fall from rigid stems. Makes a fountain all summer in a moist border. 1.2-1.5m/4-5ft. ZONE 5.

M. s. 'Zebrinus'
Graceful stems in dense clumps carry narrow green leaves, arching at the tips

Plants that keep their leaves in warm, well-drained soils
Ballota
Bergenia
Cistus
Dianthus
Eryngium agavifolium
Euphorbia characias
  subsp. *wulfenii*
Festuca
Lavandula
Libertia
Marrubium
Salvia officinalis
Santolina
Stipa
Teucrium
Thymus
Verbascum

and strongly banded at intervals with yellow; very striking as a contrasting form in the border, marvellous by water. Easy anywhere in good soil. 1.2-1.5m/4-5ft. ZONE 5.

MITELLA

M. breweri

Rounded, scallop-edged dark green leaves, arranged in neat clumps. In spring, tiny forests of pale leafless stems carry wands of minute green flowers with fringed edges. Charming on the edge of a shady path but needs retentive soil. 15cm/6in. ZONE 5.

M. caulescens

A delight in awkward shade. Thread-like stems run over the soil, forming carpets or edgings of pea-green heart-shaped leaves, with tiny palest-green flowers in spring. 8cm/3in. ZONE 5.

MOLINIA

M. caerulea subsp. *caerulea* 'Heidebraut'

Creates its own sunshine on grey autumnal days, with narrow columns of stiff straw-coloured flowering stems topped with dainty seed-heads. For sunny positions in retentive soil. 1.2-1.5m/4-5ft. ZONE 4.

M. c. subsp. *c.* 'Variegata'

One of the best variegated grasses, with short neat tufts of vividly coloured green and cream leaves sending up feathery plumes. 45cm/1½ft. ZONE 5.

MORINA

M. longifolia

A most distinctive plant for full sun and retentive soil. Forms rosettes of prickly aromatic foliage, from which rise tall stems, bearing pagoda-like chalices, set at intervals. These are packed with jade-green tubes from which spring white tubular flowers changing to crimson with age. After the flowers are finished the standing green stem with its fantastic outline is perhaps even more beautiful for green arrangements. Effective midsummer to winter. 75cm/2½ft. ZONE 6.

MYOSOTIS

M. scorpioides 'Mermaid'

Different from the spreading common water forget-me-not, this plant is very compact, covered with short-stemmed blue flowers for weeks in summer. It flourishes in retentive rich soil and full sun. 5-8cm/2-3in. ZONE 3.

NARCISSUS

N. minor 'Cedric Morris'

This unique daffodil is usually in flower for Christmas day, continuing to bloom till March. Small lemon-yellow perfectly formed daffodils with lightly frilled trumpets, a joy to pick with early snowdrops. Plant in shade to protect from narcissus fly. Needs retentive soil. 15-30cm/6-12in. ZONE 5.

N. pallidiflorus

Has a curious characteristic. The unopened buds face skywards like beaks, gradually lowering as they open pale creamy-yellow perfectly shaped trumpet flowers. Early flowering. 30cm/12in. ZONE 5

N. 'Rijnveld's Early Sensation'

Given to me many years ago by Graham Stuart Thomas. This odd hybrid earns

BELOW *Narcissus pallidiflorus*
BELOW CENTRE *Narcissus minor* 'Cedric Morris'
BOTTOM *Narcissus* 'Rijnveld's Early Sensation'

FAR LEFT *Nerine bowdenii*
LEFT *Nectaroscordum siculum* subsp. *bulgaricum*
BELOW *Nepeta racemosa* 'Walker's Low'

its place by opening very early, often in January, and continuing into March. Its flowers create a dash of colour with yellow trumpets and slightly paler 'petals'. 45cm/1½ft. ZONE 3.

NECTAROSCORDUM
N. siculum subsp. **bulgaricum (syn. Allium siculum subsp. dioscoridis)**
Curious and beautiful. On a thick stem, a pointed papery case splits to release creamy-green and faintly purple-flushed bells. As they fade, they turn upright to form fascinating seed-heads. Early summer. 90cm/3ft. ZONE 5.

NEPETA
N. racemosa 'Walker's Low'
Produces long flowering stems above silvery grey-green aromatic leaves. Dark buds and stems add to the rich effect of the strong blue flowers. May to June. 75cm/2½ft. ZONE 5.
N. 'Six Hills Giant'
Larger than the common catmint, this variety has aromatic grey-green leaves and spikes of lavender-blue flowers in midsummer. It is thought to be hardier. 75cm/2½ft. ZONE 5.

NERINE
N. bowdenii
Glorious pink trumpets in October. Winters well under a warm wall or in very well-drained soil. For full sun. 30-38cm/12-15in. ZONE 7.

OENOTHERA
O. lindheimeri (syn. Gaura lindheimeri)
Flowers in autumn when there is nothing else like it. Palest-pink flowers float for weeks among graceful branches set with small willow-like leaves. Needs full sun and well-drained soil. 75cm/2½ft. ZONE 5.

Plants that keep their leaves in cooler, shady conditions
Arum italicum subsp. *italicum* 'Marmoratum'
Asplenium
Epimedium
Euphorbia amygdaloides var. *robbiae*
Geranium macrorrhizum
Helleborus
Heuchera
Lamium
Liriope
Mitella
Ophiopogon
Pachyphragma
Pachysandra
Polystichum
Pulmonaria
Symphytum
Tellima
Vinca

OMPHALODES
O. cappadocica
Forms dense clumps of oval, slightly crinkled green leaves over which float sprays of intense gentian-blue flowers, larger than those of forget-me-not. Breathtaking in spring. A very good ground cover in retentive soil. 23cm/9in. ZONE 6.

ONOCLEA
O. sensibilis
The sensitive fern has light green, broadly segmented leaves making handsome, arching ground cover in damp or wet soil. It will also grow in the shade of trees or shrubs if not too dry, but it does tend to wander. 45cm/18in. ZONE 4.

ONOPORDUM
O. acanthium
Commonly called the Scotch thistle. A splendid feature plant that forms a rosette of huge spiny leaves copiously felted with white down. The towering flower stem is topped with pale-lilac thistle flowers from midsummer to autumn. Needs sun and good drainage. 2m/6ft. ZONE 4.

OPHIOPOGON
O. planiscapus 'Kokuryū' (syn. *O. p.* 'Nigrescens')
Arching strap-shaped black leaves make spidery clusters against the soil, a feature all year round. In summer, short sprays of tiny mauve bells appear, maturing as shiny black berries which last well into winter. Creeps slowly in well-drained but retentive soil, in sun or part shade. 25cm/10in. ZONE 8.

ORIGANUM
O. vulgare 'Thumble's Variety'
Forms a good ground-covering carpet of fresh yellow-green leaves which do not scorch in sun. Flowers white. 30cm/1ft. ZONE 6.

OSMUNDA
O. regalis
The elegant royal fern will tolerate sunshine provided its roots can reach water and does best on soil that is well fed with vegetable waste. The large flat fronds up to 1.2m/4ft tall are soft

TOP *Ophiopogon planiscapus* 'Kokuryū'
ABOVE *Origanum vulgare* 'Thumble's Variety'
LEFT *Onopordum acanthium*

coppery-brown in spring, changing again to warm tobacco shades in autumn. 1.2m/4ft. ZONE 4.

PACHYPHRAGMA
P. macrophyllum
The large, round green leaves overlap to make weed-free cover all summer. Veins and stems become purple-tinted in winter. Showy heads of these white cress-like flowers appear early in March before new leaves. Does not run and can be divided. It prefers shade and retentive soil. 30cm/1ft. ZONE 6.

PACHYSANDRA
P. terminalis
Much valued rich green carpeter for covering bare earth beneath trees or shrubs. It grows well in shade and retentive soil. Evergreen rosettes of toothed glossy leaves, insignificant white scented flowers in spring. 30cm/1ft. ZONE 4.

PAEONIA
P. 'Avant Garde'
Given to me by Eric Smith. A delicate-looking peony with enchanting pink flowers. 75cm/30in. ZONE 6.
P. daura subsp. mlokosewitschii
In early spring the buds and young leaves are a rich pinkish bronze. As they turn to soft grey-green, the buds

gradually open to full beauty, perfect bowls of cool lemon-yellow, filled with golden stamens in May. For part shade and retentive soil. 60cm/2ft. ZONE 5.

PANICUM
P. virgatum 'Rubrum'
A non-invasive, clump-forming grass, tinted red in autumn. Likes retentive soil in sun. 1.2m/4ft. ZONE 5.

PAPAVER
P. (Oriental Group) 'Royal Wedding'
A spreading perennial with bristly, green leaves and pure white flowers with a bold, crimson-black basal blotch on each petal. 1m/3ft. ZONE 3.
P. rupifragum
A lovely perennial poppy and a rare colour in the garden. Semi-double, tissue-paper petals of soft orange, in flower throughout the summer. Seeds freely. 30cm/12in. ZONE 5.

PARAHEBE
P. catarractae (white-flowered)
An excellent plant for sunny areas and retentive soil. Tidy mound of evergreen leaves, completely whitened like snow by the thousands of tiny 'bird's-eye' flower-heads in early summer. 15cm/6in. ZONE 7.

Grasses

FOR DRIER SOILS
Calamagrostis *
Festuca
Helictotrichon
Pennisetum villosum
Stipa

FOR DAMPER SOILS
Carex
Deschampsia
Glyceria
Miscanthus *
Molinia *
Panicum *
Pennisetum *

FOR SHADE
Hakonechloa
Melica
Milium

* Will also grow in an average soil, ideally in full sun.

TOP **Osmunda regalis**
LEFT **Pachyphragma macrophylla**

PENNISETUM

P. alopecuroides **'Black Beauty'**

An upright, clump-forming, deciduous, perennial grass with flat dark green leaves, turning yellow-brown in autumn, and, in summer, narrow, oblong panicles of purple-black flowers. 45cm/1½ft. ZONE 8.

P. villosum

A beautiful grass with drooping flower-heads, each a tassel of fine white hairs. Needs sun. 45cm/1½ft. ZONE 8.

PENSTEMON

P. **'Evelyn'**

Forms neat bushy plants of very narrow leaves topped with slender spires of slim flowers, rose-pink with pale striped throats. In flower all summer. Needs well-drained soil and sun. 60cm/2ft. ZONE 7.

PERSICARIA

P. affinis **'Suberba'**

Low spreading mats of neat green leaves, which turn rich russet brown in autumn and remain all winter. Spikes of pale pink flowers from midsummer to autumn. 23cm/9in. ZONE 5.

P. amplexicaulis **'Alba'**

Slim tapers of tiny white flowers smother tall bushy plants for months. Needs sun and retentive soil. 1.2m/4ft. ZONE 5.

TOP LEFT ***Persicaria bistorta*** **'Superba'**
ABOVE LEFT ***Persicaria amplexicaulis* 'Atrosanguinea'**
TOP RIGHT ***Pennisetum villosum***
ABOVE RIGHT ***Pennisetum alopecuroides*** **'Black Beauty'**

P. a. 'Atrosanguinea'
Forms large branching bushy plants
which glow with slender tapers of tiny
crimson flowers in late summer and
autumn. 1.2m/4ft. ZONE 5.

P. bistorta 'Superba'
Best in a moist soil. Massed stems carry
thick cyclamen-pink pokers; handsome
dock-like foliage. Early summer.
75cm/2½ft. ZONE 3.

P. microcephala 'Red Dragon'
Grown for its foliage. Leaves are sharply
pointed, with maroon and green
patterning and a pale white margin.
75cm/2½ft. ZONE 4.

P. vacciniifolia
This plant leafs very late in spring when
its mats of russet brown stems push
out tiny shining green leaves. By late
September it is smothered with spikes
of tiny pink flowers. 8cm/3in. ZONE 4.

P. virginiana 'Painter's Palette'
Forms low branching plants with large
oval leaves marbled in shades of cream
and green, faintly brushed with pink.
The centre of each leaf is marked with
a strong 'V'. Tiny rat-tail wisps of little
brown flowers show its relationship
with knotweeds. For sun or part shade
and good soil. 60cm/2ft. ZONE 4.

PETASITES
P. japonicus var. giganteus
While flower-arrangers love the posy-
like heads of green and white flowers
that burst through bare clay in early
spring, this is a plant for landscaping
with its huge round leaves and invasive
roots, making impenetrable ground
cover in heavy retentive soil in sun or
part shade. 1.2-1.3m/4-5ft. ZONE 5.

PHLOMIS
P. russeliana
From large weed-smothering clumps of
soft heart-shaped leaves rise stiff stems
carrying whorls of rich-yellow hooded

flowers in midsummer. The seed-heads,
whether green or dried, are equally
effective. For sun and retentive soil.
90cm/3ft. ZONE 5.

PHLOX
P. stolonifera 'Ariane'
The prostrate forms of *Phlox* are a
delight both for their weed-suppressing
habit and for their flowers, beautiful
individually or in breath-taking sheets
of colour. Spreading mats of light green
leaves are a background for loose heads
of snow-white yellow-eyed flowers. Best
in part shade and retentive soil. April to
May. 20cm/8in. ZONE 4.

P. s. 'Blue Ridge'
Prefers cool conditions, semi-shade
and a little peat. It makes good ground
cover, above which stand heads of lilac-
blue flowers with a pin-eye of orange
stamens. April to May. 20cm/8in.
ZONE 4.

PHORMIUM
P. tenax
The New Zealand flax is an all-year-
round feature plant. Huge sword-
shaped leaves form a fan-like clump. A
flower spike with dull red flowers soars
above, followed by black curving seed-
pods. 2m/6ft or more. ZONE 7.

BELOW *Phormium*
tenax
BOTTOM *Phlomis*
russeliana

PHUOPSIS
P. stylosa
Super ground cover for dry sunny soil with refreshingly bright green finely divided foliage, over which stand round pincushions stuck with pink pins. Early summer. 15cm/6in. ZONE 5.

PHYLA
P. nodiflora
A pretty trailing plant for paving or as groundcover in warm, well-drained soil. Small oval leaves cover prostrate branching stems, set in late summer with globular heads of tiny white, mauve and orange flowers. Disappears in winter but returns in spring. Has a wonderful common name – Turkey tangle frogfruit. 2.5cm/1in. ZONE 8.

PIMPINELLA
P. major 'Rosea'
Enchanting cow parsley-like plant carrying flat heads of rose-pink tiny flowers over several weeks in midsummer. Prefers ordinary to damp soil. 90cm/3ft. ZONE 5.

POLEMONIUM
P. caeruleum
Also known as Jacob's ladder. Held well above clumps of fresh green divided foliage are an endless succession of sky-blue small open bells, orange-centred. Charming, especially in a cool situation where it has sun and retentive soil; early to midsummer. 60cm/2ft. ZONE 3.
P. c. subsp. *caeruleum* f. *album*
A good white form, in flower for weeks, from late spring to late summer. 60cm/2ft. ZONE 3.
P. carneum
In early summer produces sheaves of silky pearl-pink cupped flowers, lovely as an edging plant. 45cm/1½ft. ZONE 4.

POLYGONATUM
P. × *hybridum*
This is the usual form of Solomon's seal. Close-set spreading rhizomes send up tall arching stems set with shining dark green leaves. In May they bear white-and green-flushed bells. For planting in shade or part shade in retentive soil. 75-90cm/2½-3ft. ZONE 4.
P. × *h.* 'Striatum'
This seldom-seen form has leaves that are boldly striped and edged in creamy-white. 60cm/2ft. ZONE 4.
P. multiflorum
Distinct from *P.* × *hybridum*. Shorter, more upright stems hold leaves more closely set, standing upright on slightly arched stems to show waxy blue undersides. Beneath hang small cream bells followed by berries, first green, then almost black. 60cm/2ft. ZONE 4.

POLYPODIUM
P. × *mantoniae* 'Cornubiense'
This pretty bright-green fern has very finely divided leaves. It makes excellent ground cover all the year round and is

ABOVE ***Primula bulleyana***
LEFT ***Polygonatum* × *hybridum***

useful for contrast with other simpler leaves. 30cm/12in. ZONE 5.

P. vulgare

This colonizing fern, making effective ground cover, is found growing on steep shady banks and in rocky regions of several continents. It comes in a wide range of varieties. 30cm/12in. ZONE 4.

POLYSTICHUM

P. setiferum Acutilobum Group

This easily grown fern has narrow, daintily set fronds of great elegance. It grows almost anywhere that is not too dry, but responds particularly well to cool semi-shade. 60cm/2ft. ZONE 5.

PONTEDERIA

P. cordata

The handsome pickerel weed spreads slowly out into shallow water from the boggy edge. Standing above the water are crowded stems of beautiful leaves, spear-shaped, marked with faint swirling lines and shadows, all topped with spikes of small blue flowers in late summer. 45cm/1½ft above water. ZONE 5.

POTENTILLA

P. alba

Useful ground cover for sun or light shade in retentive soil, formed by mats of soft grey-green lupin-like leaves, which are covered with orange-eyed white flowers in spring and again in autumn. 10cm/4in. ZONE 5.

P. atrosanguinea var. argyrophylla

Neat clumps of heavily silvered strawberry-like leaves are a base for branching sprays of yellow flowers with orange centres for many weeks in midsummer. Best in sun and retentive soil. 45cm/1½ft. ZONE 5.

PRIMULA

P. bulleyana

The candelabra primula will grow in shade or in full sun, if moist. Mealy stems bear whorls of bright orange flowers. Good seed-heads. May and June. 45cm/1½ft. ZONE 4.

P. denticulata var. alba

Beautiful form: white flowers with yellow eyes and large rosettes of luscious pale-green leaves. Spring. For full sun and retentive soil. 30cm/1ft. ZONE 5.

Plants for ground cover

Ajuga
Bergenia
Brunnera
Cyclamen
Epimedium
Euphorbia amygdaloides
  var. *robbiae*
Geranium endresii
Geranium macrorrhizum
Lamium
Ophiopogon
Pachyphragma
Pachysandra
Persicaria affinis
Petasites
Phuopsis
Symphytum
Tiarella
Thymus
Vinca
Waldsteinia

BELOW LEFT/RIGHT
Pontederia cordata

P. florindae

Himalayan cowslip. Must have moisture. Tall stems carry large drooping bells of softest sulphur yellow. Beautiful seed-heads dusted with luminous green. Up to 90cm/3ft ZONE 3.

P. pulverulenta

Deep wine-coloured flowers with purple eyes. A favourite bog primula for damp, shady soil. 60cm/2ft. ZONE 5.

P. veris

Our native cowslip. Rosettes of mid-green leaves and nodding clusters of pale-yellow fragrant flowers in spring. 15cm/6in. ZONE 5.

PRUNELLA

P. grandiflora 'Loveliness'

Short dense spikes of pale-violet flowers in midsummer, shaped like a dead nettle. Good edging plant or makes useful ground cover for sun and retentive soil. 15cm/6in. ZONE 5.

PULMONARIA

Also known as lungwort, pulmonarias make excellent ground cover in moisture-retaining soil, preferring partial shade. Very early to flower, regardless of weather. There is considerable variation, both from interbred seedlings and varying clones.

P. rubra

Weed-smothering clumps of large light-green leaves, unspotted, are preceded in very early spring by clustered heads of coral-red tubular flowers. 30cm/1ft. ZONE 5.

P. saccharata

Not the common lungwort. These leaves are up to 30cm/1ft long, rough-textured, dark green, variously marbled in silver and grey-green. Likes cool shade. Masses of blue and rose-coloured flowers in March. 30cm/1ft. ZONE 3.

P. s. 'Alba'

This fine form produces quantities of large pearl-sized snow-white flowers, followed by rosettes of well-marked leaves for the rest of the season. 30cm/1ft. ZONE 3.

PULSATILLA

P. vulgaris

From ferny green leaves in March emerge silky buds unfurling into huge purple flowers filled with golden stamens. Prefers well-drained soil in full sun. 25cm/10in. ZONE 5.

RANUNCULUS

R. constantinopolitanus 'Plenus'

Non-invasive. A choice plant for damp retentive soil in sun, it produces many

Plants with handsome foliage

Acanthus
Arum
Bergenia
Cynara
Darmera
Gunnera
Heuchera
Hosta
Libertia
Ligularia
Lysichiton
Onopordum
Ophiopogon
Petasites
Rheum
Rodgersia
Sasa
Trifolium
Trillium
Zantedeschia

LEFT *Rhaponticum centaureoides*

large tightly double, glossy yellow flowers, sharply green-centred. Early summer. 30cm/1ft. ZONE 6.

RHAPONTICUM
R. centaureoides
Previously known as *Centaurea pulchra* 'Major'. From a base of strong silver-grey cut leaves rise stiff stems bearing large knobbly buds of overlapping transparent silver scales which open into striking cyclamen-pink flowers. Midsummer. Requires sun and good drainage. 90cm/3ft. ZONE 5.

RHEUM
R. palmatum
The first year will see a huge weed-smothering mound of apple-green leaves that are 1m/3ft across. Stout flower stems carry branched heads of frothy white flowers in June. For sun or part shade and retentive soil. 2m/6ft. ZONE 5.
R. p. 'Atrosanguineum'
When young, its crinkled leaves are rosy purple, the topsides later turning dark green. Tall branching spires are massed with tiny cherry-red flowers in

early summer. Needs plenty of humus. 2m/6ft. ZONE 5.
R. p. var. *tanguticum*
Larger leaves of more intense rosy purple and spires of tiny white flowers in early summer. 2m/6ft. ZONE 5.

RHODANTHEMUM
R. hosmariense
Finely fingered clusters of silver-grey leaves make a comfortably low mound, carrying in winter hundreds of tight black-pencilled buds which open a few large white daisies in mild spells and then make a glorious show in spring and early summer. Needs full sun and good drainage. 30cm/1ft. ZONE 7.

RODGERSIA
These are among the finest foliage plants for marshy land, waterside or cool, damp retentive soil. Will grow in sun if soil is moist, also in shade provided soil does not dry out. They make slowly spreading rhizomes.
R. pinnata 'Superba'
Knobbly buds opening to sterile cyclamen-pink flowers. Midsummer. 90cm/3ft. ZONE 5.

ABOVE *Rodgersia pinnata* 'Superba'
BELOW *Rheum palmatum* var. *tanguticum*

R. podophylla

The young leaves are rich dark brown in spring, turning green as they expand, often copper-tinted when mature. Each dramatically handsome leaf consists of five large leaflets, broadly triangular in outline with jagged tips, arranged at the top of each stem. Unremarkable cream flowers. 60cm/2ft. ZONE 5.

ROMNEYA
R. coulteri

The Californian tree poppy has many branching stems clad with glaucous grey leaves topped with fat buds opening to huge white, tissue-paper-like flowers pinned together with a mass of yellow stamens. Well-drained soil in sun 1.8m/6ft plus. ZONE 7.

RUBUS
R. idaeus 'Aureus'

A form of raspberry. Very attractive plant for part shade and retentive soil, where there is room among shrubs or in the leaf litter beneath trees. Pale lemon-yellow leaves create a patch of sunlight where its underground shoots weave through fine leaf-mould. 25-38cm/10-15in. ZONE 5.

RUDBECKIA
R. fulgida var. deamii

Considered to be an improved variety; it is similar to R. fulgida var. speciosa, with slightly taller, rougher foliage. Late summer to autumn. 75cm/2½ft. ZONE 4.

R. f. var. speciosa

Making a bright display in autumn, it forms mounds of dark-green foliage to set off large bright-yellow flowers, with a prominent black eye. For sunny areas and retentive soil. 60cm/2ft. ZONE 4.

SALVIA
S. blancoana

In sun and well-drained soil, this choice sage makes a low spreading bush with narrow silver-grey leaves. From

Plants attractive to butterflies
Achillea
Anaphalis
Armeria
Aster
Ajuga
Calamintha
Echinacea
Echinops
Eupatorium
Hylotelephium
Knautia
Ligularia
Lychnis
Lysimachia
Nepeta
Persicaria
Phuopsis
Scabiosa
Thymus
Verbena

TOP **Rudbeckia fulgida var. deamii**
LEFT **Salvia 'Blue Spire'**

S. × superba
Clumps of rich green leaves send up stiff spikes of intense violet-purple flowers with crimson bracts in mid- to late summer. Full sun. 90cm/3ft. ZONE 5.

S. uliginosa
Worth protecting underground shoots with straw. In late September, slender leafy stems carry head-high loose spires of pure sky-blue flowers. Needs a warm sunny site with soil that does not dry out. 1.5m/5ft. ZONE 8.

ABOVE *Salvia officinalis* 'Icterina'
LEFT *Salvia × superba*

the tip shoots extend long curving sprays of soft lilac-blue flowers in midsummer. 30cm/1ft. ZONE 7.

S. 'Blue Spire'
Formerly *Perovskia* 'Blue Spire'. Makes a feature when the slender whitened stems, lightly clad in fine-cut grey leaves, appear. In late summer they are topped with long spires of lavender-blue flowers. Needs sun and good drainage. 1.2m/4ft. ZONE 6.

S. officinalis. 'Icterina'
Golden sage. The new foliage is marbled primrose, gold and sage green. Best in a warm site. 60cm/2ft. ZONE 6.

S. o. 'Purpurascens'
The young summer foliage of purple sage is a delight – soft greyish purple velvet – with spikes of purple-blue flowers in early summer. Will form a lax bush but can be kept under control by careful pruning in spring. Needs sun and good drainage. 60cm/2ft. ZONE 6.

S. rosmarinus 'Tuscan Blue'
(formerly *Rosmarinus officinalis* 'Tuscan Blue') Makes upright growth with strong blue flowers, produced even in winter. Leaves are broader than the species. Greatly admired at its best in early summer. 1.8m/6ft. ZONE 6.

SANTOLINA
S. rosmarinifolia subsp. rosmarinifolia
Drought-resisting, yet green, it forms a neat round bush of vivid green aromatic foliage, a bright setting for the lemon-yellow button flowers. Midsummer. 45cm/1½ft. ZONE 6.

SASA
S. veitchii
This ground-covering bamboo has wide blade-shaped leaves, plain green all summer, but by autumn the leaf margins become blanched straw-yellow. Only suitable for large gardens. 1.2m/4ft. ZONE 6.

SAXIFRAGA
S. × urbium 'Aureopunctata'
Also known as London pride. Richly variegated gold and green. Sprays of pale pink flowers in early summer. For part shade and retentive soil. 23cm/9in. ZONE 6.

SCABIOSA
S. caucasica 'Miss Willmott'
In flower for months throughout the summer. Large pale-cream, almost greenish-white flowers on tall stems are produced endlessly till the frosts. 75cm/2½ft. ZONE 4.

Plants attractive to bees
Allium
Campanula
Dictamnus
Echinacea
Echinops
Eryngium
Eupatorium
Helleborus
Lamium
Lavandula
Ligularia
Nepeta
Onopordum
Origanum
Persicaria
Pulmonaria
Salvia
Scabiosa
Sidalcea
Thymus

SCROPHULARIA

S. auriculata 'Variegata'

The variegated water figwort makes a spectacular foliage plant in sun or part shade. Its broad basal leaves are crimpled and richly banded in cream. The smaller leaves in branching stems are also variegated. Needs rich retentive soil. 60cm/2ft. ZONE 5.

SEDUM

S. spurium 'Green Mantle'

Makes solid ground cover, creeping stems carrying close-packed rosettes of broad green leaves. 13cm/5in. ZONE 4.

SEMPERVIVUM

There are many species and named hybrids. Some grow as wide across as a saucer, making handsome feature plants for sunny, well-drained areas. Others are tiny, suitable for crevices in the rock-garden. Among the larger ones the texture is mostly waxen, apple-green rosettes tipped with mahogany, purple, or bronze-red. There are also the 'cobweb'-covered forms, and those with incurved leaves edged with bristly hairs. To 15cm/6in. ZONE 5.

SISYRINCHIUM

S. 'Californian Skies'

Large sky-blue flowers. Foliage like a miniature bearded iris. Ideal edging plant. Divide in spring every few years to maintain vigour. 15cm/6in. ZONE 7.

S. 'Quaint and Queer'

Curiously attractive chocolate- and cream-coloured flowers spangle stiff branching, sprawling stems for months, throughout midsummer and into autumn. 40cm/16in. ZONE 7.

S. striatum 'Aunt May'

Has iris-like leaves boldy striped in creamy yellow making a perfect foil for blue flowers. Brightest when freshly divided. 45cm/1½ft. ZONE 7.

STIPA

S. gigantea

Tall stems carrying superb heads of oat-like flowers shimmer and shine as if made of beaten gold. A long-lasting feature throughout summer. Grows well in any average soil in sun. 2m/6ft. ZONE 7.

S. tenuissima

Delicate hair-fine foliage topped with silver-green flower plumes, mid-summer to autumn. Needs well-drained soil and sun. Will seed but is easily removed. 60cm/2ft. ZONE 7.

SYMPHYTUM

S. caucasicum

Clusters of grey-green pointed leaves colonize by underground stems. Horribly invasive in the wrong place, but, where allowable, it is one of the delights of spring, with arching stems carrying clusters of sky-blue tubular flowers. Best in retentive soil in sun or part shade. 60cm/2ft. ZONE 4.

S. ibericum

A handsome plant making good weed-cover in retentive soil in shade, spreading via underground shoots. Mounds of large dark-green leaves with flowers changing in spring from orange buds to creamy-yellow bells. 30cm/1ft. ZONE 5.

BELOW **Stipa gigantea**
BOTTOM **Stipa tenuissima**
OPPOSITE **Thalictrum aquilegiifolium**

TELLIMA

T. grandiflora Odorata Group
Scented form. Foliage not so deeply coloured in winter as that of the following form, but the flowers smell deliciously of old-fashioned pinks, scenting the air for yards around. Both need retentive soil in sun or part shade. 60cm/2ft. ZONE 6.

T. g. Rubra Group
An all-year-round foliage plant. Spreading clumps of round, scalloped leaves, green above, purple beneath, changing to rich red-purples and bronze in winter. In early summer there are tall spikes of pink-fringed green bells. 60cm/2ft. ZONE 4.

TEUCRIUM

T. × lucidrys
Low bushy plants for dry soils and a wonderful bee plant. Dark green glossy leaves carry short spires of small pink flowers in summer. 30cm/1ft. ZONE 6.

THALICTRUM

T. aquilegiifolium
From a basal clump of grey-green leaves, finely divided, slender purple stems carry fans of leaves, topped with large heads of fluffy rosy-lilac flowers from early to midsummer. Likes sun and retentive soil. 90cm-1.2m/3-4ft. ZONE 5.

THYMUS

T. herba-barona
Wiry mats of dark green leaves heavily scented of caraway. Pink and mauve flowers. Needs sun and good drainage. 10cm/4in. ZONE 4.

TIARELLA

All tiarellas need humus-rich soil in part shade.

T. cordifolia
Running trails of pretty, pointed green leaves form complete cover in spring. A mass of foaming creamy-white flower spikes in early summer. Grows in part shade. 23-30cm/9-12in. ZONE 4.

T. wherryi
This also has delicate spires of starry white flowers, but the leaves are like shadowed green velvet. Exquisite for months. Midsummer. 25cm/10in. ZONE 3.

TRACHYSTEMON

T. orientalis
Superb ground cover in dense shade and retentive soil. Makes an important feature with large, healthy-looking, rough green leaves forming overlapping mounds. Curious blue borage-like flowers in spring before the leaves take over. 60cm/2ft. ZONE 6.

TRIFOLIUM

T. repens 'Purpurascens Quadrifolium'
This clover is valued for its foliage, mostly four-leaved and of a striking chocolate colour. Quickly makes effective ground cover in retentive soil and sun. Typical heads of white clover flowers. 10cm/4in. ZONE 3.

Plants with good seed-heads
Acanthus
Achillea
Agapanthus
Allium
Anaphalis
Asphodelus
Carlina
Chasmanthium
Cynara
Deschampsia
Echinops
Eryngium
Galtonia
Miscanthus
Morina
Nectaroscordum
Panicum
Phlomis
Pennisetum
Stipa

TRILLIUM

Trilliums need deep rich leaf-mould soil, adequate rainfall and cool shady conditions. As the name suggests the parts of the plant are all in threes.

T. grandiflorum

Also known as wake robin. This is the best-known species with pure white flowers. Late spring. 30-45cm/12-18in. ZONE 4.

TROLLIUS

T. chinensis

Has a mass of orange stamens and slashed petals filling orange bowls. Midsummer. 90cm/3ft. ZONE 5.

T. europaeus

The wild European globe flower is unbeatable with its exquisite pale lemon globes over mounds of glossy cut foliage. Early summer. 75cm/2½ft. ZONE 3.

TULIPA

T. sprengeri

The last wild tulip to flower in late May. Olive green buds open to dazzling scarlet pointed petals on 40cm/16in stems. ZONE 5.

UVULARIA

U. perfoliata

Related to Solomon's seal and needing retentive leaf-mould soil and part shade. From arching stems dangle light lemon-yellow flowers with long twisting petals held above the leaves in spring. Makes slowly increasing clumps. 30cm/1ft. ZONE 4.

VERATRUM

V. album

Takes five to seven years to produce good plants from seed. Grow in retentive soil in sun or part shade where it produces clusters of hosta-like leaves, finely pleated like a fan. In late summer, a tall flower stem emerges, carrying a pyramidal head of little white cups shadowed with green. 1.5-2m/4-6ft. ZONE 4.

VERBASCUM

V. bombyciferum

Giant mullein. Huge rosettes, a yard across, of large white-felted grey leaves. Sends up a tree-like stem covered in white wool, supporting a candelabra-like head of yellow flowers. Biennial. For full sun in well-drained soil. Mid- to late summer. Over 1.8m/6ft. ZONE 5.

V. chaixii

Good perennial. Scarcely branched stems tightly massed with yellow or white flowers, with massive eyes. Mid- to late summer. 75cm/3½ft. ZONE 5.

VERBENA

V. bonariensis

For hot dry sunny positions with good drainage. Tall branching stems topped

TOP LEFT **Trollius europaeus**
TOP RIGHT **Tulipa sprengeri**
ABOVE **Veratrum album**

with flat clusters of small, scented mauve flowers make summer screens to view the garden through. Late summer to autumn. 1.5m/5ft. ZONE 8.

V. b. 'Lollipop'
A useful smaller cultivar. 60cm/3ft. ZONE 8.

VERONICA

V. teucrium 'Crater Lake Blue'
A good edging plant with low tufts of small green leaves and spires of vivid blue flowers. 30cm/12in. ZONE 4.

VERONICASTRUM

V. virginicum
Erect stems, with whorls of horizontal dark green leaves, topped with tapers of tiny close-set flowers, palest pink in late summer. 1.2m/4ft. ZONE 3.

VINCA

This makes useful ground cover.

V. minor f. alba
Has white flowers with small leaves marbled in light and dark green in spring and early summer. 20cm/8in. ZONE 5.

V. m. 'Argenteovariegata'
The variegation is green and white, the plants smaller. Pale blue flowers. 15cm/6in. ZONE 5.

V. m. 'Bowles's Variety'
Similar but with large blue flowers. 20cm/8in. ZONE 5.

VIOLA

V. cornuta Alba Group
Long succession of chalk-white flowers in spring and early summer with a late flush in autumn. Prefers full sun and retentive soil. 15cm/6in. ZONE 6.

V. riviniana Purpurea Group
Makes a running mass of small dark purple leaves, setting off the many light-coloured, scentless flowers. 15cm/6in. ZONE 5.

WALDSTEINIA

W. ternata
A beautiful and valuable carpeter which will flourish in retentive soil in sun or part shade, spreading its dark-lobed leaves, evergreen and glossy, to contrast with yellow strawberry-like flowers in spring. 10cm/4in. ZONE 4.

ZANTEDESCHIA

Z. aethiopica 'Crowborough'
This well-known arum lily, handsome in leaf and summer flower, grows well in sunny areas in bogs or deeply prepared soil kept moist in summer. Crowns must be protected in winter. Thrives in mud. 90cm/3ft. ZONE 8.

Z. a. 'Green Goddess'
Large green flowers with white throats, magnificent foliage. Cultivation as above. 1.5m/4ft plus. ZONE 8.

ZAUSCHNERIA

Z. canum
Also known as the humming-bird trumpet. Will stand the hottest drought. Wiry stems covered with narrow ash-grey leaves are topped throughout summer with brilliant scarlet tubular flowers. 30cm/1ft. ZONE 8.

Z. c. 'Dublin'
Scarlet tubular flowers for weeks in autumn. Small matt green leaves. For sunny well-drained areas. 38cm/15in. ZONE 8.

TOP *Verbascum bombyciferum*
ABOVE *Verbena bonariensis* 'Lollipop'
LEFT *Zantedeschia aethiopica* 'Crowborough'

Page numbers in italics refer to captions to illustrations. The Plant Directory is in alphabetical Latin name order and entries there are not indexed below. Plant names cross referenced in the index without a page number refer to entries in the Plant Directory.

A

Acer griseum 152; *A. negundo* 'Flamingo' *94, 114, 130*; *A. palmatum 82*; *A. p.* 'Atropurpureum' *130*; *A. p.* 'Sango-kaku' *154*
Achillea 12, 37, 37, 147; *A. filipendulina 12*; *A. f.* 'Gold Plate' *12*
aconite, winter SEE *Eranthis*
Aconitum 106; *A.* 'Stainless Steel' *109*
Actaea 92, 106; *A. matsumurae* 'Elstead Variety' *121*; *A. simplex* 'White Pearl' 112
Adiantum venustum 163
Agapanthus 17, 39, 46, 57, 138
Agastache 'Blue Boa' *146*
Agave americana 55, 56
Ajuga 106, 114, 126; *A. reptans 94*; *A. r.* 'Atropurpurea' *102, 105*; *A. r.* 'Burgundy Glow' *128*; *A. r.* variegated 128
Alchemilla mollis 142
algicides 81
Allium 14, 53, 55, 56, 136, 146; *A. hollandicum 39*; *A. karataviense 181*; *A.* 'Purple Rain' *134, 138, 147*; *A.* 'Purple Sensation' *46*; *A. siculum* subsp. *dioscoridis 48, 51*; *A. sphaerocephalon 46, 52*; *A. stipitatum* 'Mount Everest' *146*; *A. tuberosum 184*; *A. ursinum 156*
Aloysia citriodora 183
Alps, Swiss 11
Alstroemeria 54; *A. ligtu* hybrids 42
Amelanchier 42; *A. lamarckii 58, 156, 166, 167*
Ampelodesmos mauritanicus 54
Amsonia 'Ernst Pagels' *143, 146*
Anaphalis 147
Anemone blanda 'Bridesmaid' *142*; *A.* × *fulgens 54, 56, 104, 105*; *A.* × *hybrida* (Japanese a.) *111*; *A.* × *h.* 'Honorine Jobert' *111*; *A. nemorosa* (wood a.) *111*, 157; *A. n.* 'Robinsoniana' *162*; *A. pavonina 184*
Anemonella thalictroides 30
Angelica archangelica 78
annuals 56
Anthemis tinctoria 'E. C. Buxton' *57*
aphids 132
apple SEE *Malus*
Aquilegia 87
Argyrocytisus battandieri 104
Arisaema candidissimum 120
Armeria 184

Artemisia 42, 48, 130, 175
Arum italicum subsp. *italicum* 'Marmoratum' (syn. *A. i.* subsp. *i.* 'Pictum') 44, *45*, 116, *133*, 168; hybrid 44; *A. maculatum 44*
arum lily SEE *Zantedeschia*
Aruncus dioicus 164
ash 152, 167
aspect, sunny or shady 32
Asphodeline 42
Asphodelus albus 42, 56
Asplenium scolopendrium 126, 163, 166
Aster amellus 'King George' *14*; *A. divaricatus* SEE *Eurybia divaricata*; *A.* × *frikartii* 'Mönch' *94*; *A. novi-belgii* SEE *Symphyotrichum n.-b.*
Astilbe 24, 62, 68, 78, 93, 101, 102, 107; *A.* × *arendsii* 'Fanal' *92*; *A.* × 'Venus' *100*
Astilboides tabularis 77
Astrantia 94, 109; *A. major 102*; *A. m.* 'Sunningdale Variegated' *102*; *A. maxima 102*; *A.* 'Roma' *109*
asymmetrical triangle (Japanese design principle) *26, 27, 51*
azalea 22, 23, 24, 99

B

Ballota 42, 53, 54, 56, 181; *B. pseudodictamnus 46, 48*
Baltic parsley SEE *Cenolophium*
bamboos *32, 88, 114*; *154*; golden crook stem b. SEE *Phyllostachys aureosulcata* f. *aureocaulis 88*
bark, crushed or pulverized 87, 108, 116, 167
bean, blue-podded *15*; scarlet runner b. *15*
bedding out 54
bell heather 23
Begonia 29, 192
Bergenia 37, 37, 38, 42, 43, 46, 51, 54, 55, 106, 131, 138, 143; *B.* 'Beethoven' *103*; *B.* 'Mrs Crawford' *58*; *B. pacumbis 178*
Beth Chatto Education Trust 6, *186, 194*, 195
Beth Chatto Gardens, Elmstead Market, Essex 6; Badger's Wood 152; borders 29; Canal Bed 81, *81, 84, 88, 88, 91*; car park *39, 39, 44, 45*; container garden 186; courtyard area *192, 192*; Entrance Garden 34, 36, 37, 42, *42*, 192; E.G. border 56; 'goat path' *183*; Gravel Garden 7, *20, 13, 24, 34, 35, 37, 37, 39, 39, 45, 47, 54, 55, 56, 57, 58, 59, 60*, 61, *145, 170, 172, 177*, 184, *186*; greenhouse 184, *185, 192*; house 192; island beds *26, 39, 45, 46, 48, 91*, 106, 138; Mediterranean Garden (Dry Garden)

(SEE ALSO Scree Garden) 25, 27, 36, 38, 104, 130, 134, 172, 175, 177, *177, 181*, 183; new car park 170; north-facing Clay Bank 130; Open Walks 77, 90-94, *107*; paved garden 33; ponds 78, 195; Pump Pond *87, 194*; raised patio 192; Reflection Garden 169, 170, *171*; reservoir 130, 134, 170, *171*; Reservoir Garden 7, *84*, 88, *88*, 114, 134, *136*, 138, 141, 143, 144, *145*, 148, 149, 149, 165; Scree Garden *24*, 172-85, *172, 175, 183*, 192; Shade Garden 108-33, 138; Shady Walk *29, 103*, 108, *128*, 130, 131, 132; sun and shade beds 140; sunny borders 94; tearoom 184, 192; Visitor Information Centre 186; Water Garden *24*, 62, *63, 63, 65*, 81, *81*, 90, 143, 145, *172, 183*; wild corner 195; Willow Room *87, 186*, 191, *191, 194*, 195; Woodland Garden 7, *24, 25*, 88, 108, 143, 152-71, *54, 156, 158, 161, 163, 164, 165*, 186; W.G. ditch *160*, 168; W.G. walkway 169
Bidens ferulifolia 54, 56
birch, silver 108, 152
blanket weed 62, 78, *78*
bleeding heart SEE *Lamprocapnos*
bluebell 157
bog arum SEE *Lysichiton*
Bond, John (1932-2001) 154
bonfire waste 26, 46, 89
Boulton, Julia (née Bates) 6
bowman's root SEE *Gillenia trifoliata*
box hedges 29
Braiswick, Colchester 14
broom, Mount Etna SEE *Genista aetnensis*; pineapple b. SEE *Argyrocytisus battandieri*
Brunnera macrophylla 111
brushwood 98
buckler fern SEE *Dryopteris filix-mas*
Buglossoides purpurocaerulea 166
bulbs 48, 51, *51*, 55, 58, 95, 157; spring b. 101
Bupleurum falcatum 54
butterbur, Japanese SEE *Petasites japonicus*

C

Calamagrostis 147; *C.* × *acutiflora* 'Karl Foerster' *141*
calcium carbonate 81
California poppy SEE *Eschscholzia*
Californian tree poppy SEE *Romneya coulteri*
Calla palustris 74
Caltha 73, 82; *C. palustris 74*; *C. p.* 'Flore Pleno' *74*; *C. p.* var. *radicans 74*; *C. p.* var. *palustris 74*

Camassia 146; *C. leichtlinii 95*

Campanula 98; *C. carpatica* var. *turbinata* 99; *C. lactiflora 99*; *C. glomerata* var. *alba* 'Schneekrone' 99

candytuft SEE *Iberis sempervirens*

cardoon SEE *Cynara cardunculus*

Carex buchananii 105; *C. elata* 'Aurea' *10, 68, 81, 100,* 152

Caryopteris × *clandonensis* 'Heavenly Blue' *178*; *C.* × *c.* 'Worcester Gold' *178*

Castle Howard, N. Yorks. 152

catmint SEE *Nepeta*

CEDEX self-binding aggregate 144

celandine 62, 74, 157

Cerastium 175

Cercis siliquastrum 134, 136, 144, *144, 145, 181, 184, 185, 185*

chalk 81, 175

Chasmanthium latifolium 96, 121

Chatto, Andrew Edward (1909-99) 6, 8, *9,* 11, *99,* 152

Chatto, Beth (*née* Betty Diana Little) (1923-2018) 6, *9,* 149; *Beth Chatto's Shade Garden* 171; Gold Medal displays, Chelsea Flower Show 6, 189; *The Gravel Garden* 61; *The Green Tapestry* 6, 8, 34, 134, 143, 152, 186; *The Woodland Garden* 171

chicory 15

Chionochloa flavicans 96

'chipping' of bulbs 161

Choisya × *dewitteana* 'Aztec Pearl' *111*

Christmas box SEE *Sarcococca*

Christmas rose SEE *Helleborus niger*

Chrysanthemum 22, 136; *C.* 'Anastasia' 136; *C.* 'Emperor of China' 136

Cimicifuga SEE *Actaea*

Cistus 37, 56, 175, 176, *176; C.* × *argenteus* 'Peggy Sammons' *46*; *C. parviflorus 176*

clay 24, 26, 65, 87, 90, 134, 143; boulder c. 175

Clematis montana 165; *C. viticella* 100

clover SEE *Trifolium*

codlins and cream SEE *Epilobium hirsutum*

Col de Sevi, Corsica, France *9*

Colchester 24, 175; C. Flower Club 14

Colchicum 44, 58, 166; *C. speciosum* 141; *C. s.* 'Album' 166; *C.* 'The Giant' *167*

colour 28, 31; primary colours 31; c. schemes 30, 104

compost 89, 134, 154, 178; homemade c. 46; mushroom c. 46, 175; pot c. 192

conifers 48

containers 192

cornelian cherry see *Cornus mas*

Cornus alba Baton Rouge = 'Minibat' *68, 69*; *C. mas* 156; *Cornus sanguinea* 'Midwinter Fire' 167

Cosmos bipinnatus 'Purity' 54, 56

Cotinus coggygria 147, 168

Cotoneaster 154

cotton grass 72

cow parsley SEE *Anthriscus, Chaerophyllum*

cowslip SEE *Primula veris*; Himalayan c. SEE *Primula florindae*

Crambe cordifolia 42

cranesbill SEE *Geranium*

Crataegus persimilis 'Prunifolia' *42, 43*

creeping Jenny SEE *Lysimachia nummularia*

Crocosmia 30, 54, *147*; *C.* 'Lucifer' 30

Crocus speciosus 'Albus' 58

crops 170

crown imperial SEE *Fritillaria imperialis*

× *Cupressocyparis* SEE × *Cuprocyparis*

Cupressus arizonica 52

× *Cuprocyparis leylandii* 61; hedge 36, *36,* 38, *39,* 42, 45, 47

cuttings 192

Cyclamen 112, 116, *166*; *C. coum* 119; *C. hederifolium* 119, *119, 196*

Cynara cardunculus 28, 43, *136, 147*

D

Dactylorrhiza fuchsia 94

Dahlia 22, 29

daffodil SEE *Narcissus*

Darmera peltata 10, 64, 68, 75

dawn redwood SEE *Metasequoia glyptostroboides*

daylily SEE *Hemerocallis*

Delphinium 38, 93

desert candle SEE *Eremurus*

Deutzia 156; *D.* × *hybrid* 'Mont Rose' *133*

Dianthus 9, 28, 183, *184*

Dicentra 32, 125; *D. formosa 160*; *D. f.* 'Langtrees' *111*; *D. spectabilis* SEE *Lamprocapnos s.*

Digitalis lutea 111; *D. purpurea* f. *albiflora* 116, *138*

dog's tooth violet SEE *Erythronium dens-canis*

dogwood SEE *Cornus*

Dorchester Flower Club 15

drainage 178

drought-loving plants 25, 34, 44, 54, 175, 176

Dryopteris filix-mas 111, 126, 162; *D. wallichiana 21, 128,* 162

duckweed *88*

E

Echinacea 146

Epilobium hirsutum 82

Epimedium 106, 122; *E.* × *perralchicum* 'Fröhnleiten' *111, 117*; *E.* × *rubrum 125*

Eranthis 44, 158, *166*

Eremurus 138, 146; *E.* 'Cleopatra' *138*; *E. robustus* 42; *E.* 'White Beauty Favourite' *146*

Erigeron annuus 149; *E. karvinskianus 184*

Eryngium 147; *E. giganteum 39,* 52; *E. planum* 'Blaukappe' 146

Erysimum pulchellum 35

Erythronium 119, 133, 162; *E. californicum* 94; *E. c.* 'White Beauty' 119; *E. dens-canis* 94, 101, 102, *111,* 119, 162; *E.* 'Pagoda' 94

Eschscholzia 8; *E. californica* 56

Eucalyptus 44, 47; *E. dalrympleana 47, 48*; *E. nicholii* 61

Euonymus 167; *E. japonicas* 'Microphyllus Pulchellus' *184*

Eupatorium maculatum Atropurpureum Group *29,* 68

Euphorbia 13, 16, *16,* 30, 42, *42,* 52, 54, *54,* 175, 176, *181*; *E. amygdaloides* 'Purpurea' 128; *E. a.* var. *robbiae* 87, *91,* 105, 119, 125, 128; *E. characias* subsp. *wulfenii 20,* 39, 46, 52, 53, *53,* 55, 58, 104, 105, *174, 175*; *E. cyparissias* 'Fens Ruby' 61; *E. epithymoides* (syn. *E. polychroma*) 39; *E. e.* 'Major' 56; *E. griffithii* 'Dixter' 104; *E. g.* 'Fireglow' *91, 94,* 95, 104; *E. margalidiana 143,* 146; *E. myrsinites 178*; *E. palustris 10,* 63, *68,* 78; *E. p.* 'Walenburg's Glorie' *107*; *E. rigida 184*

evergreens *31,* 174

F

false goatsbeard SEE *Astilbe*

Fargesia nitida 114; *F. scabrida* 114

Farrer, Reginald John (1880-1920) *The English Rock Garden* 96

Fatsia japonica 31

feather grass, Mexican SEE *Stipa tenuissima*

fennel SEE *Foeniculim, Ferula*; giant Greek f. SEE *Ferula communis*

ferns 20, *25,* 32, 43, 78, 114, *122,* 126, *126,* 154, 157, *158,* 166; marsh f. 72

Ferula communis 56; *F. tingitana* 'Cedric Morris' *56*

figwort SEE *Scrophularia*

flag iris SEE *Iris pseudocorus*

fleabane SEE *Erigeron*

Flower Club movement 14, 15
flowering currant 156
foam flower SEE *Tiarella cordifolia*
foliage plants 21, 53
forget-me-not SEE *Myosotis*; water
  f.-.m.-n. SEE *M. scorpioides*
foxglove SEE *Digitalis*
foxtail lily SEE *Eremurus*
frames 189
Framlingham, Suffolk 16
French marigold 20
Fritillaria imperialis 38, 39, 56, 142, *147*;
  F. meleagris (snake's head fritillary) *68*,
  94, 102, 142; *F. persica* 48

G

Galactites tomentosa 56
Galanthus 44, 78, 94, 126, 132, 157, 160,
  161, 162, *163*, *164*, *166*; *G. caucasicus*
  141; *G. elwesii* 44, 160; *G. e.* 'Cedric's
  Prolific' 160; *G. e.* 'Mrs Macnamara'
  158, 158; *G.* 'Hippolyta' 159; *G.* 'James
  Backhouse' 158, *163*; *G. plicatus* 160;
  G. p. subsp. *byzantinus* 119
Gaura SEE *Oenothera*
Genista aetnensis 42, *43*, 47, 60; *G.
  hispanica* 37; *G.* 'Lydia' *183*
Gentiana (gentian) 9, 18, 99; *G. lutea* 95,
  99; willow g. SEE *G. asclepiadea*
Geranium 25, 95, 106, 116, 126, *126*,
  136, 168; *G. endressii* 117, 143, *160*;
  G. macrorrhizum 95, *111*, 116, 164;
  G. m. 'Album' *164*; *G. m.* 'Glacier' 164
  G.maculatum 138; *G.* 'Orion' *142*; *G.
  psilostemon* 95; *G.* Rozanne = 'Gerwat'
  94; *G. tuberosum* 142; *G. wallichianum*
  'Buxton's Variety'; 136
Geum × *borisii* 104
Gillenia trifoliata 164
Gladiolus 15, 22; *G. communis* subsp.
  byzantinus 48
globeflower SEE *Trollius*
globe thistle SEE *Echinops*
goat's beard SEE *Aruncus dioicus*
golden larch SEE *Pseudolarix amabilis*
golden oat grass SEE *Stipa gigantea*
goldenrod 12, 38
Good Easter, Chelmsford, Essex 8
gorse, Spanish SEE *Genista hispanica*
gourd *15*
grasses *17*, 28, 55, 57, 58, 82, *107*, 122,
  143, 146, 154, 157, *158*, *191*; wild g. 21
gravel 24, 38, *39*, 65, 172, 175, 184;
  g. paths 45
Great Dixter, Northiam, E. Sussex 100
Great Storm of October, 1987 33, 152
green-flowered plants 16, *16*
'green tapestry' 126, 185

green waste 148
grey-leaved plants 20, 104
Gregers-Warg, Åsa 7, 134
grit 25, 26, 89, 134, 178
ground cover 55, 87, 143, *160*, 168
gum tree SEE *Eucalyptus*; mountain g.
  SEE *E. dalrympleana*
Gunnera 63, 65, *70*, 72, 82; *G. tinctoria*
  (Chilean g.) *70*, 72, *156*
Gypsophila repens *184*; *G.* 'Rosenschleier'
  178

H

Hadleigh, Suffolk 14
hair-grass, tufted SEE *Deschampsia*
Hakonechloa (hakone grass) *macra*
  'Aureola' *29*, 105, *164*, *166*
Hamamelis mollis 116
hand-digging 46
Haplopappus coronopifolius 141
hardiness zones *196*
hart's-tongue fern SEE *Asplenium
  scolopendrium*
hawthorn 131
heathers 23
Hedera 112, 127; *H. colchica* 'Sulphur
  Heart' 131; *H. helix* 126, 128; *H. h.* f.
  poetarum 'Poetica Arborea' 128; *H. h.*,
  yellow-leaved 133
Helianthemum 141
Helleborus (hellebore) 16, 131, 138, 162;
  H. argutifolius 55, 117; *H. foetidus* *111*,
  117, 132; *H.* × *hybridus* 11, *126*, 131,
  131, 162, *166*
Hemerocallis 72, *94*, *101*
hemp agrimony SEE *Eupatorium*
Hepatica transsilvanica 119
herbaceous plants 157
Hesperantha coccinea 102
Heuchera 157, *166*
Hidcote Manor Garden, Chipping
  Campden, Gloucestershire 2
Himalayan poppy SEE *Meconopsis*
holly SEE *Ilex*
honeysuckle 165
hop SEE *Humulus*
hosepipe 168
Hosta 18, 20, 25, *25*, 32, 38, 51, 68, 74,
  78, 101, 102, *103*, 106, *107*, 108-33,
  109, *111*, *112*, 114, *126*, 132, 157, *158*,
  166, *166*, 168, *190*, *192*: blue h. 164;
  H. fortunei var. *albopicta* f. *aurea* 102;
  H. f. 'Spinners' *100*; *H.* 'Gold Standard'
  111, *114*; *H. sieboldiana* 102, *130*;
  H. s. 'Frances Williams' *109*, *128*;
  H. (Tardiana Group) 'Halcyon' *29*, *119*;
  H. undulata var. *albomarginata* 102
houseleek SEE *Sempervivum*

humus 25, 26, 38, *172*
Hyacinthoides non-scripta 116
Hydrangea 32; *H. anomala* subsp.
  petiolaris (climbing h.) 165); *H. aspera*
  Villosa Group *128*; *H. paniculata* 120;
  H. p. 'Limelight' *120*
Hylotelephium 38, *189*; *H.* 'Herbstfreude'
  43, *43*, 46; *H. telephium* (Atropurpureum
  Group) 'Karfunkelstein' *178*

I

Iberis sempervirens 176
Ilex 25, 89, 115, 125, 131, 154;
  I. × *altaclerensis* 'Golden King' 44
impulse buying 100
Ipheion 55
Iris 14, *53*, 62, 85; Bearded i. 148; *I.*
  'Benton Deirdre' *136*; *I.* 'Benton Menace'
  146; *I. foetidissima* 37, 38, 53, 128, 142;
  I. 'Jane Phillips' *35*; *I. pallida* subsp.
  pallida 13; *I. pseudacorus* 68, 75;
  I. p. 'Bastardii' 85; *I. p.* 'Variegata' 74;
  water i. 64, 77, 82;
irrigation 154, 167, 170
ivy SEE *Hedera*; common or English i.
  SEE *Hedera helix*

J

Jacob's ladder SEE *Polemonium
  caeruleum*
Jekyll, Gertrude (1843-1932) 12, 217
Jerusalem cross SEE *Lychnis
  chalcedonica*
Joe Pye weed SEE *Eupatorium*
Judas tree SEE *Cercis siliquastrum*
Juneberry SEE *Amelanchier lamarckii*
Juniperus scopulorum 'Blue Arrow'
  46, 48

K

kingfishers *194*
Kirengeshoma palmata 166, *166*
Knautia macedonica 142
Kniphofia 54, 138; *K.* 'Little Maid' 61
knotweed SEE *Persicaria*

L

lad's love 202
lady fern 205
lady's locket SEE *Lamprocapnos*
Lambert, Harry 15
lamb's ears SEE *Stachys byzantina*
Lamium 138; *L. maculatum* 133, *166*
Lamprocapnos spectabilis 93, 125, *166*
laurel 154
Lavandula (lavender) 48, 52, 53, 56, *183*
leaf blower 167
leafmould 92, 108, 116, 175

lemon balm SEE *Melissa officnalis*
lemon verbena SEE *Aloysia citriodora*
Le Nôtre, André (1613-1700) 20
Leng, Basil 161
Lenten rose SEE *Helleborus* × *hybridus*
Leucojum aestivum 'Gravetye Giant' 68
Leyland cypress SEE × *Cuprocyparis leylandii*
Libertia ixioides 141, 185; *Libertia peregrinans 184*
Ligularia 62, 63, 68, 70, 77, 78, 168
Lilium (lily) 112, 120; *L. martagon* (Turk's cap l.) 94
Limonium bellidifolium 184
ling 23
Liriope muscari 111
Lloyd, Christopher Hamilton ('Christo') (1921-2006) 100
London pride SEE *Saxifraga* × *urbium*
Louis XIV (1638-1715) 20
lungwort SEE *Pulmonaria*
Lychnis coronaria 23
Lysichiton 24, 25; *L. americanus* 72, 75, 85; *L. camtschatcensis* 76; *L.* × *hortensis* 76
Lysimachia ciliata 'Firecracker' *94*; *L. nummularia* 'Aurea' *68*, 78
Lythrum 68; *L. salicaria 81*

M

Magnolia × *soulangeana* 121, *192*, *192*
Mahonia 155
maidenhair fern 163
male fern SEE *Dryopteris filix-mas*
Maltese cross SEE *Lychnis chalcedonica*
Malus 116; *M. hupehensis* 42, 43
manure 154; farmyard m. 134, 178
maple, field 89; paperbark m. SEE *Acer griseum*
marjoram SEE *Origanum*; wild m. SEE *O. vulgare*
marrow 'Avocadella' 15
marsh marigold SEE *Caltha*
marsh thistle 65
Matteuccia struthiopteris 75, 85, *125*, *133*, *156*, 168
Meconopsis 92, *112*
Melica uniflora f. *albida* 111
Melissa officinalis 183; *M. o.* 'All Gold' 177
Metasequoia glyptostroboides 70
Mexican feather grass SEE *Stipa tenuissima*
Michaelmas daisy 12, 102, 105, 203
mildew, powdery *43*
Milium effusum 'Aureum' *111*, 121, 164
Miscanthus 63, 85, 147, *147*, *191*; *M. sinensis* 68; *M. s.* 'Dronning Ingrid'

147; *M. s.* 'Morning Light' *72*, *101*; *M. s.* 'Poseidon' *65*; *M. s.* 'Yaku-jima' 126
Miss Willmott's ghost SEE *Eryngium giganteum*
Molinia 94, *191*; *M. caerulea* subsp. *caerulea* 'Variegata' 78
Morris, Sir Cedric Lockwood (1889-1982) 13, *13*, 14, 15, 116, *136*, 146, *172*
mountain ash SEE *Sorbus*
mulch 23, 24, 148; straw m. 134
mullein SEE *Verbascum*
Myosotis 68, *136*, *144*, *152*; *M. scorpioides* 77; *M. sylvatica 111*

N

Narcissus 94, 132, *164*; *N.* 'February Gold' 161, *161*; *N.* 'Jenny' *161*; *N. minor* 141, *161*; *N. m.* 'Cedric Morris' 116; *N.* 'Rijnveld's Early Sensation' *94*; *N.* 'Thalia' 161; *N.* 'W. P. Milner' 141
narcissus fly 132
Nectaroscordum SEE *Allium*
Nepeta 13, 42, 46, *142*; *N.* 'Blue Dragon' 145; *N.* × *faassenii* 'Purrsian Blue' *140*
New Zealand flax SEE *Phormium tenax*
Nicotiana 54; *N.* 'Lime Green' *55*, 56
nitrogen 81
Nursery (Beth Chatto Plants and Gardens – formerly Unusual Plants) 16, 186, *186*, *189*; nursery stock beds *17*, 170, 189, *189*, *190*, 191; Stock Bed walk *189*, 191

O

oak, English SEE *Quercus robur*; pin o. SEE *Q. palustris*
oak posts 170, *170*
Observer newspaper 14
Oenanthe pimpinelloides 138
Oenothera lindheimeri 28, 46, 57
Omphalodes cappadocica, *122*; *O. linifolia* 35
Onoclea sensibilis 68, 72, 78, 168
Onosma alborosea 141
Ophiopogon planiscapus 'Kokuryū' (syn. *O. p.* 'Nigrescens') 105, 130
orchards 170
Origanum vulgare 177; *O. v.* 'Aureum' 177; *O. v.* 'Thumble's Variety' *46*
Osmunda regalis 68. 75
ostrich plume fern SEE *Matteuccia struthiopteris*

P

Pachyphragma macrophyllum 119, *132*, *166*
Pachysandra terminalis 132

Panicum 147
pansy 103
Papaver cambricum 119; *P.* Oriental Group 39; *P.* (O. G.) 'Cedric Morris' 13, *42*; *P. rhoeas* Mother of Pearl Group 56, *176*; *Papaver somniferum 176*
Parahebe 138
paving, council *177*
pea-stakes 98
Pearson, Dan *194*
peat 108, 116; p.-free compost 191; p.loving plants 112
Pelargonium 185, *192*, *192*
Pennisetum alopecuroides 'Hameln' *94*; *P. a.* 'Black Beauty' *147*, *149*
peppermint, narrow-leaved black SEE *Eucalyptus nicholii*
periwinkle, dwarf SEE *Vinca minor*
Persicaria 28, 62, 72, 74, 77, 78, 98, 106; *P. affininis* *94*, 98; *P. amplexicaulis* 94, 98, *98*, 106; *P. bistorta* 'Superba' 70, 84, 103; *Persicaria microcephala* 'Red Dragon' *166*; *P. vacciniifolium* 98
pesticides 191
Peruvian lily SEE *Alstroemeria*
Petasites japonicas var. *giganteus* 'Nishiki-buki' 168
Petunia 68
Phacelia tanacetifolia 144
pheasant *161*
Phlomis italica 172; *P. russeliana* 141, *147*
Phlox 136; *P. douglasii* 136; *P. paniculata* *147*; *P. p.* 'Norah Leigh' 126; *P. serrulata* 136; *P. stolonifera* 114, 132
Phormium tenax 94, 144
Phyla nodiflora 184
Phyllostachys bambusoides 88
pickerel weed SEE *Pontederia cordata*
Pieris 155
Pimpinella major 'Rosea' 146, *147*
pine 108
pink SEE *Dianthus*; maiden p. SEE *D. deltoides*
planting plans *46*, *68*, *94*, *111*, *147*, *166*, *184*
plaques 170, *170*
plastic sheeting 65
Poa labillardieri 136
Polemonium caeruleum 96; *P. carneum* 96
Polygonatum 96; *P.* × *hybridum 111*, *122*, *154*; *P.* × *h.* 'Betburg' *162*
Polypodium × *mantoniae* 'Cornubiense' 126; *P. vulgare* 126
Polystichum munitum 126; *P. setiferum* Acutilobum Group 126, *166*; *P. s.* (Divisilobum Group) 'Dahlem' *111*, *162*; *P. s.* (D. Group) 'Herrenhausen' 163

polythene 65; black p. 23
polytunnels *17*
pond liners 62
Pontederia cordata 75
pools 32, 68
Pope, Mary 15
poppy 14, 42; blue p. SEE *Meconopsis*
  Oriental p. SEE *Papaver* Oriental
  Group; Welsh p. SEE *Papaver cambricum*
Portugal laurel SEE *Prunus lusitanica*
pots 192; pot displays 192; pot topper,
  minibark 191
Potentilla 53, 138, 183; *P. argyrophylla*
  138; *P. atrosanguinea* 138; *P.* 'Miss
  Willmott' 138
primrose SEE *Primula vulgaris*
Primula 18, 31, 62, 64, 68, 82, 87, 175;
  Candelabra p. *63*, 72, 81, *84*; *P. bulleyana*
  64, 68, 81; *P. florindae* 81; *P. japonica* 81,
  84; *P. pulverulenta* 84; *P. vulgaris* 116,
  131; *P. v.* var. *alba* 117
propagation material 191
Prunus lusitanica 128: *P.* 'Shirofugen'
  100; *P.* 'Tai-haku' *65*
Pseudolarix amabilis 76, *96*, 99
Pulmonaria 25, *111*, *112*, *126*, 131, *142*;
  P. rubra 131; *P. saccharata* 131
Pulsatilla vulgaris 184
Puschkinia 55
pyrethrum (*Tanacetum coccineum*) 11

Q
Queen Anne's lace SEE *Anthriscus*
Quercus robur 25, 44, *44*, 58, 81, 89, 108,
  114, 115, 128, 132, 152, 154, *165*, *191*;
  Q. palustris 81, *87*

R
rabbits *190*
radish, varieties of 15
rainfall 108, 112
raised beds 178, *178*, 184
ramsons SEE *Allium ursinum*
raspberry SEE *Rubus*
redwood forests, Oregon 126
Rheum palmatum 82, 96
Rhododendron 22, 23, 24, 132, 175;
  R. occidentale 99; *R. ponticum* 22, *112*,
  125, 131, 154; *R.* 'Sappho' *84*
rhubarb, ornamental SEE *Rheum*
  palmatum
Rhus typhina 58; *R. t.* 'Dissecta' *168*
Robinson, William (1838-1935) 12
rock rose SEE *Cistus*
Rodgersia 74, 77, 85, 168; *R. aesculifolia*
  77; *R.* 'Herkules' *72*; *R. pinnata* 'Superba'
  122; *R. podophylla* 125; *R. tabularis*
  SEE *Astilboides t.*

Romneya coulteri 61
Rosa (rose) 15, 31; *R.* 'Bobbie James' 166;
  R. filipes 'Kiftsgate' 166; *R. glauca* 42,
  43, 138; old-fashioned r. 95, 229;
  R. 'Paul's Himalayan Musk' *165*, 166
rosemary 176
royal fern SEE *Osmunda regalis*
Royal Horticultural Society qualification
  courses 195
Rubus tricolor 132
Rudbeckia 12; *R. fulgida* *94*
rushes 82

S
Sackville-West, Vita (1892-1962) 12, 13
Saffron Walden, Essex 8
sage SEE *Salvia*; bush s. 175
Salix repens var. *argentea* 85; *S. udensis*
  'Golden Sunshine' *178*
Salvia 12, *189*; *S.* 'Blue Spire' (syn.
  Atriplex 'B. S.') 48, 185; *S. lavandulifolia*
  35; *S. nemorosa* *147*; *S.* × *sylvestris* *147*;
  S. verticillata 'Hannay's Blue' 149; *S. v.*
  'Purple Rain' *138*, *142*, 149
sand 24; sandy soil *25*, 26
Sambucus nigra f. *porphyrophylla* 'Eva'
  (syn. *S. n.* f. *p.* 'Black Lace') *138*
Sanguisorba 147
Santolina 38, 42, 56; *S. chamaecyparissus*
  48; *S. virens* 176
Sarcococca *111*, 128, 131; *S. confusa* 155;
  S. hookeriana var. *digyna* 155
Savill Gardens, Windsor Great Park,
  Berks. 154
Saxifraga (saxifrage) × *urbium*
  'Aureopunctata' *120*, 122; mossy s. 128
Scabiosa (scabious) *columbaria* subsp.
  ochroleuca 149
Schizostylis SEE *Hesperantha*
Scilla *46*, 55
Scotch thistle SEE *Onopordum*
  acanthium
scree 178
Scrophularia aquatica 'Variegata' 78
secateurs 168
sedge, Bowles's golden SEE *Carex elata*
  'Aurea'
Sedum 176, 183, 185; *S. spurium* *184*;
  SEE ALSO *Hylotelephium*
seed-heads 148
self-seeding 47
Sempervivum 9, 176, 183, *184*, 185
sensitive fern SEE *Onoclea sensibilis*
shade 111; dry s. 112
shrubs 154
shuttlecock fern SEE *Matteuccia*
  struthiopteris
silt 24, 25, 62, 90

silver-leaved plants *23*, 48
Sissinghurst Castle, White Garden,
  Kent 28
Skimmia 126, 155; *S.* × *confusa* 'Kew
  Green' 155; *S.. japonica* 166, *167*;
  S. j. 'Rubella' *31*
Smith, Eric (1917-86) 212, 237
smoke bush SEE *Cotinus coggygria*
Smyrnium perfoliatum 87
snowdrop SEE *Galanthus*
soft shield fern SEE *Polystichum*
  setiferum
Solomon's seal SEE *Polygonatum*
Sorbus glabriuscula 167; *S. pseudo-*
  hupehensis 167
Southernwood 202
spacing of plants 101
spangle grass SEE *Chasmanthium*
  latifolium
spindle bush SEE *Euonymus*
Spiraea japonica 'Goldflame' *166*
spotted orchid SEE *Dactylorrhiza fuchsii*
spurge SEE *Euphorbia*; wood s. SEE *E.*
  amygdaloides
Spry, Constance (1886-1960) 14
squash *15*
Stachys byzantina 42, 46, *136*, *138*; *S. b.*
  'Cotton Boll' *174*
staking 98
Stewartia pseudocamellia 125
Stipa barbata 61; *S. gigantea* *23*, 28, *28*,
  44, *46*, 57, *183*; *S. pseudoichu* 147; *S.*
  tenuissima 39, *46*, *52*, 60
stone chips 167
stonecrop 176
straw 38; s. mulch 134
subsoiler 46
succulents *185*, 192, *192*
sumac, stag's horn SEE *Rhus typhina*
sun rose 56
sustainable planting 191
swamp cypress SEE *Taxodium*
  distichum
Symphyotrichum novi-belgii 'Heinz
  Richard' *94*
Symphytum 168

T
Tanacetum parthenium 'Aureum' 132
Tarragon, French 202
Taxodium distichum 65, *83*, *88*, *109*
teasel SEE *Dipsacus*
telegraph wire 166
Tellima 92, *112*; *T. grandiflora* 119
Teucrium × *lucidrys* 46
Thalictrum 98, *143*, 147; *T. aquilegiifolium*
  118; *T. flavum* subsp. *glaucum* 103;
  T. delavayi 98

Thomas, Graham Stuart (1909-2003)
136, 234
Thymus (thyme) *46*, 52, 53, 176, 183,
184, 185; golden-leaved t. 141;
T. pulegioides 'Bertram Anderson' 177;
T. vulgaris 'Golden King' 177
Tiarella 51, 92, 114; *T. cordifolia* 78,
111, 121
tidying-up 43
Titchmarsh, Alan *194*
toadflax SEE *Linaria*
toetoe grass SEE *Cortaderia richardii*
Trachystemon orientale 132
tree poppy, Californian SEE *Romneya
coulteri*
Trollius 68, *74*, 84; *T. × cultorum* 'Helios'
63
Tulipa (tulip) 31, 55; *T. linifolia* Batalinii
Group *184*
tussock grass SEE *Chionochloa*
twitch grass 11

U

Underwood, Pamela Richenda Cubitt
(Mrs Desmond U.) (1910-78) 14, 16
University of Essex, Colchester *194*

V

vegetables, unusual 15
Veratrum 96; *V. album* 95, *169*;
V. californicum 152, 158, 168; *V. viride*
95
Verbascum 14; *V. bombyciferum 20, 23,*
36, 47, 48, *51*, 56, *172*; *V. chaixii 52*
Verbena bonariensis 48, 57, 146;
V. macdougalii 'Lavender Spires'
146
Veronica 138
Versailles, France 20
vervain SEE *Verbena*
Viburnum 154; *V. davidii* 129;
V. plicatum 'Mariesii' 82
Vinca 168; *V. major* 116; *V. minor* 112,
126; *V. m.* 'Bowles's Blue' 85, 116;
V. m. 'Variegata' 116
Viola 103; *V. cornuta* (horned v.) 103,
128; *V. odorata* 132; *V. riviniana*
Purpurea Group 105, 132;
V. septentrionalis 128
violetta 103

W

wake robin SEE *Trillium grandiflorum*
Waldsteinia ternata 120
Walkden, Christine *194*
walls, house 32
Ward, David 7, 34, 152, 172
Warley Place, Essex 13

water figwort SEE *Scrophularia
aquatica*
waterlily 62, 78
waterside plants 68
weed control 46, 148
weeding 116
weedkiller 85
Weigela florida 'Foliis Purpureis' *111*

wildflowers 22
Willmott, Ellen (1858-1934) 13
willow 65, 77, 78, 89; weeping w. 77
willowherb SEE *Epilobium,
Chamaenerion*
wine cask 68
wood fern, Wallich's SEE *Dryopteris
wallichiana*
woodland plants *30*
Wooster, Steven 7
Workshops, plant and gardening 195

Y

yew 108, 128
Yucca 51; *Y. gloriosa* 39; *Y. nobilis 183*

Z

Zantedeschia aethiopica 77;
Z. a. 'Crowborough' *72*
Zeppelin, Gräfin Helen von Stein
(1905-95) 162
Zauschneria californica 177
Zinnia, double 11

Publishers' Acknowledgments

We would like to thank the following:

Julia Boulton and her team, **David Ward**, **Åsa Gregers-Warg** and **Jacob Pettersson**, at **Beth Chatto's Plants and Gardens** for their respective contributions in bringing this revised and updated edition to fruition and for being so consistently and uncomplainingly cooperative; **Anthony Paul**, for having brought the idea for the original book to Beth and for seeing it through to print so many years ago; **Steven Wooster** for his consistently brilliant photography and long-term commitment to recording Beth's garden as well as for his graphic eye; **Tony Lord** for his attention to the intricacies of plant nomenclature and for creating the index.

And last, but by no means least, to Beth herself for having given up her time all those years ago to explain via a series of recorded interviews, why she, and her gardens, were so special. It was a privilege to work with her on the resulting manuscript and we hope that her philosophy and ideas continue to inspire generations to come.

Plan of Beth's Gardens

The sketch plan below shows the main areas of interest at Beth's gardens. The Gravel Garden has replaced the original Entrance Garden.

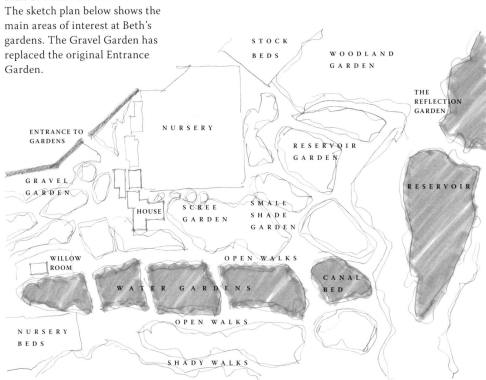

STOCK BEDS

WOODLAND GARDEN

THE REFLECTION GARDEN

ENTRANCE TO GARDENS

NURSERY

RESERVOIR GARDEN

RESERVOIR

GRAVEL GARDEN

HOUSE

SCREE GARDEN

SMALL SHADE GARDEN

WILLOW ROOM

OPEN WALKS

CANAL BED

WATER GARDENS

NURSERY BEDS

OPEN WALKS

SHADY WALKS